MW01101067

Contemporary Anthropology of Religion

Series Editors
Don Seeman
Department of Religion
Emory University
Atlanta, GA, USA

Hillary Kaell
Department of Anthropology
School of Religious Studies
McGill University
Montreal, QC, Canada

Contemporary Anthropology of Religion is the official book series of the Society for the Anthropology of Religion, a section of the American Anthropological Association. Books in the series explore a variety of issues relating to current theoretical or comparative issues in the study of religion. These include the relation between religion and the body, social memory, gender, ethnoreligious violence, globalization, modernity, and multiculturalism, among others. Recent historical events have suggested that religion plays a central role in the contemporary world, and Contemporary Anthropology of Religion provides a crucial forum for the expansion of our understanding of religion globally.

More information about this series at
https://link.springer.com/bookseries/14916

Marc Roscoe Loustau

Hungarian Catholic Intellectuals in Contemporary Romania

Reforming Apostles

Marc Roscoe Loustau
Journal of Global Catholicism
Catholics & Cultures Program
College of the Holy Cross
Worcester, MA, USA

Contemporary Anthropology of Religion
ISBN 978-3-030-99220-0   ISBN 978-3-030-99221-7   (eBook)
https://doi.org/10.1007/978-3-030-99221-7

This Palgrave Macmillan imprint is published by the registered company Springer Nature Switzerland AG.
The registered company address is: Gewerbestrasse 11, 6330 Cham, Switzerland

To Amy

A NOTE ABOUT ORTHOGRAPHY, NAMES, AND PLACE NAMES

I use standard Romanian and Hungarian orthography.

I identify public figures by name, especially when discussing their published works. When it is unclear whether individuals are public figures, I err on the side caution. For instance, all members of the Csíksomlyó choir are identified by pseudonyms. I also use pseudonyms for individuals who explicitly requested that their identities be protected.

For place names, I use the model established by Brubaker et al. (2007). I use official place names as determined by the governing legal regime of the period in question. For example, I use the "Csík Valley" when discussing the era of Dualist Austro-Hungarian rule in Transylvania. I change this place name to the "Ciuc Valley" for the interwar decades and then, from the post-World War II period until the present.

Csíksomlyó is the only the exception to this convention. I use the Hungarian place name throughout because it refers to both a place and an event, as in "the annual Csíksomlyó pilgrimage."

Acknowledgements

I am grateful to the colleagues who both supported and exhorted me while I was writing this book. Mathew Schmalz and Tom Landy at the College of the Holy Cross provided wise counsel and pedagogical mentorship. Members of Holy Cross's Department of Religious Studies were engaged interlocutors about their own groundbreaking research projects. The Sociology and Social Anthropology Department at Central European University supported a semester's residency, and I continue to benefit from the relationships I made while in Budapest. A post-graduate school conversation with Michael D. Jackson about intellectualism as a vocation was both personally and theoretically impactful. I remain grateful for Michael's friendship.

The editorial staff at Palgrave -Macmillan were patient, skilled, and helpful. Hilary Kaell and Don Seeman, editors of the Anthropology of Religion book series, have been friends and champions of my research. I received the support of several generous institutions without which I could not have finished this book: Harvard University and Harvard Divinity School, the American Council of Learned Societies, the Unitarian Universalist Association's Panel on Theological Education, the Center for Theologically Engaged Anthropology, and the Working Group on Lived Religion in Eastern Europe and Eurasia. The Catholics & Cultures Program at the College of the Holy Cross has kept me connected to a vibrant intellectual community after offering me a generous Post-Doctoral Fellowship in 2016.

Over the years, friends, family, and religious communities offered valuable encouragement as I pushed ahead with this text and also pursued public scholarship: István Cziegler, Kate Y. DeConinck, Robert and Nóra Ferencz, Chris and Regina Walton, Nicolie Loustau, Sarah Langer and Rachel Fichtenbaum, Nathan and Amira Shulman, Abraham and Jaclyn Miller-Barbarow, the members of the Minns Lectures Steering Committee, King's Chapel and First Church in Boston for the gift of their pulpit and faithful guidance, Stephen and Liz Kendrick, Johannes, Leena, Devendra, and Anvidha Loustau, Kate Dugan, Kate and Ethan Handelman, Linda and Tom Dickey, Frank Karioris, Ezgican Özdemir, Alice Horning, Anne Loustau, Cayla Saret, Julia Hamilton and Adam Shive, Ari Shapiro, Erick Verran, Dan McKanan, James Bielo, Sara Williams, the editorial staff at *America: The Jesuit Review*, Allan Oliveira, Leah Varsano, Ariela Lovett, Cathy Wanner, Joel Robbins, Elizabeth and Jim Epstein, Sherill Stroschein, Zsuzsa Csergő, Frank Clooney, Valentina Napolitano, John Brooks and Laura Brooks Partain, Ben Legg, Emil Moldovan, Nándor Bárdi, Stefano Bottoni, Dénes Kiss, Seth and Amy Izen, and Deborah McConnell.

I am deeply indebted to the people I met in Transylvania and at the Our Lady of Csíksomlyó shrine.

My wife, Amy Loustau, once coined the phrase "book bonanza" to describe one of my marathon writing sessions. According to my dictionary, a bonanza is also a sudden increase in good fortune. That is an accurate description of what happened to me the first time we met.

My father, John A. Loustau, took such pride in the books he published at the end of his life. May his memory be a blessing.

Praise for *Hungarian Catholic Intellectuals in Contemporary Romania*

"In this intimate ethnographic account of the inner lives of Catholic thinkers and practitioners among the Hungarian-speaking minority of Romania, Marc Loustau humanizes theology for a discipline that has often treated it with suspicion. He sympathetically examines these local intellectuals' ethical and pedagogical dilemmas after the demise of state socialism and the uneven rise of consumerism on both sides of a culturally and ideologically conflicted border. This is a rich account of the sufferings and satisfactions, the rewards and reversals, of religious vocation under unending, shape-shifting siege."

—Michael Herzfeld, *Ernest E. Monrad Research Professor of the Social Sciences emeritus, Harvard University, USA*

"This is an exciting book. Loustau has given us a sustained exploration of the lives of engaged Catholic theologians who lead important educational and charitable projects among the Hungarian minority population of Romania. The first full length ethnography to take the intellectual life and practice of important Christian thinkers as its focus, the book is a milestone in the growing conversation between anthropology and theology. Along the way, the book also speaks powerfully to those interested in issues of volunteerism and right wing populism, both subjects appearing in fresh ways under Loustau's superb ethnographic eye. Written with great energy, this book should find a wide audience."

—Joel Robbins, *Sigrid Rausing Professor of Anthropology, University of Cambridge, UK*

"This exceptional study of Hungarian Catholics in Transylvania looks at how a minority's intellectual tradition is forged and transformed in the long 20th century. Bringing back 'intellectuals' as key actors in the relationship between state, church and minority politics it contributes to broader discussions about civic cultivation/ education, Christianity and nationhood in Central and Eastern Europe, and sheds light on the roots of contemporary Hungarian right-wing populism. Loustau's study of theologians and pedagogical institutions bridges historical analysis with a rich ethnography of Catholic devotionalism, provoking anthropologists to rethink their engagement with Christianity and theology in a more radical manner."

—Vlad Naumescu, *Associate Professor of Sociology and Social Anthropology, Central European University, Austria*

"In this fascinating book, Marc Loustau has managed the feat of conveying the contours of theological debates among Hungarian Catholics in Romania over the past century, with astounding mastery of the language and its nuances. He then pairs this account with the perspective of Hungarian-Romanian Catholic clergy and congregants today, as they grapple with challenges to their values that emerge from the necessity of appealing to their (wealthier) Hungarian ethnic kin, who come from Hungary on touristic pilgrimages to the "old lands." Highly recommended for anyone interested in how longer-term religious doctrine both affects and is affected by faith as it is practiced."

—Krisztina Fehérváry, *Associate Professor of Anthropology,*
University of Michigan, USA

"An important contribution not just to the study of Hungarian speaking communities but to the ethnography of intellectuals and their work. Loustau's skill as an ethnographer is reflected in a thematically rich discussion that is firmly grounded in Transylvanian life. His Conclusion and Epilogue will also surely spark broader—and necessary—discussions about the aims and scope of the anthropology of Christianity itself."

—Mathew N. Schmalz, *Professor of Religious Studies,*
College of the Holy Cross, USA

"Marc Loustau's fascinating account of a Hungarian Catholic tradition of intellectual life in Transylvania is both rich and strange. How has such a minority group survived, pre- and post- Communism, in Romania, and had such cultural and ethical impact in rural communities? The 'thick description' that Loustau provides makes a significant contribution to the burgeoning literature in 'Christian anthropology', and he is not afraid to engage theology itself to clarify how the idea of 'collaboration' between the divine and human has animated the movement. This study is as ethnographically meticulous as it is methodologically sophisticated."

—Sarah Coakley FBA, *Norris-Hulse Professor of Divinity* emerita,
University of Cambridge, UK

"Putting God's 'collaborative presence' at the centre, Loustau very aptly moves beyond ethical subject-centred readings of Transylvania Hungarian Catholicism to show the living practices of its theologians, educators, orphanage networks and choirs, and of knighthood orders and its relics. Loustau's critical ethnographic and theological engagement with affects of love, penitence, atonement and pride in the animation and subversion of missions, in a patronage and priestly charisma that reckons with the anxiety of post-socialist capitalist desires timely shows that a creativity of the Church's sacramental body can challenge a pervasive catholic humanitas paradigm, for too long complicit with European populist, exclusionary formations of cultural otherness."

—Valentina Napolitano, *Professor of Anthropology, University of Toronto, Canada*

CONTENTS

CHAPTER 1

Introduction: An Intellectual Tradition of Our Own

EXPANDING THE TRANSYLVANIAN HUNGARIAN INTELLECTUAL TRADITION

In late 2010, the Catholic priest Csaba Böjte, born into an ethnic Hungarian family in Romania, stood before reporters outside the parliament building in Budapest. He was in the Hungarian capital to accept a government award and announce a plan to collect donations via the state tax system. He called it a turning point for the Saint Francis Foundation (SFF), his Romania-based network of children's homes: "Over the last eight years, I have accepted no awards of any kind," he explained; "[a]fter all, this work is mine as a Transylvanian Hungarian" (Magnificat.ro 2010).[1] "Eight years" referred to the period during which a left-wing socialist party governed Hungary. Böjte was thus expressing a view, popularized by Hungarian political conservatives, that Hungary's left-wing socialists had neglected to support Romania's 1.5 million ethnic Hungarians while they were in power. During this period of apparent state abandonment, the SFF had come to symbolize ethnic minority intellectuals' responsibility to serve their own community.[2]

Times were changing, though. Earlier that year, Hungary's right-wing Fidesz Party had won a landslide electoral victory, partly by promising to support the Hungarian educational system in Romania. Böjte himself had spent the eight years of left-wing rule producing movie documentaries,

M. R. Loustau, *Hungarian Catholic Intellectuals in Contemporary Romania*, Contemporary Anthropology of Religion, https://doi.org/10.1007/978-3-030-99221-7_1

books, and radio and television programs appealing for such help. With new government accolades and access to the state's donation system that allowed citizens to set aside 1% of their taxes for specific charitable organizations, it seemed this effort was paying off. Still, Böjte was not ready to claim victory. He finished the speech on a hopeful but cautious note, suggesting that he anticipated further challenges. "Quite possibly," he concluded, "this is a sign that I am heading in the right direction."

Where I carried out fieldwork in a Hungarian ethnic minority enclave in Romania's Ciuc Valley, there is a vibrant state-funded Hungarian-language educational system, which receives additional support from the Hungarian government; but upon arriving in the area I also found a number of thriving educational NGOs that provide pedagogical assistance to rural Transylvanian Hungarians. In addition to Brother Csaba and his orphanages (Chap. 3), I researched a parish choir (Chap. 4), a knighthood order that models itself after lecture societies (Chap. 5), and a competing orphanage network run by a former Catholic priest (Chap. 6). The teachers I worked with thought of "serving the people" (népszolgálat), or volunteering to educate the rural populace, as the hallmark of a distinctively Transylvanian Hungarian pedagogical mode and rationale, and also the foremost sign of their ethnic minority and ethical self-consciousness.

With this cohort of volunteer rural intellectuals as my primary research subjects, this book is about a generation of teachers, their ethical and theological beliefs about intellectual service, and the opportunities and challenges they face as they reconstitute and expand these ideas to reach new audiences of volunteers. In more concrete terms, it is about a generation of Hungarian-speaking Catholic theologians from the 1930s and how their writings about reforming the Transylvanian Hungarian educational system are inspiring contemporary educators; and then how these educators, including Brother Csaba, further adapt these theologians' ideas to help other volunteers experience God's presence as a colloquy to performing charitable work in Transylvanian villages.

The basic premise of this ethnographic study of theologians' contributions to an educational reform initiative is that theologians ought to be understood and studied as intellectuals. I believe that the idea that contemporary theologians are influential educators and agentive, but certainly not all-powerful and self-sufficient, shapers of a national public culture will be theoretically generative for and open up subsequent trajectories of research in two social scientific fields: the anthropology of intellectuals and the anthropology of Christianity. The phenomenon of intellectuals construing a practice of rural educational service as "our own" intellectual tradition harkens back to Zygmunt Bauman's influential claim that every definition of the intellectual is always self-reflexive, constructive, and delineative. Whenever intellectuals write about intellectualism, says Bauman, "[it] is an attempt to draw a boundary of their own identity," a notion that in turn emerges from a sociological tradition identifying intellectuals with the project of guarding postcolonial national traditions and cultural knowledge (Bauman 1987b: 8; Coser 1965; Parsons 1969; Shils 1972).[3]

With the acknowledgment that intellectualisms always include and exclude, Bauman also points helpfully to the "conflict paradigm" that has greatly influenced the anthropology of intellectuals (Giesen 1998: 7–8). Intellectuals' agency arises in relationships between unequal sociostructural groups—an association between intellectualism and social contestation embedded in other characterizations of intellectual practice that refer to speaking truth to power (Said 1994; Spivak 1988) and inhabiting fields of knowledge production and authorization (Bourdieu 1991; Boyer 2003, 2005). A social and hermeneutic approach like Bauman's, as applied to this project about a group of Catholic theologians and educators, has the benefit of drawing attention to the content of Transylvanian Hungarian intellectuals' ideas—in this case, about the basis of selfhood—while also emphasizing the dynamics of power and domination that come into play in the formal practice of drawing social and group boundaries.

In the Transylvanian Hungarian intellectual tradition, as contemporary Catholic theologians construe it, ethnic minority selfhood takes shape in and through not only a rural populace or "people," but also a historically and socially situated mode of divine presence. Throughout this book, I call this "collaborative presence." In Chap. 2, I describe how interwar period Catholic theologians took up a notion of "collaborative presence" in conversation with their Reformed (Calvinist) colleagues, who preceded them in calling for a voluntaristic notion of pedagogical authority apt to the needs of the post-World War I Transylvanian Hungarian ethnic minority.

Catholics drew on the natural law ethical tradition as it appeared in Pope Pius XI's (1857–1939) authoritative theological statements to argue that educators work collaboratively with God in divinely ordained natural and social groups. God is present in a specific mode—in slow, patient, and arduous ethical labor to cultivate and perfect human beings in and through certain divinely ordained natural groups. Human beings perform their ethical action in these same groups. They labor in and through the same natural and social processes that manifest God's labor: thus, "collaborative presence." In this book's ethnographic chapters, I demonstrate that today

Catholic theologians continue to resinstrumentalize this notion of collab-orative presence in their agentive interventions in Hungarian national culture.

By highlighting this notion of collaborative presence, I build on Bauman's work and argue that talk about serving the people is a way that ethnic minority intellectuals reflect on the nature and basis of their iden-tity. However, by highlighting how Catholic theologians struggled to inject their own practice of revealing divine presence into an emerging ethnic minority intellectualism, I preempt Katherine Verdery's argument, in her classic work on Romanian nationalist historians, that intellectuals are engaged in a competition for cultural representativeness (Verdery 1991: 284–6). In short, presence comes before representation.

I make a similar move to use the intellectual practice of contemporary Catholic theologians to break open the anthropology of intellectuals' restrictively political appropriation of the Marxian-Gramscian tradition. To the extent that Catholic theologians have been included as a distinct social group worthy of study in this field, anthropologists have debated whether Catholic theologians are "radicals" who support revolutionary movements or, in Gramsci's view, "traditionalists" who advocate for a return to a medieval age of political economic organization (Gunderson 2010; Burdick 1998; Gramsci 1972; Feierman 1990: 26). By tracking the notion of divine presence, my account both complicates and cuts transversely across this unhelpfully polarized view of Catholic theologians' agency in public culture. Beyond both Bauman and Marx-Gramsci lies the cultural creativity of contemporary Catholic theologians who, when they urge readers to manifest their ethical and national self-consciousness in serving the people, carry with them the assumption that ethical and national self-hood emerges where human and divine activity mingle and collaborate.

This is not to say that the history of intellectuals in Europe, the social and political conditions of that process of intellectual self-definition, is irrelevant to understanding how Catholic theologians contribute to Transylvanian Hungarians' educational reform initiatives. To rephrase my argument vis-à-vis the anthropology of intellectuals: If we are to take Transylvanian Hungarian Catholic theologians' ideas about vocation on their own terms and follow where they lead, then we ought to emphasize just as much how intellectual self-creation transcends the work of safe-guarding tradition to become a socially and historically embedded process of boundary-crossing, boundaries that themselves were constructed within a modernizing discourse about church history, institutional form, and authority.[4]

When Hungarian-speaking theologians in Transylvania began demanding far-reaching reforms for their educational system, research on the history of the church and confessional polemics were closely related. The notion of reform by recreating an ideal period of Christian practice—the church of the early apostles—was associated with a post-Reformation understanding of ecclesiastical historical development in which the apostolic age acquired vital explanatory importance for anti-Catholic disputation. By the early twentieth century, generations of Protestant thinkers had argued that prior to the Reformation the Catholic Church had erred by embracing cultural and institutional decadence (Eire 2016; Cameron 2012; Bollbuck 2021; Bauer 2021). Catholics who wanted to make common cause with Protestants toward reforming educational institutions had to overcome skepticism from within their own community. To make their own mark on the emerging Transylvanian Hungarian intellectual tradition, they had to confront the tendency among some Catholics to react against calls for a new apostolic church—that is, for reforming ecclesiastical institutions—by closing ranks against "foreign" Protestant outsiders.

Bauman's claim that Eastern European intellectuals adopt an "inherently missionary" relationship toward the rural masses, which he compares to a "state of war against the 'lower' [culture]," also fails to capture the fact that rural teachers' work takes shape both in relation to the otherness they encounter among the peasantry and also in the equally destabilizing, if more ambiguously foreign, presence of Hungarian state representatives and ordinary Hungarian citizens (1987a: 173; see also Kligman and Verdery 2011). Following Bauman in viewing an intellectual tradition as a process of social identification, inclusion, and exclusion, I do not offer a substantive definition of the peasants. Rather than identifying peasants with smallholding farmers, I understand the peasantry—the "people" in the appellation "serving the people" (népszogálat) or the "folk" of "folk educator" (népnevelő)—to be a relational concept: whomever stands on the outside of the boundary drawn by intellectuals in their search for identity. In Steven Feierman's words, the concept of the peasant should open up "exploration of the relationship between the rural population and dominant strata," rather than speculation about the term's concrete demographic referent (1990: 24–5; see also Verdery 1983, 2003; Kligman and Verdery 2011).

Just as much, this social boundary should not be understood as fixed or even clear. In Chap. 4, for example, members of a parish choir, urban intellectuals who themselves were born and raised in villages, imagine the work of changing peasants' worship habits properly as a transformation they first made in their own lives. Transylvanian Hungarian volunteer teachers are even encouraged to encounter the peasant other in their own embodied and biographical selfhood. More importantly, Transylvanian Hungarian village teachers like Brother Csaba also conduct their pedagogy under the watchful and evaluative gaze of Hungarian citizens living within Hungary's borders, the people I call "Hungarians from Hungary."

I argue that contemporary consumer culture, which leads Transylvanian Hungarian intellectuals to defer to the authoritative tastes of Hungarians from Hungary, mediates ethnic minority intellectuals' effort to cultivate young peasants into virtuous village teachers, leading to a variety of unintended consequences for everyone involved. To grasp the social and institutional processes for negotiating the meaning of intellectual practice—meanings that go far beyond the righteous confidence of colonial missionaries or soldiers at war—I argue that we must break open the social relational locus of Eastern European pedagogical practice beyond the teacher-peasant binary.

Reforming Apostles

Although Transylvanian Hungarian public discourse is increasingly dominated by the notion that rural pedagogical volunteerism is a crucial manifestation of collective ethical self-consciousness, only recently have anthropologists begun focusing on the ideas through which Christians express and negotiate group identities. From Mathew Engelke writing about Zimbabwe's Friday Apostolics, who seek a live and direct relationship with God, to Joel Robbins on Papua New Guinean Pentecostals, who demur that belief cannot be shared, in Courtney Handman's words, "the refusal of sociality has become a central predicate of contemporary views of the Christian subject" (Handman 2015: 10; Engelke 2007; Robbins 2007).[5] In North American and European social contexts, anthropologists have also tended to see Christians as ethical arch-individualists. While studies of Christians' politics show that conservative Evangelicals use individual prayer to shape the national body, Handman has filled this lacuna with a cogent analysis of the ecclesiological logic, especially the idea of "the invisible and visible church" that lies behind Papuan New Guinean Pentecostals' practice of schism, or forming splinter denominational groups (Handman 2015: 56–60).[6]

My intervention into this emerging branch of research on groups and institutions within the anthropology of Christianity is a reminder that Christians' debates about institutional form are always caught up in modernizing discourses about the history of Christianity that define the apostolic period as authoritative. Additionally, during the interwar period, arguments for reforming the church by restoring its institutions to what they were during the age of the first apostles—claims that authority in the church should be based not on executing church doctrine but rather, like the apostles, on enacting a calling—were strongly associated with Protestant anti-Catholicism.

I argue that Catholics helped make the notion of serving the people authoritative by crossing confessional boundaries, in the process actively reconstructing practices of interconfessional polemics that had long shaped ideas about church institutional form. Thus, while Handman finds a Christian cultural logic behind Guhu-Samane Christians' tendency to deal with conflict through the formation of new denominations, such an account would be inadequate in the case of Transylvanian Hungarian Catholics for its inability to explain why certain institutional forms—in her case, denominations; in mine, apostolic house churches—become authoritative models for structuring new forms of Christian sociality. What is required, therefore, is an account of how Christian actors make particular imaginings of Christian groupism seem persuasive at certain socio-historical junctures.

Populist and national projects of Christian cultural and institutional reconstruction—like the effort to reform Transylvanian Hungarians' educational system—are provisional, partial, and unstable; they are subject to appropriation and reinstrumentalization by multiple institutions, leaving leaders wondering if the movement is serving their interests anymore.[7] Even as individuals profess their dedication to a movement, they often doubt privately, questioning their methods and if they will eventually achieve their goals. Seldom do reform initiatives receive funding solely from one institution that determines the norms by which failure and success are judged. Instead, such movements cross multiple social fields, which can shift relationships between differing groups of participants to reveal latent but destabilizing inequalities.

In the case of the effort to revive the Transylvanian Hungarian intellectual tradition, consumer culture and tourism is one such field. When Hungarians from Hungary approach Transylvanian Hungarian NGOs with a willingness to serve, they come as savvy consumers and tourists—wealthier ethnic kin secure in and eager to perform their middle-class status. Village intellectuals understand that many Transylvanian Hungarians perform menial labor for middle-class consumers, as construction workers, waiters, or door-to-door salespeople. But resentment about deferring to consumers' wishes can alienate the two groups and threaten to limit the support Hungarians from Hungary are prepared to give.

Throughout this book, I strive to show that the revival of the Transylvanian Hungarian intellectual tradition, which is populist by virtue of its core concept that the rural "people" are the basis of national self-hood, is subject to the same destabilizing conditions as many other reform movements. Recent research on Christian populist nationalism has how-ever yielded few signs that such movements are unstable and ever-in-progress. The right-wing Christian populist movements that have emerged in Europe since 2010 caught many social scientists off-guard, leading scholars to make claims about the nationalization (Ádám and Bozóki 2016), politicization, (Zúquete 2017), or hijacking of Christianity (Marzouki et al. 2016).[8] Furthermore, the anthropology of Christianity has lagged behind nationalism studies and political science in studying Christian populist nationalism, allowing scholars in these disciplines to set the parameters of research on this topic by drawing anthropologists into semantic debates over what *Christianity, populism,* and *nationalism* should refer to (see Brubaker 2011).

Using these terms, scholars have speculated about a good, pure, power-less, and universal Christianity, one that exists untouched by the state, as distinct from the politicized and corrupted Christianity of populist nation-alism.[9] Anthropologist Harry Englund's observation regarding the pre-scriptive thrust of ostensibly descriptive research on religious politics is apt here: Implicit in this body of literature is the belief that "[religion's] return to the public realm made it imperative to put the lid back on Pandora's box before religious passions would infuse the domains of public life" (Englund 2011: 1). Crypto-normative secularization theory also seems to inform influential theoretical statements about Christian intellectuals' role in the creation of national formations: Both Bauman and historian Bernhard Giesen strike a functionalist note when they write that intellec-tuals use nationalism to atavistically reject modernity, to construct the nation as a replacement religion complete with the pre-modern age's epis-temic certainty (Bauman 1987b: 90–5) and immutable group boundaries (Giesen 1998: 12).

Critics have charged that when scholars speculate about nationalism as a replacement religion, they rarely spend critical effort giving an empiri-cally cogent defense of whatever goes by the name "religion." The "reli-gion" that nationalism supposedly takes over is often essentialized, ahistorical, and reductive to such a degree that it is better to understand it not as an accurate description of actually existing Christian and national intellectual and social practice but rather as a product of the secular and liberal Enlightenment's paranoid fantasies about religious and political others (Omer 2015; Santiago 2012). By alternatively raging against or lamenting the return of Christianity to national politics, nationalism studies and political science have done little else than reframe the normative assumptions of secularization theory, demanding there be a functional differentiation of Christian and political institutions while claiming to document its demise.[10]

Instead of expressing fury or grief that theologians are involved in— indeed, are leaders of—Christian nationalist and populist movements, I try to understand the actual practice of their involvement as a form of creative religious agency that takes shape within the broader field of post-socialist consumer culture. In Chap. 3, I describe how Csaba Böjte uses an intimate tone to reveal God laboring beside spiritual seekers from Hungary who are serving Transylvanian Hungarian peasants. The Franciscan friar defers to the seekers' consumer preferences while also reviving that experience of God's presence associated with the Transylvanian Hungarian intellectual tradition.

This mediation through consumer culture also makes leaders in the Transylvanian Hungarian intellectual tradition subject to various unintended consequences, including social inequalities that have the potential to destabilize bonds of national solidarity between Transylvanian Hungarians and Hungarians from Hungary. Driven by secularization theory's implicitly moralistic categories, the latest research on Christianity, nationalism, and populism in Europe either overlooks such creativity or reinterprets the whole process in crass instrumentalist terms as the right-wing Hungarian government's effort to legitimize its rule. Such reinterpretations render religious agency unrecognizable on its own terms and badly misreads the dynamics of Transylvanian Hungarian Catholics' complexly deferential and agentive engagements in and with Hungarian public culture.

VIRTUES, VOLUNTEERS, CREATIVITY

Historian Nándor Bárdi has argued that the Transylvanian Hungarian intellectual tradition is a type of virtue ethics, a program of self-cultivation toward a culturally defined notion of the good life. In words that echo anthropologists' understanding of the core questions of the virtue ethics tradition, Bárdi writes that interwar Transylvanian Hungarian intellectuals sought to draw students, themselves future intellectuals, into a process of interrogating their personal becoming. The ethnic minority intellectual should ask, "not just who I am, but rather who should I become, what should direct my life, and how should I live so that I can accomplish the end that has been set out for me" (2015: 24).[11]

The former question sought out scientific knowledge of an immutable national character and essence, while the latter ones were directed toward emergent self-knowledge. The answer to these ethical investigations emerged, according to the interwar architects of the Transylvanian Hungarian intellectual tradition, in the task of teaching the people. Rural educational service—a perfect crucible for cultivating virtues like dedication, persistence, and responsibility—was the supreme act of self-conscious national subjects cultivating themselves toward the good.

Elements of this individualistic reading circulate in Transylvanian Hungarian public discourse, influencing the contemporary revival of the ethnic minority intellectual tradition; however, amid a growing effort by anthropologists to expand our understanding of the Christian practice of sociality, I note the manner in which interwar Catholic intellectuals defended a concept of vocation that allowed for institutional subjects to express God's call according to their naturally ordained properties and goals. In addition to emphasizing the servant intellectual's virtuousness, Catholic theologians argued that the Church itself, *qua* institution, had a distinctive divine vocation to teach the rural populace.

In the process of developing this premise—that God calls institutions to serve and thus accomplishes a reform process that returns the Church to a primitive, apostolic Christian sociality—they also adapted a post-Reformation modernizing discourse on the history of Christianity into the Transylvanian Hungarian Church. Catholic intellectuals still refer to village education as both an individual and institutional calling; and while this is to a certain degree a contradiction in terms, it is a contradiction they inherited as part of the bargain their theological forebears struck in order to play a part in reforming the Transylvanian Hungarian educational system.

In her monograph about a similar case of voluntaristic service, Andrea Muehlebach uses a study of an Italian state-supported eldercare program to construct a genealogy of Catholics' theological contributions to the neoliberal state's moral imaginary. In the process, Muehlebach seeks to demystify the Italian government's claim that the "vibrant culture of volunteering [is] supposedly 'natural' to the northern Italian territory" (2012: 113). In my research, I found that similar statements, when articulated by the right-wing Hungarian state, do indeed mystify the state's use of unpaid labor not only to integrate Transylvania's Hungarian educational system into the government's bureaucracy but also to lay claim to a border-transcending Christian national cultural identity.

Ciuc Valley intellectuals sometimes worry about whether the Hungarian state oversells their skills when officials appropriate their pedagogy for these different ends, and I document a case in which an ethnic minority teacher justifies walking away from educational NGO when it seems that others have betrayed the organization's mission in the process of seeking state patrons. While Muehlebach's genealogy illuminates how Catholic theologians' intellectual creativity unintentionally developed neoliberalism into a moral position, the neoliberal state's appropriative capacity also unfolds at this other level: within volunteers' understated affective expressions of misgiving as well as their post hoc verbal rationalizations. Indeed, ethnographic acuity is just as essential as genealogical insight in the study of neoliberal volunteerism, since the state extracts volunteers' labor by constructing face-to-face interactions as privileged contexts for performing voluntary service. In Muehlebach's case, these everyday interactions constitute relationships of caring presence for the elderly, while in mine they are relationships of educational cultivation for rural peasants.

However, I argue that the Marxian language of neoliberal "victimization" and "rebellion," which has influenced both Muehlebach's book and other accounts of state-supported volunteerism, should take a backseat as we develop a robustly detailed account of both the self-contradictions of volunteers' affective life and everyday voluntary practice's multiple and ambiguous meanings.[12] On one hand, middle-class and urban Transylvanian Hungarian volunteer teachers do not act like rebellious and exploited victims toward the Hungarian state. On the other, they do not uncritically cheer the Hungarian government's effort to appropriate their labor for its own agenda.

Instead, they apprehend their somewhat in-between position—not quite helplessly dependent on the state and not quite able to determine the state's goals—in expressions of halfhearted approval and anxious, skeptical laughter. For example, the singers in the volunteer parish choir I describe in Chap. 4 accepted a right-wing Christian political party's offer to pay for the choir to tour Hungary but laughed about a party leader's ridiculously hyperbolic statement that they were famous throughout Europe as a crowning achievement of Hungarian Christian culture. Beyond rebellious opposition to the state, volunteers laughed, harbored misgivings, and combined an internally oriented sense of inadequacy with an externally oriented uncomfortable awareness of authoritative others' unrealistic expectations. The very success of the historical genealogy of Catholic theology's contributions to neoliberal morality makes it more necessary to develop equally effective ethnographic accounts of the everyday contexts in which the state enacts its appropriation, a need in response to which I offer my own attempt at a fulsomely thick description of Transylvanian Hungarian volunteers' ambiguous affects and unfolding meanings.

In this chapter, I have referred repeatedly to creativity; I take creativity to be a socially situated human practice, which, in the Transylvanian Hungarian case that I am concerned with in this book, intellectuals take up in those social situations when they are made aware of the educational reform movement's instabilities. Partly because the effort to remake the Transylvanian Hungarian educational system is a work in progress and new initiatives to teach the people are mediated across multiple social fields—including and especially post-socialist consumer culture—educational leaders often find themselves occupied by doubts as well as practical uncertainties. Indeed, the Transylvanian Hungarian intellectual tradition's architects of the early twentieth century seemed to anticipate both the unintended consequences and creative processes educators are frequently caught up in. Interwar Catholic theologians spoke to village teachers about trials, setbacks, and hardships; they demanded tirelessness and resourcefulness in the face of inevitable failures; and they praised virtues like persistence and loyalty. The virtuous intellectual, Bárdi writes, showed "commitment to the work that they have taken on and Christian perseverance in bearing its difficulties" (Bárdi 2015: 26).

Like Catholic theologians of the interwar period, today's Transylvanian Hungarian Catholic writers exhort teachers to see their own responses to these challenges as tests of personal virtue, signs of the nation's mature self-consciousness, and, as I show in my ethnographic chapters, opportunities to reveal God's collaborative presence. This is one way that volunteer educators engage the instabilities that afflict and animate their educational initiatives. While some intellectuals find ways to ignore these doubts, others invent dramatic new pedagogical initiatives that prove they still have a calling; still others fill new positions in educational NGOs that seek to grow their programs. I use *creativity* to refer to these and other efforts that on an interpersonal level open up possibilities for teachers to defend, sustain, and reformulate their vocation, even as this creative labor also strengthens their identification with the region-wide movement to reform the ethnic minority educational system.

My inclination to take seriously the social consequences of intellectuals' doubt, the instability of their reform initiatives, and the creativity that seeks to envelop and contain these phenomena leads me to part ways with an influential body of anthropological literature on Christian intellectuals after socialism. Over the last thirty years, anthropologists working in various Eastern European states—such as Romania until 1989, governed by officially atheist socialist regimes—have made insightful use of the method of historical ethnography to explain how socialist-atheist culture has influenced religious revivals in the region.[13] Anthropologists have written about how socialism affected levels of religious knowledge (Lindquist 2006; Pelkmans 2009; Abrahms-Kavunenko 2015; Højer 2009); types of religious folklore (Hann and Pelkmans 2009; Peyrouse 2004); relations between priests and believers (Halemba 2015); religious concepts (Ssorin-Chaikov 2008); the general understanding of what religion is about (McBrien and Pelkmans 2008; Steinberg and Wanner 2008); relations between local practice and politics (Kligman 1988); and how people understand their roles within religious institutions (Halemba 2015; Abrahms-Kavunenko 2012). The field's central problematic, according to anthropologist Douglas Rogers, is "the question of whether present-day phenomena are best understood as holdovers or legacies of the socialist past or responses to new circumstances" (Rogers 2009: 299).

One response to this problematic has been to conduct historical research about a particular religious practice in order to judge its relative degree of novelty or conventionality—a way of asking how meanings and practices change when they are taken up in new cultural contexts. For a while, this historical ethnographic approach to post-socialist religion was highly generative, but today much research in this field feels like an infinite historical regress in search of precedents.

To avoid this fate, I have taken up the latter of Rogers's questions. Thus I write about the revival of an interwar tradition under the new conditions of post-socialist consumer inequality; in Chap. 4 I describe how parish choir members embody the ethical value of civilization they learned in socialist-era cultural institutions, cultivating this civilization as a means of reforming the central act of worship in the Catholic Church: the sacrament of the Mass. However, I do so without the assumption built into the very way Rogers frames the inquiry, that anthropologists have the final say in determining whether a religious practice is new or old, or that by answering this question, we have fully accounted for the potential meanings a practice may come to have for religious subjects.

Adopting Elizabeth Hallam and Tim Ingold's "pathways" approach to studying creative processes seems more evocative of the anthropology of intellectuals' inherently self-reflexive, intersubjective complexity, a complexity that would destabilize any attempt I might make to step outside Transylvanian Hungarian intellectuals' field of debate to impose my determination about how the past actually shapes the meaning of a religious practice. Hallam and Ingold propose, "to follow the paths along which such [creative] projections take shape." (Hallam and Ingold 2007: 3). Besides tracking the choir's reorientation of a socialist-era civilizing practice, this leads me in other chapters to present biographical narratives about village teachers who, for various reasons, saw their educational initiatives disrupted, distorted, or displaced; I then describe, based on my own on-site observation, how these intellectuals took account of, responded to, and sought to continue the work of intellectual service in light of their failures.

The subject matter of Chap. 4, a church choir's engagement with the atheist regime's civilizational ethics, evokes Sonja Luehrmann's influential study of intellectuals "recycling" socialist pedagogical methods, what she refers to as "the laborious process by which people transform these skills, habits [...] and make them usable in a context for which they were not intended" (2005: 44). Where I part ways with Luehrmann is her claim that, amid the collapse of the Soviet Union and the declining political power of teachers' unions, intellectuals shored up their weakened social and economic position by joining churches and reorienting their skills (Luehrmann 2005: 41). I argue that the question of religious volunteerism's benefits should not be measured externally as a social fact of group economic standing but rather within religious intellectuals' engagement with authoritative forms of cultural otherness. In Chap. 3, for example, I show how Brother Csaba addresses the question as to whether village teachers ought to anticipate rewards for their service; he does so in order to meet, though also change, the expectations of authoritative spiritual consumers in Hungary.

In the end, I question the assumption that post-socialist religion should either help or hurt its followers, choosing instead to follow the architects of the Transylvanian Hungarian intellectual tradition in exploring how intellectuals strive to sustain their activity, to maintain their work in socially recognizable and authoritative ways. An interwar theologian who helped imagine the Transylvanian Hungarian intellectual tradition once wrote that the academic journal he helped found, *Transylvanian School*, "is the journal for those who instead of giving in to a death-like exhaustion, embrace the driving fever of [pedagogical] work" (Márton 1934: 106). In other words, in the face of every educator's inevitable shortcomings, virtue lies not in economic benefits but rather persistence. Thus, the goals intellectuals embrace—to make "our own" Transylvanian Hungarian intellectual tradition, help future generations of intellectuals identify with it, revive it under new conditions, and address it to new populations— sometimes accord with but often swing free of individuals' efforts to improve their class position; that is, to count the benefits and costs of religious participation.

While Luehrmann refers to the laborious process of recycling atheist pedagogy and even quotes former Soviet atheist teachers confessing their sins and requesting forgiveness, she claims that these petitions have no social impact on Christian intellectuals' pedagogy since their churches believe that history is predestined (2011: 72). This interpretive move is a breathtaking dismissal of lived experience in favor of official doctrine, but it also betrays Luehrmann's own thesis that recycling atheist pedagogy is laborious, since dealing with sin, guilt, and doubt is surely also work. Given Luehrmann's thesis about laboring to make the transition from atheism to Christianity, that she does not give a fuller account of these moments is an oversight and shows us the limitations of projects that attempt to explain successful outcomes of the transition from socialism. As a result, it does not ask how the work of repairing Christian revival movements' deep instabilities devolves, as a manifestation of power, onto certain socially situated groups of individuals. By highlighting the creativity involved in responding to the unintended consequences of institutions' educational initiatives, I hope to provide this field of study with several counterexamples and a corrective reemphasis.

PLAN OF THIS BOOK

My argument that Catholic theologians are, in fact, intellectuals extends across five chapters, a conclusion, and an epilogue. Chapter 2 is a historical review of how "serving the people" became an organizing concept in the emergent Transylvanian Hungarian intellectual tradition, while the subsequent four chapters comprise the book's ethnographic heart. Each of these chapters has a title that indicates the ethical virtue that the group in question cultivates in and through intellectuals' educational practice: For the SFF's children's homes, love; for Catholic parish choirs, composure;

for the Knighthood Order of the Holy Crown, courtliness; and for a separate orphanage network, the Black Sheep Foundation, penitence.

In the concluding chapter, I describe how these educational organizations and their leaders have fared since I completed my fieldwork. I tell this story based on the organizations' responses to an article I published in the U.S.-based Catholic magazine, *America: The Jesuit Review*, urging Pope Francis to denounce right-wing nationalist populism during his 2019 visit to Transylvania. In the Epilogue, I excerpt from my ethnographic field journal in an extended mediation on scholarly identity. These writings were informed by fieldwork in communities that engage in Catholic prayer practices and recent theoretical innovations in theologically engaged anthropology.

In Chap. 2, "Vocation," I examine the discursive and imaginative space created by the journal *Transylvanian School*, founded by prominent Catholic intellectuals in the 1930s, and track the journal's role in the post-World War I formation of the Transylvanian Hungarian intellectual tradition. In the second half of the chapter, I consider how two institutions, dormitories and choirs, became hallmarks of the tradition's effort to recreate the ecclesiastical institutions of the early Christian apostolic age. I rely on primary source materials by those interwar Catholics today identified with the Transylvanian Hungarian intellectual tradition; in particular, I highlight the historical contexts for their use of Protestant theological tropes, most notably the return to the primitive and pure apostolic form of Christianity. Against a historical background in which this was a central trope of Protestant-Catholic boundary-constituting polemics, the journal *Transylvanian School* not only erected boundaries around a project of intellectual self-definition but also created processes for risky interconfessional conceptual borrowing and adaptation.

In Chap. 3, "Love," I take Brother Csaba's orphanages to be successors to the dormitories Catholic theologians envisioned during the interwar period. Brother Csaba himself is the foremost contemporary interpreter of the Transylvanian Hungarian intellectual tradition, which he updates by encouraging Hungarians from Hungary to volunteer at his orphanages. I conduct a socially situated analysis of the content and theological poetics of Brother Csaba's published works aimed at this group. I extend my findings using an ethnographic account of a volunteer garden renovation project that I attended at a SFF orphanage. As a participant with a group from Hungary, I observed Brother Csaba organize the event, help us demolish, dig, and plant, and give twice-daily lectures. This ethnographic data drives my account of the creativity enacted in this outreach effort: the revelation of a Catholic mode of collaborative presence in spiritual seekers' personal lives.

Chapter 4, "Composure," offers an up-close look at Catholic parish choirs, which interwar educators once promoted as the keystone institutional vehicle for cultivating emotional forms of ethnic minority solidarity. I use observations from my time spent as a member of the Csíksomlyó Catholic shrine's volunteer choir. Composed yet emotionally dynamic and intense musical expression, or virtuous singing, was interwar choirs' goal. Today, teaching Catholics to sing virtuously also enables them to carry forward the socialist-era project of civilizing the peasantry, an effort that constitutes a mode of ethical creativity. Along the way, the Szekler cultural revival, promoted by the Transylvanian Hungarian-dominated county government, threatens to destabilize virtuous singing when the choir finds itself drawn into performances of "uncivilized" rural masculinity.

Chapter 5, "Courtliness," looks at a Transylvanian Hungarian teaching group, the Knighthood Order of the Holy Crown. As another example of creativity agency to sustain and expand the Transylvanian Hungarian intellectual tradition, the Knighthood Order's members organize village lectures about King Stephen (975–1038), a Hungarian saint and monarch who converted his kingdom to Christianity. By using small-scale events in rural locales to teach King Stephen's virtuous courtliness, I argue that they thus extend the cult[14] to Transylvania by injecting it with the Transylvanian Hungarian intellectual tradition's primitive institutional forms, which harken back to the apostolic age, as well as its characteristic ethical themes.

This chapter's latter half presents an ethnographic biographical portrait of Emil, a former director of his village's House of Culture. Before taking this educational position, Emil had previously worked in a now-shuttered copper mine. Together, we turned his biographical narrative about petitionary prayer into a university lecture that I presented in Hungary; but in the process, Emil struggled to convert an account of his working-class identity into a story that would solidify his new intellectual identity. Eventually, he renounced the narrative altogether. I argue that this renunciation was a creative response through which Emil deepened his identification with the Transylvanian Hungarian intellectual tradition.

Chapter 6, "Penitence," returns to the present-day version of the urban dormitories for rural students imagined by interwar Catholic theologians. In this case study, I examine another Transylvanian orphanage network, the Black Sheep Foundation. I examine a new initiative by the NGO's founder, Father Pál, to erect a shrine to the Holy Crown of King Stephen on a hillside at Csíksomlyó. This project, conducted by a group of volunteers Father Pál recruited from Hungary, took place after the Catholic Archdiocese of Transylvania (Alba Iulia) suspended Father Pál from the priesthood. Although in interviews he referred to the shrine as a "place of penitence," its overlarge design effectively muted this ethical message; and while the Archdiocese's punishment gave Father Pál a new appreciation for the value of public performances of atonement, he was also aware that post-socialist Hungarians are reluctant to submit themselves to priests' demands for penitence. To get around these contradictions and still exhort Hungarian audiences to perform labor for their sins, he made his call to penitence an optional aspect of visitors' journey to the hillside site.

FIELDWORK AND METHOD

My fieldwork centered on groups of Transylvanian Hungarian Catholic educators in Romania's Ciuc Valley. Sixty kilometers long and ten kilometers at its widest point, the Ciuc Valley is formed by the Olt River, which flows southward through the eastern Carpathian Mountains. I was initially based in the Ciuc Valley's largest city, Miercurea Ciuc, with a population of 40,000. Over 90% of the valley's total population of 109,478 identified themselves as Hungarian on the 2011 census, with the remaining 10% identifying as Romanian (Kozán 2013).[15] Transylvania's overall Hungarian population is equally divided between Catholics and Protestants, with the census reporting 600,000 Reformed (Calvinist) believers and half a million Catholics (Negruți 2014). In contrast, nearly 95% of Ciuc's population is Catholic. Ciuc Valley villages are even more homogenously Hungarian, and for the second portion of my fieldwork I relocated to a rural settlement with a census population of 6000, including twenty-four ethnic Romanians (Erdélystat.com 2020).

The Ciuc Valley is also known as an enclave of ethnic Szeklers, a group that during the Habsburg Empire enjoyed legal privileges as colonists and imperial border guards.[16] Over the nineteenth century, the Hungarian state within the Austro-Hungarian Empire successfully integrated Hungarian-speaking Szeklers into a national society.[17] The contemporary sense of Szekler cultural distinctiveness emerged in the last century via a state-driven ethnic cultural revival the history of which I outline in Chap. 4. The revival that most shaped Ciuc Valley residents' practice of identifying with Szekler culture was spearheaded by county-level socialist government administrators in Miercurea Ciuc. Today's Szeklers are part of a larger Transylvanian Hungarian community making up approximately 6% of Romania's overall population.

In the epilogue, "Witnessing the Rosary's Voice," I offer an extended reflection on the Catholic practice of praying the Rosary and its influence on my method for researching in a community that combines petitionary prayer with evangelism. I relocated to the Ciuc Valley for extended fieldwork in September 2009, where I remained until January 2012. I returned for the summer of 2012 and then again multiple times in 2013 while in residence at Central European University in Budapest, Hungary. I conducted interviews on site again in 2016 and 2018. Finally, I did archival research in the National Archives of Hungary in Budapest as well as archdiocesan archives in Transylvania.

In addition to extensive participant observation, I conducted approximately one hundred formal interviews with intellectuals of all kinds: government employees, elected officials, teachers, archdiocesan leaders, and priests. The organizations that I write about welcome volunteers, and as a result, I had little difficulty overcoming institutional barriers to access. Language posed an informal barrier to participant observation. I conducted fieldwork in both Romanian and Hungarian with both Romanian- and Hungarian-speaking Catholics. In Ciuc Valley Catholic institutions, Hungarian is the language of pedagogy, which made Hungarian my dominant fieldwork language. I have no Hungarian ancestry; I spoke Hungarian with an accent unusual to my acquaintances' ears and which they often had a hard time placing. After three years of daily use, I also became proficient in the Ciuc Valley's distinctive repertoire of colloquialisms, rhythms, and styles. A volunteer from Budapest once tried to locate my linguistic practice by guessing that I was a Hungarian from Hungary who was pretending to be from the Ciuc Valley (and not quite succeeding). When people would eventually learn that my grandfather, from whom I inherited my last name, was French and Catholic, this made sense in the same terms that have traditionally made Catholic religious affiliation an element of ethnocultural belonging.

I also introduced myself as an anthropologist (*antropológus*) and an ethnologist (*néprajz kutató*). I received my graduate training at Harvard Divinity School in a theology and religious studies program where my direct professional mentors were anthropologists. Within a Transylvanian Hungarian context, where several well-known Catholic priests have done ethnographic research, this intellectual background seemed reasonable enough to the people I spoke with (Daczó 2000; Loustau 2021). It proved confusing only when they then assumed I would have the same methods and goals of ethnologists, and would want to meet with headscarf-wearing old ladies to record Hungarian national genres of folk songs and stories.

I was raised Unitarian Universalist. Although there is an indigenous Transylvanian Hungarian Unitarian Church, which made this category familiar to many Ciuc Valley Catholics, it also inspired some to evangelize in a manner not altogether different from Transylvanian Hungarians' ethical outreach to their ethnic kin. Much of my fieldwork took place at the Ciuc Valley's Csíksomlyó Hungarian national shrine to the Virgin Mary. Some Miercurea Ciuc-based devotees of Our Lady of Csíksomlyó view the Rosary, a type of memorized prayer text recited while holding a string of prayer beads, as an evangelistic tool. Like Catholic women around the world, devotees see the evangelistic dimension of this practice in relation to intimate social bonds—as a way to express their sense of obligation to family members and a means to help lackadaisically faithful husbands, sons, and relatives become devout (Peña 2011; Kaell 2014). From this practice, it was a short leap to see me, an unmarried Protestant man, as an evangelistic target; after one of my first choir rehearsals at Csíksomlyó, a member invited me to the group in her Miercurea Ciuc neighborhood. While I did not convert, I got to know members of these groups well and they became an important social network early in my fieldwork.

Rightfully, the discussion I include in the epilogue should begin here, for the epilogue picks up this thread about identity, method, and Catholic prayer. Certainly, you are free to read the book sequentially, starting next with Chap. 2. But you might also skip ahead to read the epilogue before the rest of the book; the epilogue not only draws out this methodological thread, but gives it a twist. While the preceding paragraphs are a highly conventional account of fieldwork method in the anthropology of Christianity, such accounts are profoundly reductive.[18] The notion that overcoming barriers to access depends on how one's identity fits cultural categories is a limited and limiting way to think about the practice of writing ethnography in a Catholic community that uses Marian petitionary prayer for evangelism.

The epilogue shows that insights from the anthropological engagement with theology open up new avenues for witnessing to divine presence in ethnographic field journaling. Reading ahead to the epilogue will hopefully make the other chapters richer, helping them to develop new and still more redolent meanings. I suspect your understanding of the text will be deeper—perhaps like some of those who visited Father Pál's Holy Crown shrine found a richer spiritual experience when they happened on the diminutive sign instructing them to offer penitential acts. So I invite you to flip forward, if you feel like it.

NOTES

1. Although Brother Csaba started founding orphanages in the early 1990s, the Saint Francis Foundation was formally registered as an NGO in 2002 (Hungarian Catholic Mission 2011).
2. This was, of course, a contestable claim. From another perspective, the left-wing government had provided significant financial support for a network of educational NGOs in Romania. After 2010, Fidesz simply shifted funding to different organizations. For example, early on during my fieldwork, Fidesz stopped funding the Hungarian University Institute of Cluj (Kolozvári Magyar Egyetemi Intézet), which was attached to Cluj's official state (multilingual) Babeş-Bolyai University. Fidesz then shifted this money to Sapientia University while installing political allies as directors of this separate Hungarian-language university in Romania. In general, Fidesz began supporting organizations under its direct control and, following through on its promise to support Christian education, also shifted funding to church-based institutions like Brother Csaba's SFF.
3. Bárdi, Filep, and Lőrincz seem to take the latter position based on their view that the Transylvanian Hungarian intellectual tradition is dedicated to the preservation and protection of the community's own cultural life (2015: 22).
4. This approach is over and against claims by anthropologists like Feierman that peasant intellectuals are characterized not by their thought but by their social position (Feierman 1990: 5).
5. In the anthropology of ethics, the subjective turn was born out of the Aristotelian tradition of virtue ethics as interpreted by Catholic theological ethicist Alasdair McIntyre and philosopher Michel Foucault, who famously defined ethics as the self's relation to itself: how we "govern" our conduct in an effort to "transform oneself into the ethical subject of one's behavior" (1990: 27). Zigon's (2007, 2008, 2009a, b, c, d, 2013, 2014) work on "remaking moral subjectivity" in post-Soviet Russia exemplifies research from a variety of ethnographic contexts in which anthropologists have identified the individual self as pedagogy's primary locus. See also Throop and Mattingly 2018; Mattingly 2012; Kleinman 2006; Laidlaw 2013; Hirschkind 2006; Mahmood 2004; Faubion 2001, 2011.

6. For examples of studies of evangelical Christian prayer and nationalism, see Bialecki 2017; O'Neill 2009.
7. These points draw on research on Catholic social movements by Burdick 1998.
8. See also references to quasi-religious radical ideologies (Szilágy 2011; Buzogány and Varga 2018); religiously inflected populist styles (Levy 2018); sacralization of the nation and people (Minkenberg 2015; Koesel 2014; DeHanas and Shterin 2018); culturalization of religion (Brubaker 2017); or religious interventions into politics and policy (Grzymala-Busse 2015). This is not to mention scholars who embrace an analogical approach—which compares nationalism to religion but ends up radically reducing these socially and culturally diverse phenomena. In Brubaker's words, "Because both 'nationalism' and 'religion' can designate a whole world of different things, few statements about nationalism per se or religion per se, or the relation between the two, are likely to be tenable, interesting or even meaningful" (2011: 2).
9. See, for instance, Ádám and Bozóki's claim that, "Christianity in this context rather signifies a degree of social conservatism and traditional nationalism than expressing any substantive religious reference" (Ádám and Bozóki 2016: 108).
10. Documenting social scientists' moralistic outrage at Christian theologians' involvement in conservative politics suggests that we should reconsider Bauman's thesis about the shifting role of intellectuals in post-modernity. Modern intellectuals were state-embedded legislators and crafters of political policy, Bauman argued, whereas the declining significance of the nation-state under post-modernity has turned intellectuals into interpreters of free-flowing cultures (Bauman 1987b). This distinction between political legislators and apolitical interpreters remains relevant today to the extent that liberal secular social scientists deploy it as a moral demand incumbent upon conservative Christian intellectuals.
11. See Laidlaw 2002, 2013; Mattingly 2012, 2013; Lambek 2008; Zigon 2008; Zigon and Throop 2014; Faubion 2001.
12. Muehlebach writes about eldercare volunteers who experience such misgivings, yet in her account of an NGO's training session for prospective volunteers, she describes how trainees feel unease and claims that their questions to their teacher are a "minor rebellion" (2012: 128). This vignette, in a section subtitled "Doubt," exemplifies at an ethnographic level Italy's "often unruly, skeptical citizenry" (2012: 129). However, these terms problematically over-render volunteers' discomfort. If rebellion is not categorically different from doubt, the two are quantitatively different and that to a highly significant degree.

13. Agnieszka Halemba has characterized the study of religion after socialism as the study of "the differential impact of socialism on various aspects of religious life" (2015: 15).
14. While cult has taken on a pejorative sense, for Catholics it remains a technical appellation meaning the shared practice of devotion to a saint. I use "cult" in the latter sense.
15. Alongside the Saxon (Lutheran) church, Transylvania's Hungarian churches were recognized as "received" churches, in which their clergies benefited from full and equal rights. Romanians, who constituted a majority of Transylvania's entire population by the mid-eighteenth century, had no equivalent rights and those denominations closely associated with Romanians (Orthodox, Greek-Catholic) remained "tolerated" (Verdery 1983).
16. In addition to Szeklers, German-speaking Saxons and the nobility were the three recognized *nationes* of Transylvania (a term that meant something different than our contemporary "nations"), each of whom enjoyed collective political rights, liberties, and immunities as colonists and border guards for the kingdom (Brubaker et al. 2007: 58).
17. Historical documents suggest that by the sixteenth century Szeklers had linguistically assimilated into the wider Hungarian-speaking population of Transylvania (Brubaker et al. 2007: 59).
18. The formula for the typical "Methods" section goes like this: An informant asks the anthropologist about ethnic and religious identity; the anthropologist's response makes sense according to the informant's categories; there are a few complications; but these do not prevent the anthropologist from fitting in, making friends, and eventually conducting a successful research project. End of section. See, for instance, Luehrmann 2011: 21–2; Kaell 2014: 23–24; Lester 2005: 28–29.

References

Abrahms-Kavunenko, Saskia. 2012. Religious 'Revival' After Socialism? Eclecticism and Globalisation Amongst Lay Buddhists in Ulaanbaatar. *Inner Asia* 14 (2): 279–297.
———. 2015. The Blossoming of Ignorance: Uncertainty, Power and Syncretism Amongst Mongolian Buddhists. *Ethnos* 80 (3): 346–363.
Ádám, Zoltán and András Bozóki. 2016. State and Faith: Right-Wing Populism and Nationalized Religion in Hungary. *Intersections: East European Journal of Society and Politics* 2 (1): 98–122.

Bárdi, Nándor. 2015. A népszolgálat genezise és tartalomváltozása. In *Népszolgálat: A közösségi elkötelezettség alakváltozatai a magyar kisebbségek történetében* [Service to the People: The Elementary Forms of Community Commitment in the History of the Hungarian Minority], eds. Nándor Bárdi, Tamás Gusztáv Filep, and József D. Lőrincz, 11–48. Pozsony: Kalligram Kiadó.

Bárdi, Nándor, Tamás Gusztáv Filep, and József D. Lőrincz. 2015. Bevezető [Introduction]. In *Népszolgálat: A Közösségi Elkötelezettség Alakváltozatai A Magyar Kisebbségek Történetében* [Service to the People: The Elementary Forms of Community Commitment in the History of the Hungarian Minority], 2–10. Pozsony: Kalligram Kiadó.

Bauer, Stefan. 2021. The Uses of History in Religious Controversies from Erasmus to Baronio. *Renaissance Studies* 35 (1): 9–23.

Bauman, Zygmunt. 1987a. Intellectuals in East-Central Europe: Continuity and Change. *East European Politics and Societies and Cultures* 1 (2): 162–186.

———. 1987b. *Legislators and Interpreters: On Modernity, Post-Modernity and Intellectuals*. Cambridge: Polity Press.

Bialecki, Jon. 2017. Eschatology, Ethics, and Ēthnos: Ressentiment and Christian Nationalism in the Anthropology of Christianity. *Religion and Society* 8 (1): 42–61.

Bollbuck, Harald. 2021. Searching for the True Religion: The Church History of the *Magdeburg Centuries* Between Critical Methods and Confessional Polemics. *Renaissance Studies* 35 (1): 100–117.

Bourdieu, Pierre. 1991. *Homo Academicus*. Stanford: Stanford University Press.

Boyer, Dominic. 2003. Censorship as a Vocation: The Institutions, Practices, and Cultural Logic of Media Control in the German Democratic Republic. *Comparative Studies of Society and History* 45 (3): 511–545.

———. 2005. *Spirit and System: Media, Intellectuals, and the Dialectic in Modern German Culture*. Chicago: University of Chicago Press.

Brubaker, Rogers. 2011. Religion and Nationalism: Four Approaches. *Nations and Nationalism* 18 (1): 2–20.

———. 2017. Between Nationalism and Civilizationism: The European Populist Moment in Comparative Perspective. *Ethnic and Racial Studies* 40 (8): 1191–1226.

Brubaker, Rogers, Margit Feischmidt, Jon Fox, and Liana Grancea. 2007. *Nationalist Politics and Everyday Ethnicity in a Transylvanian Town*. Princeton: Princeton University Press.

Burdick, John. 1998. *Blessed Anastacia: Women, Race, and Popular Christianity in Brazil*. New York: Routledge.

Buzogány, Aron, and Mihai Varga. 2018. The Ideational Foundations of the Illiberal Backlash in Central and Eastern Europe: The Case of Hungary. *Review of International Political Economy* 6: 811–828.

Cameron, Euan. 2012. *The European Reformation*. Oxford: Oxford University Press.

Coser, Lewis. 1965. *Men of Ideas: A Sociologist's View*. New York: Free Press.

Daczó, Árpád. 2000. *Csíksomlyó titka: Mária-tisztelet a néphagyományban* [The Secret of Csíksomlyó: Marian Devotionalism in Folk Tradition]. Miercurea Ciuc: Pallas-Akadémia.

DeHanas, Daniel Nilsson, and Marat Shterin, eds. 2018. *Religion and the Rise of Populism*. London: Routledge.

Eire, Carlos. 2016. *Reformations. The Early Modern World, 1450–1650*. New Haven: Yale University Press.

Engelke, Matthew. 2007. *A Problem of Presence: Beyond Scripture in an African Church*. Berkeley: University of California Press.

Englund, Harri. 2011. *Christianity and Public Culture in Africa*. Athens: Ohio University Press.

Erdélystat.com. 2020. Csíkszentdomokos. (Sândominic). http://statisztikak.erdelystat.ro/adatlapok/csikszentdomokos/1446

Faubion, James. 2001. Toward an Anthropology of Ethics: Foucault and the Pedagogies of Autopoiesis. *Representations* 74: 83–104.

———. 2011. *An Anthropology of Ethics*. Cambridge: University Press.

Feierman, Steven. 1990. *Peasant Intellectuals: Anthropology and History in Tanzania*. Madison, Wis.: University of Wisconsin Press.

Foucault, Michel. 1990. Morality and Practice of the Self. In *History of Sexuality Vol. 2: The Use of Pleasure*, ed. Robert Hurley. New York: Vintage Books.

Giesen, Bernhard. 1998. *Intellectuals and the Nation: Collective Identity in a German Axial Age*. Cambridge: Cambridge University Press.

Gramsci, A. 1972. *Selections from the Prison Notebooks of Antonio Gramsci*. New York: International Publishers.

Grzymala-Busse, Anna. 2015. *Nations Under God: How Churches Use Moral Authority to Influence Policy*. Princeton: Princeton University Press.

Gunderson, C. 2010. "The making of organic indigenous-campesino intellectuals: catechist training in the diocese of San Cristóbal and the roots of the Zapatista uprising", Coy, P.G. (Ed.) *Research in Social Movements, Conflicts and Change* (Research in Social Movements, Conflicts and Change, Vol. 31), Emerald Group Publishing Limited, Bingley, pp. 259–295. https://doi.org/10.1108/S0163-786X(2011)0000031011

Halemba, Agnieszka. 2015. *Negotiating Marian Apparitions: The Politics of Religion in Transcarpathian Ukraine*. Budapest: Central European University Press.

Hallam, Elizabeth, and Tim Ingold, eds. 2007. *Creativity and Cultural Improvisation*. London: Routledge.

Handman, Courtney. 2015. *Critical Christianity: Translation and Denominational Conflict in Papua New Guinea*. Berkeley: University of California Press.

Hann, Chris, and Mathijs Pelkmans. 2009. Realigning Religion and Power in Central Asia: Islam, Nation-State and (Post)socialism. *Europe – Asia Studies* 61 (9): 1517–1541.

Hirschkind, Charles. 2006. *The Ethical Soundscape: Cassette Sermons and Islamic Counterpublics*. New York: Columbia University Press.

Højer, Lars. 2009. Absent Powers: Magic and Loss in Post-Socialist Mongolia. *JRAI* 15 (3): 575–591.

Hungariancatholicmission.com. 2011. Hungarian Catholic Mission – Deva Foundations. http://www.hungariancatholicmission.com/charity/devafoundations.htm. Accessed December 3, 2021.

Kaell, Hillary. 2014. *Walking Where Jesus Walked: American Christians and Holy Land Pilgrimage*. New York: New York University Press.

Kleinman, Arthur. 2006. *What Really Matters*. Oxford: Oxford University Press.

Kligman, Gail. 1988. *The Wedding of the Dead: Ritual, Poetics, and Popular Culture in Transylvania*. Berkeley: University of California Press.

Kligman, Gail, and Katherine Verdery. 2011. *Peasants Under Siege: The Collectivization of Romanian Agriculture, 1949–1962*. Princeton: Princeton University Press.

Koesel, Karrie J. 2014. *Religion and Authoritarianism: Cooperation, Conflict, and the Consequences*. Cambridge: Cambridge University Press.

Kozán, István. 2013. Népszámlálás: a hargitaiak 85 százaléka magyar [Census: Residents of Hargita County are 85 percent Hungarian]. *Szekelyhon.ro*. http://www.szekelyhon.ro/aktualis/csikszek/pontafolytatodhatnak-a-kitiltasok. Accessed 23 June 2014.

Laidlaw, James. 2002. For an Anthropology of Ethics and Freedom. *Journal of the Royal Anthropological Institute* 8: 311–332.

———. 2013. *The Subject of Virtue: An Anthropology of Ethics and Freedom*. Cambridge: Cambridge University Press.

Lambek, Michael. 2008. Value and virtue. *Anthropological Theory* 8 (2): 133–157.

Lester, Rebecca. 2005. *Jesus in Our Wombs: Embodying Modernity in a Mexican Convent*. Berkeley: University of California Press.

Levy, David. 2018. The Impulse to Orthodoxy: Why Illiberal Democracies Treat Religious Pluralism as a Threat. In *Religion and the Rise of Populism*, ed. Daniel Nilsson DeHanas and Marat Shterin, 58–72. New York: Routledge.

Lindquist, Galena. 2006. *Conjuring Hope: Magic and Healing in Contemporary Russia*. New York: Berghahn Books.

Loustau, Marc R. 2021. Belief Beyond the Bugbear: Propositional Theology and Intellectual Authority in a Transylvanian Catholic Ethnographic Memoir. *Ethnos: A Journal of Anthropology* 86 (3): 492–509.

Luehrmann, Sonja. 2005. Recycling Cultural Construction: Desecularisation in Postsoviet Mari El. *Religion, State, and Society* 33 (1): 35–56.

———. 2011. *Secularism Soviet Style: Teaching Atheism and Religion in a Volga Republic*. Bloomington: Indiana University Press.

Magnificat.ro. 2010. Böjte atya: Ha egymillió ember csak 1 eurót adományozna….
Magnificat.ro. https://www.magnificat.ro/portal/index.php/hu/szent-ferenc-alapitvany/rk-mainmenu-315/sajtinmenu-311/5335-boejte-atya-ha-egymillio-ember-csak-1-eurot-adomanyozna. Accessed 25 Nov 2020.

Mahmood, Saba. 2004. *Politics of Piety: The Islamic Revival and the Feminist Subject.* Princeton: Princeton University Press.

Márton, Áron. 1934. Ugartörés előtt. *Erdélyi Iskola* (2): 1–2. Available online at https://ispmn.gov.ro/uploads/012Marton_Aron_Ugartores_elott.pdf

Marzouki, Nadia, Duncan McDonnell, and Olivier Roy, eds. 2016. *Saving the People: How Populists Hijack Religion.* New York: Oxford University Press.

Mattingly, Cheryl. 2012. Two Virtue Ethics and the Anthropology of Morality. *Anthropological Theory* 12 (2): 161–184.

———. 2013. Moral Selves and Moral Scenes: Narrative Experiments in Everyday Life. *Ethnos: Journal of Anthropology* 78 (3): 301–327.

McBrien, Julie, and Mathijs Pelkmans. 2008. Turning Marx on His Head: Missionaries, 'Extremists' and Archaic Secularists in Post-Soviet Kyrgyzstan. *Critique of Anthropology* 28 (1): 87–103.

Minkenberg, Michael. 2015. *Transforming the Transformation? The East European Radical Right in the Political Process.* London: Routledge.

Muehlebach, Andrea. 2012. *The Moral Neoliberal: Welfare and Citizenship in Italy.* Chicago: The University of Chicago Press.

Negruți, Sorin. 2014. The Evolution of the Religious Structure in Romania Since 1859 to the Present Day. *Revista Română de Statistică* 6: 46–70.

Omer, Atalia. 2015. Modernists Despite Themselves: The Phenomenology of the Secular and the Limits of Critique as an Instrument of Change. *Journal of the American Academy of Religion* 83 (1): 27–71.

O'Neill, Kevin Lewis. 2009. *City of God: Christian Citizenship in Postwar Guatemala.* Berkeley: University of California Press.

Origo.hu. 2019. "Böjte Csaba: Arra születtünk, hogy a szolgáló szeretet által az élet mellett döntsünk" ["Böjte Csaba: We Are Born to Stand on the Side of Life Through the Love of Service]. *Origo.hu,* September 6. https://www.origo.hu/itthon/20190906-bojte-csaba-arra-szulettunk-hogy-a-szolgalo-szeretet-altal-az-elet-mellett-dontsunk.html. Accessed 1 Dec 2019.

Parsons, Talcott. 1969. 'The Intellectual': A Social Role Category. In *On Intellectuals,* ed. Peter Rieff, 3–26. Garden City: Doubleday.

Pelkmans, Mathijs, ed. 2009. *Conversion After Socialism: Disruptions, Modernisms and Technologies of Faith in the Former Soviet Union.* New York: Berghan.

Peña, Elaine A. 2011. *Performing Piety: Making Space Sacred with the Virgin of Guadalupe.* Berkeley: University of California Press.

Peyrouse, Sebastien. 2004. Christianity and Nationality in Soviet and Post-Soviet Central Asia: Mutual Intrusions and Instrumentalizations. *Nationalities Papers* 32 (3): 651–674.

Robbins, Joel. 2007. Between Reproduction and Freedom: Morality, Value, and Radical Cultural Change. *Ethnos* 72 (3): 293–314.

Rogers, Douglas. 2009. *The Old Faith and the Russian Land: A Historical Ethnography of Ethics in the Urals.* Ithaca: Cornell University Press.

Said, Edward. 1994. *Representations of the Intellectual: The 1993 Reith Lectures.* London: Vintage.

Santiago, Jose. 2012. Secularisation and Nationalism: A Critical Review. *Social Compass* 59 (1): 3–20.

Shils, Edward, ed. 1972. *The Intellectuals and the Powers, and Other Essays.* Chicago: University Chicago Press.

Spivak, Gayatri Chakravorty. 1988. Can the Subaltern Speak? In *Marxism and the Interpretation of Culture*, ed. Cary Nelson and Lawrence Grossberg, 271–313. London: Macmillan.

Ssorin-Chaikov, Nikolai. 2008. Evenki Shamanistic Practices in Soviet Present and Ethnographic Present Perfect. *Anthropology of Consciousness* 12 (1): 1–18.

Steinberg, Mark D., and Catherine Wanner, eds. 2008. *Religion, Morality, and Community in Post-Soviet Societies.* Bloomington: University of Indiana Press.

Szilágy, Tamás. 2011. Quasi-Religious Character of the Hungarian Right-Wing Radical Ideology. An International Comparison. In *Spaces and Borders: Current Research on Religion in Central and Eastern Europe*, 251–264. Berlin: Walter de Gruyter.

Throop, Jason, and Cheryl Mattingly. 2018. The Anthropology of Ethics and Morality. *Annual Review of Anthropology* 47: 475–492.

Verdery, Katherine. 1983. *Transylvanian Villagers: Three Centuries of Political, Economic, and Ethnic Change.* Berkeley: University of California Press.

———. 1991. *National Ideology Under Socialism: Identity and Cultural Politics in Ceaușescu's Romania.* Berkeley: University of California Press.

———. 2003. *The Vanishing Hectare: Property and Value in Postsocialist Transylvania.* Ithaca: Cornell University Press.

Zigon, Jarrett. 2007. Moral Breakdown and the Ethical Demand: A Theoretical Framework for an Anthropology of Moralities. *Anthropological Theory* 7 (2): 131–150.

———. 2008. *Morality: An Anthropological Perspective.* London: Bloomsbury Academic.

———. 2009a. Developing the Moral Person: The Concepts of Human, Godmanhood, and Feelings in Some Russian Articulations of Morality. *Anthropology of Consciousness* 20.1 (March): 1–26.

———. 2009b. Morality and Personal Experience: The Moral Conceptions of a Muscovite Man. *Ethos* 37.1 (March): 78–101.

———. 2009c. Morality Within a Range of Possibilities: A Dialogue with Joel Robbins. *Ethnos* 74.2 (June): 251–276.

———. 2009d. Phenomenological Anthropology and Morality. *Ethnos* 74.2 (June): 286–288.

———. 2013. On Love: Remaking Moral Subjectivity in Postrehabilitation Russia. *American Ethnologist* 40.1 (February): 201–215.

———. 2014. Attunement and Fidelity: Two Ontological Conditions for Morally Being-in-the-World. *Ethos: A Journal of Anthropology* 42 (1): 16–30.

Zigon, Jarrett, and C. Jason Throop. 2014. Moral Experience: Introduction. *Ethos: Journal of the Society for Psychological Anthropology* 42 (1): 1–15.

Zúquete, Jose Pedro. 2017. Populism and Religion. In *Oxford Handbook of Populism*, ed. Cristobal Rovira Kaltwasser, Paul A. Taggart, Paulina Ochoa Espejo, and Pierre Ostiguy, 445–466. Oxford: Oxford University Press.

CHAPTER 2

Vocation

TRANSYLVANIAN SCHOOL

In 2016, I attended the opening of a new dormitory, the Áron Márton Center for Talent Cultivation, built for rural schoolchildren to attend schools in Miercurea Ciuc, a city in one of Transylvania's ethnic Hungarian enclaves. The dormitory was named for a Catholic priest, Áron Márton (1896–1980), who rose to prominence in the Transylvanian Hungarian community in the 1930s by proposing a far-reaching reform of the ethnic minority's educational system (Barabás 2016). A short walk from the dormitory, the Áron Márton High School also commemorates his educational contributions. If you turn right and toward the city center from the High School's front doors, a five-minute walk will take you to a bust and plaque commemorating the birthplace of Márton's foremost interwar period collaborator, the sociologist József Venczel (1913–1972). Walking the other way on the main road toward Şumuleu Ciuc, ten minutes later you arrive at another student dormitory. This one features a life-size statue of another interwar Transylvanian Hungarian educational innovator, Pál Péter Domokos (1901–1992), who was born in this village on the city's outskirts before becoming one of the Transylvanian Hungarian community's most renowned ethnomusicologists and choral leaders.

© The Author(s), under exclusive license to Springer Nature Switzerland AG 2022
M. R. Loustau, *Hungarian Catholic Intellectuals in Contemporary Romania*, Contemporary Anthropology of Religion, https://doi.org/10.1007/978-3-030-99221-7_2

Márton, Venczel, and Domokos came of age as educators after World War I, and during this period contributed decisively to an enduring perspective on the ethical mission and purpose of ethnic minority education, what I call the Transylvanian Hungarian intellectual tradition. Until 1919, the Hungarian state had controlled Transylvania's educational system. As part of the post-World War I Treaty of Trianon, named for the French chateau where it was signed, Romania was granted sovereignty over

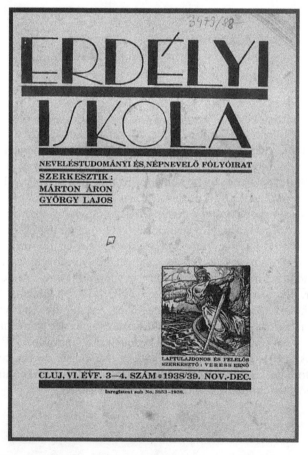

Cover of *Transylvanian School* issue featuring József Venczel's article, "Bishop Áron Márton's Educational System"

Transylvania and Hungarians in the region became an ethnic minority. After the Romanian government closed Hungarian schools and fired Hungarian teachers who refused to take an oath of loyalty to the state, Márton and Venczel founded a journal, *Transylvanian School*, to outline their plans for a new ethnic minority educational system and then invited Domokos to contribute articles about music pedagogy.

By examining these writings in *Transylvanian School*, I outline the parameters and core concepts of the Transylvanian Hungarian intellectual tradition. I also set up my later arguments by describing the Transylvanian Hungarian intellectual tradition's primary social types: village educators, the rural "folk" or "people" (*nép*), and the entrepreneurial middle class. While these types are reimagined within changed social conditions by the tradition's contemporary inheritors, throughout I argue that the central tensions expressed by theories of intellectualism saturated the social imagination of Transylvanian Hungarian intellectuals of the interwar period: vocation versus professionalization, identification versus differentiation, civilization versus nature, and institutional form versus practice. I also argue that Catholic intellectuals' contributions to the project of crafting an ethnic minority intellectual tradition centrally involved not just the construction of boundaries, as in Zygmunt Bauman's influential formulation, but also dangerous border-crossings to identify with previously suspect—that is, foreign—Protestant theological sources and ideas.

I resituate the creative process in intellectual practice out of the bounded and solipsistic social spaces, debating clubs and monks' isolated cells, where anthropologists of Europe have typically gone to study it (Boyer 2005; Giesen 1998). I look to sites of intellectual production—in this case, the journal *Transylvanian School*—where Catholic intellectuals simultaneously turned inward to construct a sense of Transylvanian Hungarian selfhood while crossing confessional boundaries to engage with otherness. Grasping what is at stake in acts of intellectual creativity ultimately requires a hermeneutic sensitivity to interpreting ideas and a social awareness of structure and context. In Chap. 2, for instance, I lay out the conceptual and doctrinal sources for contemporary theologians' educational reform initiatives. As such, the discussion of theological ideas about the presence God in the work of grace may sound abstract to some anthropologists' ears.

However, focusing on the content of theological ideas is a necessary intervention in the anthropology of Christianity. This is not only because, as Andrea Muehlebach observes before an extended summary of Catholic social teaching on political economy, "It seems Catholicism has become good to think with in these neoliberal times"; but also because the anthropology of Christianity has had a marked tendency to embrace concepts like "sensational form" and "semiotic ideology" that privilege form, style, and performance over the content of Christians' thought (Muehlebach 2012: 92; see Meyer 2015; Keane 2007). While attending to the substance of Christian theology, I do not neglect social context, instead situating meanings in relation to modernizing discourses about the history of the church that, in the twentieth century, defined the characteristic ecclesiastical institution of the apostolic age to be both authoritative and polemically anti-Catholic. Interwar Catholic theologians took up the mantle of modernity by embracing institutional reform in this Protestant mode, but adapted accounts of the apostolic age to reflect Catholic concerns and expectations.

The first section of this chapter traces the emerging demographic, economic, and political conditions that led a new generation of Protestant and Catholic theologians to develop a collective identity as Transylvanian Hungarian ethnic minority intellectuals. They shifted away from a state-centered vision of the teaching profession, in which their authority was based on the ability to execute government policy. Instead, they embraced rural teaching as a vocation.

In the second section, I look at interwar intellectuals' writings about two ethnic minority institutions, dormitories and choirs, where I conducted some of my fieldwork. Here, I treat institutions as key tropes in the production of a social imaginary. In the process, I go beyond conventional anthropological accounts of intellectual nationalism, where institutions are understood to be the brick-and-mortar loci of professional practice (Boyer 2005: 53) or functional engines of social reproduction (Giesen 1998).[1]

By referring to dormitories and choirs as "apostolic institutions," interwar Transylvanian Catholic intellectuals identified themselves with the Protestant modernist trope of reform through a return to a primitive and pure Christianity. At the same time, by calling dormitories and choirs "nurseries of virtue," these scholars drew on arguments in authoritative papal theological documents to include these groups alongside other naturally ordained social institutions. Márton, Venczel, and Domokos used these institutions to engage in a cross-confessional synthesis enacted through simultaneous differentiation and identification.

In the final section, I turn my focus to the relationship between ethnic minority intellectuals and the Hungarian middle class, noting how interwar intellectuals recognized the bourgeoisie's ethnic minority self-consciousness by affording them a specific educational role in Transylvanian Hungarian dormitories. Today's Transylvanian Hungarian educators recruit volunteers who demonstrate their middle-class status with their authoritative consumer taste. Through highlighting this difference, I set up my narrative in later chapters to describe how Transylvanian Hungarian intellectuals formulate new appeals to volunteer Hungarians from Hungary, adapting a tradition marked as their own in conversation with their cross-border ethnic kin's ambiguously familiar, definitively authoritative desires and expectations.

The architects of the Transylvanian Hungarian intellectual tradition are noted for criticizing other ethnic minority intellectuals for crossing national borders to work with Romanian state officials. Still, as anthropologist Tom Bolyston has argued for the process of forming Orthodox Christian monastic identity, "prohibition is always accompanied by mediation" (Boylston 2018: 2). I seek to understand what interwar Catholic architects of the Transylvanian Hungarian intellectual tradition risked in such mediations and why they felt the risk was worth it.

A Revision of Our Own

The post-World War I Hungarian state's vastly reduced role in Transylvania's educational system came as a great shock to the intellectuals who would go on to craft a Transylvanian Hungarian intellectual tradition. In contemporary historian Nándor Bárdi's words, "the Hungarian state [in the 1920s] disappeared out from behind the backs of the Transylvanian Hungarian community" (2015: 11). Over the course of 1919, Hungary's governing social democratic coalition gave way to a short-lived Bolshevik revolutionary government and widespread political violence, which lasted until Romanian soldiers invaded as far as Budapest (Case 2009: 25–7). Then in the 1920s, Hungary struggled to integrate a large body of exiles from the areas of the former Austro-Hungarian Empire now under the control of successor nation-states. Many of these refugees were former government bureaucrats: teachers, lawyers, professors, and cultural officials.[2]

The Hungarian state's preoccupation with political, economic, and cultural problems within its own borders endured long into the interwar period. Historian Stefano Bottoni writes that, rather than help Transylvanian Hungarians to develop a new sense of mission as an ethnic minority, these exiles simply tried to recreate and preserve their former lifestyle in Hungary—for instance, by building a reproduction Transylvanian Hungarian village in an area near the new border with Romania (Bottoni 2013: 498).

In the absence of an effective Hungarian state to counter the post-War Romanian government's nationalizing educational policies, Transylvanian Hungarian intellectuals began searching for not only new means of support but, more deeply, a new and distinctive educational rationale and understanding of pedagogical authority. Before the War, Transylvanian Hungarians had largely relied on state and religious schools to provide Hungarian-language education and intellectuals were civil servants enacting the political policies of the Dualist Hungarian state.[3] After taking over Transylvania in the 1920s, according to Bárdi's statistics, "the Romanian state shut down more than two-thirds of Hungarian elementary and secular schools, and three-fourths of middle schools and teacher accrediting institutes" (Bárdi 2013: 255). The state demanded remaining teachers use Romanian as the official language of instruction and severely limited the work of Transylvanian Hungarian cultural organizations, when it did not shut them down entirely.[4] After the faculty of Transylvania's largest university resigned en masse rather than swear a loyalty oath to the Romanian state, many left to a newly founded university in exile in Hungary, leading Transylvanian Hungarian intellectuals to worry that future college-bound students from the ethnic minority community would likewise move abroad to pursue educations and careers.

Against the backdrop of their insecurity about the effectiveness and durability of the weakened Hungarian state's support as well as their suspicion of the nationalizing Romanian state, Transylvania's Reformed (Calvinist) theologians began questioning the rationale that had underwritten the Dualist Hungarian state's educational policies—the policies Transylvanian Hungarian intellectuals, as civil servants, had implemented during the pre-War period. The Dualist state had asserted that its assimilationist educational policies would resolve national tensions by creating a homogenous nation-state, in much the same way that they claimed the nationalizing Romanian state was now trying to create a unified populace through education (Brubaker et al. 2007: 73–5). In the early 1930s, László Dezső, a theologian at Cluj-Napoca's Reformed (Calvinist) seminary, wrote, "With the help of superficial intellectual and other factors we wanted to make everyone Hungarian, but we ended up forgetting about our own selves" (Dezső 1997: 79). Dezső faulted the pre-War Hungarian government for being so focused on linguistically assimilating Transylvania's non-Hungarian ethnic groups that the intellectuals who implemented these policies fell out of touch with "ourselves," by which he meant the Transylvanian Hungarian peasantry that, in the interwar period, was viewed as the authentic source of the new ethnic minority community's culture (see Hitchins 2007).

Like Dezső, Catholic intellectuals also drew on this notion that teaching children to speak a language produced a superficial awareness of shared national belonging, in contrast to a deeper and enduring emotional basis for national solidarity. In the 1930s, ethnomusicologist Pál Péter Domokos wrote that Catholic parish choirs help foster ethnic solidarity because they demand a level of emotional attachment that transcends linguistic competence: "Having a shared language produces only a unity of understanding," Domokos wrote, "This is a one-sided unity, but we need an emotional unity" (1938: 139). Without saying so explicitly, his argument takes aim at the Romanian state, then instituting policies requiring Romanian as the language of instruction, as well as at the Dualist-era Hungarian state whose intellectual civil servants had also enforced assimilationist educational policies.

This turn toward voluntaristic pedagogical service was also born of a growing satisfaction with competing efforts, embraced by other Transylvanian Hungarian intellectuals, to strengthen ethnic minority identification. During the interwar period, an idea that became known as "Transylvanism" gained popularity among intellectuals who sought to create cooperative scholarly and culture-building initiatives among Transylvania's various ethnic groups. These Transylvanists, according to historian Keith Hitchins, believed that Transylvania has a unique history and an identity all its own that makes it a Switzerland-style space of harmonious ethnic coexistence (Hitchins 2007: 90–5). Its leading Transylvanian Hungarian proponents in the 1920s were a small group of young sociologists whom the Romanian rural sociologist Dimitrie Gusti had invited to join his government-funded research institute, which was in the midst of conducting a series of social scientific surveys of Romanian villages.

Bárdi contextualizes Transylvanism as the Transylvanian Hungarian intelligentsia's "outward-facing stance," which is accurate at least regarding intellectuals' attitude toward political institutions (2015: 10). Transylvanist rhetoric about harmonious coexistence and peaceful cooperation was aimed at the Romanian state and international institutions that provided valuable material support for undertaking Gusti's cross-ethnic intellectual exchanges; but some of the same interwar intellectuals also grew frustrated with Transylvanism's inability to effect lasting institutional change—for instance, persuading the Romanian state to fund research institutes run by and for ethnic minority intellectuals.[5] Reformed (Calvinist) and Catholic theologians led a turn to the concept of vocational intellectualism after other Transylvanian Hungarian political and intellectual leaders, so Márton and others claimed, had failed to change state policy via international arenas established by the Communist Party and League of Nations (Bárdi 2015: 14).[6]

While the Transylvanists used the sociological survey methods of the period to live in and get to know Transylvanian Hungarian villages—responding to Dezső's jab about forgetting ourselves—Márton and his allies adopted an ethical rather than scientific approach to these engagements and even derided the sociological pursuit of objective knowledge for neglecting the ethnic minority community's needs. They were inspired partly by Reformed (Calvinist) theologian Sándor Makkai who wrote, in his 1931 essay "A Revision of Our Own," that the task of national renewal required identifying and cultivating a new generation of ethical intellectuals who felt called to return to and educate rural communities.[7] Reformed (Calvinist) theologian Sándor Tavaszy also declared that, "For us, we must become neither a political, economic, nor racial community but rather in the first place an ethical community" (1936: 435). By 1937, the leading Protestant and Catholic advocates of a Transylvanian Hungarian intellectual tradition were ready to issue a programmatic statement outlining this ethical approach to cultivating national intellectuals and gathered in the city of Târgu Mureş for a congress to write this declaration.

Many of the virtues that today's Transylvanian Hungarian Catholic intellectuals praise—love, humility, poverty, commitment, loyalty, patience, and justice (quoted in Bárdi 2015: 23–5)—are the same that appear in what would become known as the Vásárhely Declaration, after Târgu Mureş's Hungarian name. Bárdi notes delegates' praise for composure and sobriety, which were supposed to be evident in virtuous intellectuals' attitude toward politics and public discourse. The Vásárhely Declaration emphasized that virtuous intellectuals would demonstrate a love of hard work, capacity for sacrifice, and sense of responsibility as they strove to develop the Transylvanian Hungarian peasantry's national and ethical self-consciousness (Bárdi 2015: 24–5).

While the border changes that accompanied the transfer of sovereignty over Transylvania to the Romanian government affected Protestants and Catholics alike, Transylvania's Catholics were alone in losing the confidence of numerical superiority among the Empire's Hungarian population. At the end of the previous century, Catholics had made up the largest Hungarian-speaking denomination by population, over 10.5 million (49%) to the Reformed (Calvinist) Church's approximately 2.6 million

(13%).[8] This gave way to an equal division between Reformed (Calvinist) and Catholic believers in the ethnic minority community that remains in place today.

In the late nineteenth century, Catholics from the Ciuc Valley sometimes deployed rhetoric about defending this predominantly Catholic region against heretical Protestant outsiders, especially when prompted by conflicts over shifts in state educational policies that disadvantaged their privileged position. One Franciscan friar based in Csíksomlyó offered this angry rebuke:

> It is the hope of those Protestants who were transplanted here that the Enlightenment that was introduced through them will conquer Csík [Ciuc] for Calvinism. But it was completely thwarted because despite all their nasty gossip the ancestral Catholic Szeklers of the Csík-Gyergyó [Ciuc-Gheorgheni], Háromszék [Trei Scaune], and Udvarhely [Odorheiu] regions, not to mention Marostorda [Mureş-Torda] County, were not shaken from their faith. (Quoted in Mohay 2009: 153)

Writing in 1892, he was responding to the Hungarian state's attempt to enforce a decree that a child of a mixed marriage must inherit the religion of the parent of the same gender. This law was passed to speed the end the Catholic Church's status as the official state church, whereas before all children who had at least one Catholic parent were required by law to be baptized into the Catholic Church.

The term "Enlightenment" (*felvilágosodás*), which the friar used to derogate Protestantism, was used specifically in debates over the proper basis of religious authority. Enlightenment, according to historian János Rada's study of nineteenth-century Hungarian pamphlet tracts, had "broad connotations of sectarianism, laicism, and anticlericalism" (Rada 2020: 24). Protestant writers were especially fond of warning about the Catholic clerical hierarchy's attempts to gather political power. They decried Catholic "ultramontanists," who believed in the pope's absolute authority and which had been defined in 1870 within the dogma of papal infallibility; and linked the Catholic hierarchy's desire for political power to the process by which Christianity had degenerated into fanaticism and mysticism (Rada 2020: 22). All these problematic features of Christianity, liberal Protestant believed, would be eliminated by the advance of Enlightenment within the church.[9]

The leading Catholic advocates of a Transylvanian Hungarian intellectual tradition, Márton, Venczel, and Domokos, were born in the Ciuc Valley at a time when the issue of clerical authority inspired local Catholics to defend resentfully the region's Catholic identity and brand Protestants as foreign invaders; after the War, however, as they sought to join the effort to reimagine pedagogical authority beyond implementing Hungarian state policy, they were confronted by a new situation of numerical parity with the Reformed (Calvinist) Church.

While Bárdi writes about interwar minority intellectuals' different rhetoric for outsiders and insiders—an argument echoing Bauman's claim that all intellectualisms draw a boundary that "splits the territory into two sides"—the notion that these Transylvanian Hungarian intellectuals were

Father Áron Márton

primarily concerned with the work of drawing social distinctions and differences tends to reduce the boundary-crossing creativity involved in projects of national awakening (Bauman 1987a: 23).[10] For Catholic intellectuals, joining the project of cultivating an ethical ethnic minority community posed specific confessional challenges they overcame by crossing the border that the issue of clerical authority raised between Protestantism and Catholicism.

Márton, Domokos, and Venczel faced suspicion in their natal milieu, where they would have been familiar with anti-Protestant messages that simultaneously portrayed the Ciuc Valley as a Catholic bastion. What is more, the Catholic Church's central hierarchy in Rome was no less suspicious of Protestantism. Pope Pius XI, who held resentful anti-Protestant views, led the global Catholic Church during the interwar period. While Transylvanian Hungarian Catholic intellectuals praised and cited his theological reflections on Catholic pedagogy, they also had to contend with the pope's views that led him to denounce Protestants as "heretics" and his threats to excommunicate Catholics who became members of the institutions of Europe's emerging ecumenical movement.[11]

In a move that ran counter to Ciuc Valley Catholics' tendency to be suspicious of Protestants, Márton and Venczel published a series of articles urging intellectuals to return to a materially primitive kind of pedagogical practice exemplified by the early Christian apostles and then revived in the early nineteenth century by a Danish Lutheran intellectual, Frederik Grundtvig.[12] While Venczel admitted that Grundtvig is a "foreign man," he urged Transylvanian Hungarians to see him as "one of our relatives" (Venczel 1938: 362). "In his devotion," Venczel wrote, "the great Danish preacher, Frederik Grundtvig, is the servant educator's role model, an exemplar of feverish innovation" (1938: 217).

Despite this reference to kinship, Márton and Venczel looked to Grundtvig not because the Danish and Transylvanian Hungarian peoples shared some kind of racial or characterological foundation—both popular tropes of interwar Eastern European intellectual reflection on nationhood—but rather because they shared an analogous post-imperial political condition (Trencsényi 2010). Márton noted that in the early 1800s, Grundtvig confronted a comparable situation after Denmark had gone bankrupt and the colonies formerly under its rule had either gained political independence or been turned over to other imperial powers. Like the victors at the World War I peace conferences debated whether Hungary should exist, so also Europe's early-nineteenth century dominant nations debated whether Denmark should remain a sovereign state (Venczel 1938: 363).

In the wake of the post-War redrawing of Europe's political boundaries, many intellectual and political leaders in Eastern Europe worried over their nation-states' right to exist, what historian Zoltán Nagy calls a region-wide existential crisis (Nagy 2017: 74). In Hungary, state-supported intellectuals took action on the international stage, mounting campaigns of "cultural diplomacy" that extolled Hungary's rich history, natural beauty, or technological advancement (Nagy 2017). In contrast, Márton and his cohort praised Grundtvig for adopting a local approach that did not depend on winning the favor of international institutions.

Grundtvig looked to the earliest Christian preachers and patterned himself after dedicated and humble itinerant apostles who awakened the first believers' faith and founded simple church institutions called "house churches." Grundtvig encountered the rural poor, Venczel wrote, and taught them in "tiny forest hovels" (*apró kunyhók*). The nineteenth century intellectual decided to spend his life in isolated villages and, despite the difficulties of living in these humble circumstances, stayed to enact his pedagogical calling. This type of difficult, even exhausting apostolic-style pedagogy did not phase the dedicated teacher. Thus, Transylvanian Hungarian intellectuals praised Grundtvig for his sense of responsibility and persistence, which helped him overcome enact his calling by "living and teaching among the people of the nation" (1938: 220). "The spirit of the apostles drove him to work," Venczel writes of Grundtvig, "[He] wandered, taught, exhorted, and served" (1938: 362).

This portrait of a poor wandering intellectual inspiring the peasantry to national self-awareness through face-to-face pedagogy is a striking contrast to the spectacles of monarchial pageantry, pomp, and grandeur that, in interwar Budapest, the Hungarian state was using to persuade the populace to identify with a renewed imperial nation. In Hungary during this period, Catholic intellectuals were instrumental in organizing celebrations of the cult of King Stephen, Hungary's first Christian monarch, who reigned until 1038. Historian Paul Hanebrink documents how Catholic Church officials held pride of place during the annual public processions of King Stephen's relics through Budapest, dramatically demonstrating their ability to control the levers of state in the name of defending Christian Hungarian culture against its enemies (Hanebrink 2006: 112). Although Márton was an ordained Catholic priest like his politically active colleagues in Hungary, he valorized intellectual exemplars who employed humbler means to change Hungarian culture.

Besides Romanians, over the course of the 1930s, Transylvania's Jewish community also came to be identified with the non-Hungarian groups that, according to theologian László Dezső, an earlier generation of intellectuals had focused too much on in their zeal "to make everyone Hungarian." Hanebrink writes that, over the course of the 1930s, public rhetoric about defending, protecting, and reforming Christian Hungarian culture focused increasingly on Jews, construing them as enemies and outsiders (Hanebrink 2006). In Transylvania, the Jewish community was located predominantly in cities (Brubaker et al. 2007: 75–6). Hungarian-speaking Jews were thus implicitly excluded from the educational revival through serving the people, since interwar theologians identified the people with the rural populace. As I will soon demonstrate by turning to Pál Péter Domokos's writings about the Hungarian musical tradition, the conversation convened by the journal *Transylvanian School* was not isolated from the racialization of debates about how to revive Christian Hungarian culture. Racial discourse entered into this conversation in debates about the relationship between Hungarian and Roma musical traditions, even if the racialized essentialization of boundaries between Hungarian, Roma, Jewish, and Romanian groups in Transylvania did allow for surprising mediations across Protestant and Catholic confessional boundaries.

While interwar writers like Márton and Venczel seemed to draw a distinction between apostolic educators and intellectuals who seek to implement state policy (or use state institutions to organize monarchial spectacles full of pomp and grandeur), contemporary intellectuals attempt to overcome the divide between the Transylvanian Hungarian intellectual tradition and King Stephen's cult. In Chap. 5, I examine the Knighthood Order of the Holy Crown, a group of volunteer rural teachers trying to revive the devotional tradition in rural Transylvanian Hungarian communities. This group is innovating village educational events about the Holy Crown during which they cultivate noble virtues. In the process, I argue, they help identify the Transylvanian Hungarian intellectual tradition, with its focus on voluntary rural education and pedagogical virtues, and King Stephen's cult.

As sociologist Bernhard Giesen writes in *Intellectuals and the Nation*, discourse about national renewal is inherently ethical, imagining the nation awakening like an individual maturing toward self-sufficient action

(Giesen 1998: 1–2). While Márton reflected this ethical preoccupation, he did not echo Giesen's talk of individualistic self-sufficiency but rather explored the theme of God's collaborative laboring in and with human communities, arguing that this ethical version of divine presence, what I call "collaborative presence," was evident in the lives and pedagogical activities of vocational intellectuals. Yet this claim required Márton to bridge seemingly irreconcilable theological traditions, since the papal documents that he drew on to develop his account of collaborative presence identified him with the intellectual authority of the Catholic hierarchy that, in the nineteenth century, Hungarian Protestant advocates of Enlightened reason had used to denounce the Catholic Church.

In the pages of *Transylvanian School*, Márton published interpretations of two authoritative papal statements of Catholic doctrine addressing education and social reform, *Divini Illius Magistri* [On Christian Education of Youth] (1929) and *Quadragesimo anno* [The Fortieth Year] (1931). Márton found this statement of the pedagogical task from *Divini Illius Magistri* especially compelling: "The proper and immediate end of Christian education is to collaborate with divine grace in forming the true and perfect Christian."[13]

Márton's writings about human action as collaboration with God's grace draws on Catholicism's natural law tradition to describe the natural and embodied matrix for the creative work of pedagogical formation and perfection. As understood in the natural law tradition, grace is slowly, patiently, and arduously working to perfect human beings in and through the three communities that God has ordained by nature: the family, the Church, and civil society. Education is one and the same as the processes for perfecting human beings proper to these naturally ordained social groups. Moreover, grace works creatively in the *natural* processes proper to these communities.

Fecundity, for example, is God's grace at work in the family.[14] Pius XI wrote that in the community of the Church, the sacraments, which take up the material qualities of objects and bodies in the process of sanctifying the faithful toward salvation, "have an immense educational value." The natural law tradition describes a form of human ethical action, within a natural matrix and in collaboration with God's grace, to perfect human beings in virtue. Attending to this Catholic theological understanding thus reveals the limitations of Giesen's influential view that intellectuals "naturalize" the nation—attach national characteristics to seemingly immutable biological characteristics—to place it beyond "the range of practical action and deeper than societal change" (1998: 28).

Márton used his article titles to redefine rural education as an eclectic profession along the lines of early Christian apostolic preaching. He wrote about, for example, "The Expanded School" (*A Kiszélesített Iskola*) and "The School with Doors Wide Open" (*Iskola Kitárt Ajtókkal*). Likewise, he encouraged priests to step outside the doors of their churches and volunteer in charitable organizations, to teach not only doctrine but also arts, economics, and physical education.[15] He embraced apostolic opportunism as the calling card of the village intellectual: "The task of organizing [the Transylvanian Hungarian minority community]," he wrote, "is defined by whatever type of social, economic, or cultural role necessity and opportunity put before us" (Márton 1935: 68).

With these exhortations, Márton expressed a skepticism toward professional specialization that resonated with the eclecticism espoused most famously by Central Europe's Romantic intellectual movement. While anthropologist Dominic Boyer takes a social structural view of Romantic intellectuals' antipathy to professionalization, arguing that in the case of these German intellectuals such heterogeneous activities evince an underlying "relatively low degree of organized professionalism," apostolicity was, for interwar Catholic intellectuals, a strategic conceptual move within a dialectic of identification and differentiation.[16] By praising apostolic intellectuals' eclecticism, they identified themselves with the Protestant modernist trope of reform through a return to a primitive and pure Christianity while emphasizing authoritative papal theological documents that described ethical pedagogy as the work of naturally ordained social institutions.

By popularizing Pope Pius XI's views and adapting them to promote educators' calling to serve Transylvanian Hungarian villages, did Márton reconcile his two loyalties: to both a particular nation and the universal church? This enduring trope of social scientific research on Catholicism is good as far as it goes but also problematic for its adaptation into crypto-moralistic Eastern Europeanist political scientific analysis (Fejérdi 2016). While Bialecki (2017) and other anthropologists studying North American Christian populist nationalism can dismiss political scientists' arguments as irrelevant simply because these scholars belong to another discipline, anthropologists of Eastern Europe do not have this luxury, since political science departments dominate professional knowledge regarding Christian populist nationalism, even as political scientists often promote the hackneyed notion that a good, pure, and apolitical universal Christianity should be distinguished from the corrupt version used by right-wing politicians.[17]

Beyond its role in smuggling such moralizing distinctions into social scientific analysis, this trope ultimately flattens out Catholic intellectuals' creativity and agency, which, in the case of interwar Transylvanian Hungarian Catholics, emerges in a subtle pattern of engagement with Protestant ideas like reorganizing contemporary institutions after the model of the Christian church of the apostolic age.[18] Indeed, Márton, Venczel, and Domokos were motivated to overcome late-nineteenth century Hungarian Catholics' antagonism toward Protestants with an eye to building bridges to the confessional group that claimed equal numbers of Transylvanian Hungarian adherents. Their creative action, emerging in the debates they convened in *Transylvanian School*, was not opposed to the necessities of historical legacy or demographic facts but rather took up history and demography simultaneously as conditions for and targets of such action (Hallam and Ingold 2007).

Imagining Institutions: Dormitories and Choirs

In the mid-1930s, Márton and Venczel began imagining a new type of residential educational institution, the Collegium Transylvanicum, to be replicated in Transylvania's various urban centers. In a 1935 article about the dormitories, Venczel writes about the institution in a speculative and imaginative mood, calling the Collegium Transylvanicum a kind of "fairytale castle." Rather than a criticism, Venczel uses this observation as a starting point and framework for inviting intellectuals to join him in performing imaginative work. "Collegium Transylvanicum," he calls out, "Let's speak about it as if the walls were standing, as if life were already rushing about inside, as if it already existed" (1935: 181)!

Collegium Transylvanicum would be an institution specifically designed to cultivate village teachers driven by a vocational self-consciousness. "[It is for] the educated on their way to becoming new educators," Venczel wrote (1935: 181). Márton and Venczel's choice of names for the dormitory, Collegium Transylvanicum, seems to confirm Giesen's claim that institutions serve the development of intellectual ideologies by defining a distinctive knowledge production and formation into a differentiated and separate social group (1998: 45). The name Collegium Transylvanicum, for instance, accorded with Márton and Venczel's desire to create a

Transylvanian Hungarian intellectual cohort that would transcend cross-cutting intra-regional identifications.

Márton had already put this policy into practice while serving as pastor to university students in Cluj, abolishing the Catholic students' association's practice of grouping students by Transylvania's subregions. According to historian Judit Ozsváth, Márton believed that, "if it continued to offer young people the opportunity only to meet with people from a single area, they would be unprepared for shared work [for the Transylvanian Hungarian community]" (Ozsváth 2017: 371). In the process, he deemphasized allegiances to the predominantly Catholic areas that the previous generation of intellectuals—like the Franciscan friar who had warned his fellow Ciuc Valley residents about invading Reformed (Calvinist) "foreigners"—had rallied in the name of opposing the Protestant Enlightenment (Mohay 2009: 153).

Márton and Venczel modeled the Collegium Transylvanicum after the residential dormitories of the British public-school system. During the interwar period, Hungarians on both sides of the border were enthusiastic about adopting British aristocratic entertainments, but Márton abjured consumption and fashion to focus instead on the capacity of England's educational institutions for cultivating not only ambition and the desire for excellence but the self-sacrificial virtues of rural intellectual servants.[19] "[The institution] imposes on the young person that dual life mission to be the best in one's profession but at the same time that there is a commitment not to forget to work diligently for the interests of the nation" (Márton 1935: 134). Before they returned to their villages to dedicate themselves to others' welfare, students would practice mutual responsibility in the dormitory. Residential dormitories inculcate, according to Márton, a sense of responsibility and care for others as well as students' capacity for self-governance (Ozsváth 2012: 109).

Ozsváth, writing about Márton's pastoral work with university students in Cluj, explains that in this period Márton was already trying to embody Collegium Transylvanicum's egalitarian ethos: "[Márton] saw his main task, besides deepening their faith, to be the development of [students'] apostolic spirit." Márton portrayed the British elite public-school dormitory as an apostolic institution insofar as it was an egalitarian social form in which young residents took responsibility for cultivating virtue in each other. In this, the dormitory was like the nonhierarchical "house church" of Christianity's apostolic age. Itinerant preachers came and went, leaving individual Christians, in the absence of formal ranks and authorities, with the responsibility to care for each other.

Venczel imagined that the dormitory would be an open social space for its cohort of students who had come from the countryside to study in the city. Although most of the dormitory's beds were to be reserved for students, "several guestrooms will be open for business professionals passing through the city." These individuals could be expected to offer students training seminars in their areas of expertise. Venczel invites readers to picture stepping through the dormitory's front door and hearing, "filtering out from the large lecture hall the sound of a presentation on economics" (1935: 181). This openness would be conferred on teachers in their intellectual attitudes, especially their ability to offer diverse instruction. Once they returned to their villages, Márton had imagined opening their school to teach a variety of disciplines. Collegium Transylvanicum would perform its ethical cultivational work at the intersection of rural and urban cultures, a matrix for encountering otherness that Venczel imagined in an apostolic vein as intellectuals teaching young peasants in direct, face-to-face interactions.

While Giesen's account of educational institutions is illuminating for focusing on their important role in distinguishing intellectuals from other social groups, reproducing intellectual cohorts over time, and conferring upon them durable and distinct attitudes, this emphasis on the function of institutions is ultimately reductive; imagining institutions becomes the mere efficient execution of a preexisting plan, a kind of mental social mechanics. What gets lost in Giesen's functionalist account is interwar Catholic intellectuals' ambivalent desire to have Transylvanian Hungarian educational institutions be both Protestant and Catholic at the same time; that is, they tried to put a Catholic spin on seemingly anti-Catholic Protestant ideas, of one's individual calling and of reform as a return to a pure apostolic practice that predates the Catholic Church's distorting and decadent introduction of hierarchy into Christianity.

As first articulated by Transylvanian Hungarian Reformed (Calvinist) theologians, a calling was a highly individualistic ethical relationship with God. Reformed (Calvinist) theologians of the post-War period were reviving what is known as the tradition of "command ethics," which construes power as God's defining characteristic and identifies this power with God's irresistibly commanding will for the human subject (McKenny 2021). Thus, Bárdi accurately describes this original version of the intellectual's vocation when he calls it a "life-command...whose historical source is

God's will" (Bárdi 2015: 22). A calling is not only God's command but also anti-institutional, insofar as it is a revelation in the individual that explosively intervenes to disrupt hierarchical social formations. Thus, the paradigmatic vocational servant for Transylvanian Hungarian Reformed (Calvinist) theologians was the preacher crying out from the wilderness who induced others to make a radical break from their past, thus disregarding—or even tearing down—existing institutions and the forms of authority they promote (see Imre 1938).

In contrast, Márton declared that teaching the people is not an individual task but first and foremost "the Church's natural calling." God reveals God's self in the institution of the Church, he wrote, insofar as "the Church has a general mission to teach" (1933: 32). The social effects of the human action through which Transylvanian Hungarian educational institutions will manifest God's calling is not—as in the Reformed (Calvinist) imaginary—destructive, disruptive, or purifying. Rather, it is collaborative, perfecting, and creative. Collaborative reform was the way Catholic intellectual institutions would demonstrate their authority by working with, in, and alongside God's presence, which the pope had taught was always already at work to order natural and social relations.

An anthropological and ethnographic account of intellectual institutions goes beyond Giesen's functionalist account also by studying the unintended consequences of institutional form, for the openness that Márton and Venczel imagined for their dormitory, when applied to the contemporary successor institutions of the Collegium Transylvanicum, serves as a matrix for the formation of patron-client relationships between students and the founders of these institutions. In Chaps. 3 and 6, I describe my fieldwork with the Catholic priests who lead orphanages that circulate rural students into urban schools and then send them back to teach in villages. Like Márton, these priests cultivate face-to-face relationships with the children who live in these institutions. In the Collegium Transylvanicum, business leaders were supposed to visit and donate to students' education by lecturing on economics, and the founders of today's Catholic dormitory take up this attitude of openness to outside volunteers. Contemporary versions of Márton and Venczel's outside visitor-volunteers are often consumerist, cultured, and urbane middle-class Hungarians who are nevertheless encouraged to visit residential educational institutions, meet the children who live there, and donate labor and money.

While these priests echo Márton in saying that personal relationships cultivate students' calling to service, in practice the students treat Márton's successors as wealthy sponsors who can use their influence with visiting volunteers to dispense jobs and other benefits; the institutions foster vertical patron-client relationships that are driven by a desire to accumulate what anthropologists call "wealth in people" (Scherz 2014: 7–10). It is unclear if Márton ever imagined his Collegium Transylvanicum as a generator of such hierarchical relationships or even himself as a patron. Today, patron-client exchanges intersect these institutions and are fueled by them. This forms the thrust of my observation of everyday practice within these institutions.

The Romanian Hungarian Musical Association (*Romániai Magyar Dalosszövetség*), according to Bárdi, was the most influential—widespread with member choirs throughout Transylvania—cultural organization founded in the post-World War I years (Bárdi 2013: 440). In a 1938 article in *Transylvanian School*, "Hungarian Folk Music and Our Choral Cultivation," the Transylvanian Hungarian and Catholic parish choir director Pál Péter Domokos outlined the movement's vocational rationale, the argument that nationally minded music instructors should feel called to serve by teaching in Transylvanian Hungarian villages. Domokos called choirs the perfect institution for building Transylvanian Hungarians' ethnic minority unity because they promote voluntary collaborative action:

> It is an exemplary tool of solidarity. Many gather together to realize some kind of goal, which individuals – no matter how talented – cannot accomplish alone. Here, everyone's work is equally important. (1938: 138)

Like Márton and Venczel, who argued that the dormitory's essence was egalitarian, Domokos believed that choirs pooled individual effort to accomplish a necessary shared task.

Earlier, I noted that Domokos argued that emotional solidarity was a firmer basis for national identity than shared language. He also disavowed the emotional timbre of Roma musical traditions. He tried to distinguish Transylvanian Hungarians' ability to combine sentiment and composure from what he derided as Roma musical traditions' violent emotional dynamism, which he called "a distorted version of Hungarian music" (Domokos 1938: 136). Domokos drew on a distinction between "natural" and "cultured" national attitudes. In European national imaginaries, according to Giesen, the natural attitude appears to be crude, rough, and sloppy while the cultured is refined, controlled, and composed (Giesen 1998: 76).

Furthermore, Hungarian national musical professionals like Domokos have long associated Roma music with music consumed for entertainment in urban settings.[20] This is an association that also informs his comments about musical sentimentality.

Domokos pragmatically mapped these racial and national distinctions onto the key interwar socio-spatial division between village and city while imagining how rural choirs can call forth a composed yet fervent national sentiment in urban audiences. In his article, Domokos praised the distinctively serious Hungarian emotional style that he sought to cultivate in village choir members. He described singing groups' entrance to one of the Romanian Hungarian Musical Association's recent events: "Dressed in folk costumes, the village groups processed in a disciplined manner, wordlessly, expressionlessly like statues. From their eyes it shone forth that they had learned the lesson" (1938: 141). Domokos claims that the groups' entrance set every audience member's heart to thumping.

In his view, village choirs are not only the objects of pedagogical cultivation, or in Bauman's words "raw material on which future [civilizing] action was yet to impress its form" (1987b: 83); village choirs are also the subjects of a missionary intervention. They have a calling to teach urban Transylvanian Hungarian communities. In Chap. 4, which features ethnographic material from my fieldwork with parish choirs like the ones that Domokos taught in the 1930s, I show how today's urban choir members likewise imagine themselves to be on a rural mission. They are teachers who, having undergone an urban education, are now out to reform the musical and liturgical sensibilities of rural Catholics.

Yet, like Domokos, they also perform for urban audiences in Hungary, thus redirecting the flow of pedagogy as it had been imagined by Márton and Venczel who were preoccupied with motivating teachers to return to villages. Domokos's description also reveals how the social position of the audience decisively shapes the meaning and interpretation of the pedagogical encounter. As I show, when today's Transylvanian Hungarian musical pedagogues perform in cities across the border, they also put urban audiences in the position of determining the success of their work to cultivate villagers' emotional identification with the Transylvanian Hungarian minority community.

POST-MATERIALISTIC TOURISTS

While interwar figures developed the vision of an ethical ethnic minority, one that need not depend on a supportive state to cultivate a virtuous community, contemporary inheritors of the Transylvanian Hungarian intellectual tradition are increasingly aware that the post-2010 right-wing Hungarian government encourages Hungarians from Hungary to contribute valuable resources to Transylvanian educational projects. The intellectuals on whom I focus in the following chapters are attracted to this support. Yet vocational service is rooted in values like hard work, seriousness, and sacrifice that, in some circumstances, interfere with the expectations that Hungarians from Hungary bring with them about what they will experience in Transylvania. In later chapters, I show how these differences can lead to misunderstandings and lingering resentments with the potential to destabilize intellectuals' appeals for support. But in order to understand what Hungarians from Hungary expect from Transylvania, we must first consider the historical context in which these desires emerged: the late-socialist period, when Hungarian citizens embraced, though not without reservations, a new socialist consumer culture.

Hungarians developed an interest in the individual pursuit of spiritual enlightenment amid conditions fostered by what the Hungarian government called its New Economic Mechanism. This set of reform policies dovetailed with several system-wide transformations that saw state socialist countries abandon open military and political conflicts with the West in favor of market supremacy, an economic stance that also influenced the Romanian government's official discourse throughout the 1970s (Apor 2013; Lampland 1995). The Hungarian government embraced this pursuit with special verve, developing what came to be known as "goulash communism" to compensate for its weakened political legitimacy after calling on the Soviet army for help in brutally suppressing an anti-Communist revolution in 1956.

In the 1970s and '80, the Hungarian state earned the allegiance of its citizens through public celebrations of the country's distinctiveness as the most Western and consumerist of the Eastern Bloc states. "Hungarians of the professional classes," Krisztina Fehérváry writes, "by-and-large experienced the decade [of the 1980s] as a time of increasing economic freedoms, including opportunities for private profit and greater access to desirable consumer goods" (Fehérváry 2013: 150). Travel restrictions to Austria were reduced and many Hungarians went abroad on shopping excursions (Chelcea 2002; Huseby-Darvas 2001; Wessely 2002). Others from around the Eastern Bloc visited Hungary for leisure tourism (Böröcz 1993: 88). In the eyes of its neighbors, Hungary came to be regarded as a paradise of consumer affluence.

But as early as the late 1960s, Hungarian philosophers and social scientists were already criticizing consumerism for encouraging materialism.[21] Hungarians grew more interested in what sociologist Zsuzsanna Bögre calls "post-materialistic values" during the same period that sociologist Miklós Tomka observed Hungarians' increasing religious diversity (Bögre 2016: 202). Tomka felt that the government's official statistics on this phenomenon, which failed to recognize more than two categories, "religious" and "not religious," did not reflect Hungary's emerging reality. As a result of this, he began tracking what he felt constituted a new type of religious attitude prevalent among baby-boomer Hungarians. He dubbed this attitude "religious in his/her own way," and subsequent generations of sociologists have explored its various similarities to what Western European and North American sociologists call the "seeker attitude" (Bögre 2016; Hegedűs and Rosta 2016; Sutcliffe 2008).

Bögre found that Hungarians of the post-1989 period who choose to describe themselves as "religious in his/her own way" often respond positively to statements like, "I am seeking what I am seeking" and "I am seeking to experience God" (Bögre 2016: 207). Other similarities with the seeker attitude include skepticism toward materialism; emphasis on cultivating selfhood as one's personal journey; and openness to combining Christianity with Eastern religions, esotericism, and the occult.

While affirming the value of peace, harmony, authenticity, and honesty, Bögre writes that their "search is directed to their inner self and focuses on their personal world" (2016: 207). As seekers, Hungarians understand themselves to be on a lifelong mission, and their target audience is their own selves. They affirm a universal and perpetual duty to grow and learn while embracing a succession of life projects that facilitate this process. They search among different religious groups, based on their personal need for growth and commitment to post-materialistic values, consuming religion in the mass-media marketplace so long as it facilitates psycho-spiritual growth and learning. With this emphasis, they reconcile such consumption with their post-materialistic values.

Finally, they associate seeking with personal crises like drug addiction and divorce (in Bögre's words, this is when "the order of everyday life comes into question" [2016: 202]). Seekers' willingness to center the journey of the self in personal life crises takes shape against the historical background of the New Economic Mechanism. Spiritual seeking is anti-materialist and thus a personal path that allowed Hungarians to stand apart from socialist values, even though, according to sociologist Péter Apor, it was the New Economic Mechanism itself that taught them to "[construe] everyday life as the most important domain for articulating the difference between capitalism and socialism" (Apor 2013: 30).[22]

Post-materialist desires for authentic community also shaped popular views of life in Transylvania, leading many Hungarians to visit this region in search of peasant culture and peasants whose lifestyles reflected Hungarians' desire for exemplary non-materialistic lifestyles.[23] Early in the 1970s, Hungarians began showing up at urban night clubs where exiles from the Transylvanian Hungarian minority taught them folk dances set to traditional Hungarian music. According to anthropologist László Kürti, what became known as the dance-house movement (*táncház mozgalom*) gained popularity among young people who had soured on consuming Western popular music.[24]

The dance-house movement grafted the desire for authentic community onto a political dissatisfaction with the socialist government's official hands-off policy toward Hungarian minorities of neighboring states (Brubaker et al. 2007: 125). The most prominent dance-house movement musicians were Transylvanian Hungarians who had gone into exile in Hungary and called for solidarity with Transylvania's Hungarian minority amid reports that the Romanian state was pursuing aggressive assimilationist policies (Kürti 2000: 114). Transylvanian Hungarian villages came to be objects of fascination and desire for those spurred by their involvement in the dance-house movement to travel in search of non-materialistic values as well as national solidarity and Hungarian heritage.

Hungarians also sought out particular Transylvanian landscapes deemed magical as part of this anti-consumerist search for authenticity. The folk cultural revival helped invest several Ciuc Valley natural sites with characteristics of magical beauty (Kürti 2000: 112–4). Chief among these were the Ciuc Valley itself viewed from high atop Harghita Mountain, the hay meadows around Ghimeş, and the volcanic crater of Lake Saint Anna, located at the valley's southern end. In their writings on these sites, Transylvanian Hungarian sociologists Juliana Bodó and Zoltán Bíró describe visiting Hungarians' mythical imaginary, a contradictory picture of magical rurality and modern technological advancement featuring bathing fairies, sleeping meadows, and the latest tractor technology (Bodó

1991: 67; Bíró and Bodó 1992). As with many aspects of Hungarians' views about Transylvania, the notion that these sites host fairytale-style adventures reflects the distinctiveness of Hungarians' own experience and their effort to grapple with the New Economic Mechanism's valorization of materialist consumerism.

In the 1980s, the regime's official television network broadcast an immensely popular animated series, *Hungarian Folktales* (Magyar Népmesék), that featured among other stories an unmarried peasant man who cut down a forest tree that transforms into a fairy; a village's childless woodcarver who sculpts a statue that subsequently comes to life; and a demon that materializes out of nowhere to lead a prince lost in the woods.[25] The folk cultural revival had the effect of assimilating the supernatural, the mystical, and the whimsical into authoritative scientific intellectual disciplines like ethnology in the same way that medical science in post-Soviet Russia, according to Galina Lindquist, became allied with "an explosion of interest in the paranormal, magic, New Age, and occult" (Lindquist 2006: 9).

Hungarians carried this desire for "the enjoyment of the exotic" with them across the border into Transylvania; Catholic priests who conducted fieldwork on Transylvanian Hungarian music, dance, and religious traditions rubbed shoulders with ethnologists who, like Lindquist's Russian New Age doctors, styled themselves as both scientists and neo-shamans and mystics (Kürti 2015). In contrast to a "Westernized, urbanized, and consumeristic Hungary," anthropologist Margit Feischmidt writes, "[tourists] viewed Transylvania as 'other,' exotic, close to nature, and traditional" (2005: 14).

If Hungarians from Hungary view Transylvanian Hungarians as inhabitants of a magical world, representatives of an authentic culture, and exemplars of post-materialistic values, Transylvanian Hungarians look back at rich cousins whose wealth is manifest in their authoritative taste, including a taste for post-materialistic goods like beautiful views, warm hospitality, and magical experiences. This dynamic is partly the result of Hungary's distinction as the envy of Eastern Bloc consumers, a status underscored by Romania and Hungary's divergent economic paths through the 1980s. While the latter was becoming known as a consumerist paradise, Romania suffered from consumer shortages as the state sold the majority of domestic production—including basic food necessities—to pay down its foreign debt. Romania's Hungarian community remained keenly aware of these divergences. Not only did Hungarians go searching for beauty and solidarity in Transylvania, but Transylvanian Hungarians themselves went to Hungary in search of consumer goods to bring back to Romania (Bodó 1996, 2008).

Certainly, the fact that the state distributed opportunities for travel through Party and workplace bureaucracies has contributed to a broad sense that consumption is an index of the state's care for the collective of national citizens. But the distinction between Eastern European state-centered consumer culture and Western European individualistic and market-driven consumer culture should not be overstated. Not every act of consumption explicitly indexes state policies. But many Transylvanian Hungarians do believe that consumer taste reveals shared differences, especially class differences that divide them from Hungarians from Hungary. For instance, during the 1990s, it was their ethnic kin's consumer taste that grabbed the attention of Transylvanian Hungarians when they moved to Hungary for work, typically in hotels, shops, and restaurants in customer-facing positions and where they likewise were at the behest of Hungarian consumers' demands (Brubaker et al. 2007: 316–20; Bodó 1996, 2008; Fox 2009).

After socialism, the growth of Hungary's village tourism industry and the expansion of labor migration out of Romania only deepened the authoritative status of Hungarians' post-materialistic desires. Hungarian sociologists have described a "second wave" of tourism to Transylvania that built on and expanded the range of the folk cultural revival-inspired traffic of the 1970s (Bakó 1998: 129; Szilágyi 2007). The Csíksomlyó Pentecost pilgrimage event was emblematic of the timing and scale of this growth: from 1990 until 1994, the event involved approximately 2000 participants who could fit in the shrine church and its adjoining courtyard (Losonczy 2009). After 1994, the annual event has grown to 100,000, most of whom come from Hungary.[26] After visiting Csíksomlyó, many continue on to Lake Saint Anna to explore the area's beauty or to Ghimeş to express solidarity with Hungarians living in the village at the border of the Dualist-era Hungarian state.

Certainly not all who come to Transylvania share the same motivations; not even all pilgrims to Csíksomlyó have the same goals. But parsing tourists into different types and categories is reductive, since individual travelers have multiple motivations and can choose to identify with some goals over others depending on which they achieve during the trip.[27] My portrait of Hungarians from Hungary as solidarity-pursuing, nature-adoring, and experience-consuming religious seekers is perhaps also reductive. Compared to the typological approach, though, it does less to prevent us from attending to the ways that Transylvanian Hungarians reconstruct these visitors' ambiguous desires and then make use of these constructions to their own ends. Ultimately, Transylvanian Hungarians' effort to work with their ethnic kin's expectations is productively generated by tourism's fundamentally unequal class dynamic, which holds true whether Hungarians from Hungary come looking for heritage, solidarity, nature, or folk culture.

CONCLUSION

Krisztina Fehérváry describes how, throughout the 1980s, Hungarian citizens embraced nature, play, spontaneity, and fantasy as an explicit rejection of socialism's focus on "adult productivity, responsibility, and sacrifice" (2013: 162). The conflict between post-materialistic values—including Hungarians' spiritual seeker attitude—and the Transylvanian Hungarian intellectual tradition could not be clearer; as Bárdi points out, interwar minority intellectuals were obsessed with sacrifice and responsibility. Village teachers, in particular, were supposed to follow Grundtvig's apostolic model of self-denial, hard work, and dedication. The 1937 Vásárhely Declaration praised humility, poverty, sobriety, and persistence.

Before 1937, Reformed (Calvinist) theologians exhorted servant intellectuals to "put aside every individual interest and dedicate all your strength in service [to the community]" (quoted in Bárdi 2015: 26). The latter principle only clarifies the conflict. Modern Hungarians' seeker attitude is inherently individualistic, valuing religious communities that provide supportive acceptance and shunning those that seek to control or impose limitations. In Bögre's words, "members of this group are searching for an authentic interpretative framework that fits their lives," and they turn away when religious leaders do as Márton did, when he called for the country to model the self-abnegating lifestyles of the early Christian apostles (2016: 208).

In the first decade of the new millennium, Transylvanian Hungarian intellectuals confronted the reality that the message of vocational service, which had initially motivated their program of post-socialist charitable renewal, might impede their plans to broaden their volunteer support base in Hungary. Exhorting Hungarian audiences of religious seekers to embrace the virtues of vocational service might turn them off rather than win their support. The next chapter begins with a story about the NGO founder who appeared in the first pages of this book, Brother Csaba Böjte, in the period when he was confronting this problem—as he began to appeal to Hungarian audiences for assistance in expanding his network of Catholic children's homes in Transylvania.

NOTES

1. Márton, Domokos, and Venczel, as heroic creators of "our intellectual tradition," took on the potentially ethically polluting work of crossing borders to borrow from antagonistic others, much like the heroes of other European national resistance movements are often both praised and derided as "thieves" (Herzfeld 1985: 135; 1987, 2005). Hungarian historian Nándor Bárdi states that Transylvanian School established "a distinct position within Hungarian right-wing politics for leading Transylvanian intellectuals" (2015: 14), I go beyond this analysis that ties the intellectual project to class competition to control the state. My creativity-centered approach also problematizes Eastern Europeanist anthropology's conventional strategy to treat public Christianity as symbols and rhetoric that legitimize state policies. Catholic theologians do much more to shape Hungarian public culture than retroactively affirm preexisting political initiatives; the notion of legitimacy radically reduces Catholic actors' proactive influence on Hungarian public life. For examples among prominent Eastern Europeanists, see Verdery 2000 and Hann 2011. For alternatives that draw on concepts of creativity, see Köllner 2016, Abrahms-Kavunenko 2012, 2015.

2. After the Romanian government replaced the faculty and student body of Cluj-Napoca's Hungarian university with an entirely Romanian population, these Hungarian intellectuals relocated to a new university near the Romanian border in Szeged (Brubaker et al. 2007: 98; Livezeanu 1995). Meanwhile, the Hungarian state also supported refugee cultural production through exile-centered organizations, including the Association of Szekler University Students (Székely Egyetemi és Főiskolai Hallgatók Egyesülete) based in Szeged (Bottoni 2013: 490).

3. While a critical caricature of the state-embedded intellectual, this account echoes definitions of intellectual practice as the execution of technocratic functions in bureaucratic roles. See Bell 1973; Gella 1976; and Gouldner 1979.

4. While in the 1920s the Hungarian state did begin surreptitiously funding and advising Transylvanian Hungarian school institutions as part of its "Eastern Action" initiative (Keleti Akció), the generation of interwar ethnic minority intellectuals retained an enduring sense that they needed to rely on their own resources, convinced that, to paraphrase Bárdi, the

Hungarian state might once again disappear out from behind their backs (1996: 90–95).

5. Hitchins writes that Transylvanism's advocates "relied on the power of good ideas and reasoned debate to achieve their ends" but in the end struggled to found institutions capable of either carrying their ideas into practice or influencing the Romanian state (Hitchins 2007: 96).

6. Parliamentary politician Árpád Paál, for one, had ardently supported Transylvanism until negotiations broke down in the mid-1920s over a new national educational law (Bárdi 2015: 14).

7. Dezső's argument for a distinctively Transylvanian Hungarian approach to revision was also a response to the Hungarian state, which by 1927 had embraced an official policy of "revising" the postwar treaty through the legal mechanisms of the post-War international order. Revisionism in both forms was opposed to irredentism, or changing political borders through military force (Nagy 2017: 4; see also Brubaker et al. 2007: 84; Hanebrink 2006: 125). Makkai also declared his allegiance to the ethnocultural and ethical notion of the minority community: "Not only in politics, but also in culture, social life, family and individual, not only in the physical, but also in the spiritual, spiritual, moral sense, these Hungarian sins and these Hungarian virtues are fighting a life-and-death struggle within us, also in this Hungarian generation" (1931).

8. See Mutschlechner 2022.

9. See also Protestant-Catholic tensions over official commemorations of historical events in which their churches played major roles, perceived by many to marginalize the Catholic Church from speaking on behalf of the nation (Klimo 2003; Hanebrink 2006).

10. See also Giesen 1998: 45–7.

11. Pope Pius XI offered this condemnation in his encyclical *Mortalium animos* (1928).

12. In the immediate post-War years, Transylvania's Catholic bishop had already taken steps to undermine this view that Calvinism is a "transplanted" faith, a foreign adversary intent on conquering Ciuc Valley Catholics. In a statement submitted to the League of Nations, Bishop Kálmán Majláth collaborated with leading Protestants on a declaration of grievances against the Romanian state and formed an Interdominational Committee to coordinate the churches' educational political advocacy. But Márton, Venczel, and Domokos faced the challenge of developing a Catholic rationale for ecumenism within an altogether different sphere of activity: The young cohort of intellectuals to which they belonged favored cultivating an ethical nation and they were skeptical about the prospect of appealing to international regimes based around minority rights. See Bárdi 2013: 104.

13. Pius XI writes that this is the statement from the encyclical that is of "great-est importance." Márton quotes it in a 1947 essay for *Transylvanian School* called, "The Contemporary Tasks of the Transylvanian School." See Ozsváth 2012: 77.

14. Pius XI observed in *Divini Illius Magistri* that, "God directly communi-cates to the family, in the natural order, fecundity, which is the principle of life, and hence also the principle of order." All subsequent references are from Pope Pius XI 1939.

15. Again, he was following from Pius XI, who stated, "[Education] also includes the great number and variety of schools, associations and institu-tions of all kinds, established for the training of youth in Christian piety, together with literature and the sciences."

16. Boyer's interpretation, while flawed, still does more to acknowledge intel-lectuals' agency than Bauman's view that intellectuals' appeals to the past are active utopian imaginings, expressions of a nostalgic longing in a struc-tural condition of anomie (Bauman 1987b: 25).

17. Writing specifically about the Transylvanian Hungarian intellectual tradi-tion, historians Bárdi, Fülep and Lőrincz state that a national calling posits its own particular end and form of human perfection, whereas a Christian calling "proclaims the universal and unitary service of God's will" (2015: 24). See also Ádám and Bozóki's claim about the Hungarian right-wing party Fidesz's 2011 constitution: "In contrast to the Constitution of 1989, the Fundamental Law of 2011 serves as expression of a secularized national religious belief system: a sort of paganized, particularistic understanding of the universalistic spirit of Christianity" (2016: 108).

18. Venczel, for instance, appreciatively criticizes Makkai's "Revision of Our Own" in his article "Metamorphosis Transylvaniae" (Venczel 1991). His starting point is the complaint that Makkai's essay has inspired individual prophet figures but failed to effect a substantial collective change.

19. See O'Sullivan 2018.

20. For instance, see a 1947 essay by Domokos's contemporary and fellow ethnomusicologist, Béla Bártok (1947).

21. Chris Hann observed in 1991 that "There was a widespread feeling among non-Catholics as well as Catholics that, with the long consumer boom now clearly over for Hungarians, the church had an opportunity and a duty to preach a renewal of spiritual values" (1991: 18).

22. In his study of Hungarian religious tourists, Pusztai remarks on the central role of their "quest for meaning" (2004: 189–92).

23. The notion of authentic community is a leitmotif of philosophical, theo-logical, and social scientific reflection throughout the late-socialist period. Ágnes Heller rose to prominence in the early 1970s by arguing that the

individual can find a meaningful purpose in life only within the framework of authentic communities (Apor 2013: 25–7).

24. See, for instance, Kürti's comment that the dance-house movement appealed to "young fans who would otherwise have been obsessed with Western popular music" (Kürti 2000: 138). For more on the dance-house movement, see Lange, who writes about the movement's notion of authenticity that, "Many participants and observers have reflected upon the intense and absorbing nature of the revival as something that participants felt was 'real' rather than urban and denatured" (2014: 42).

25. The stories are "A háromagú tölgyfa tündere," "Fából faragott Péter," and "Abeles-kobeles."

26. Hungarian ethnologists and Church officials insist even this number is an underestimate (see Mohay 2009).

27. Kaell (2014) makes this point. Although scholars of religion in North America religion have taken this observation to heart, many Hungarian anthropologists remain mired in a sterile debate about whether Hungarian visitors fit a certain type of heritage, religious, ecological, or rural tourist (see Feischmidt 2005: 13; Losonczy 2009).

References

Abrahms-Kavunenko, Saskia. 2012. Religious 'Revival' After Socialism? Eclecticism and Globalisation Amongst Lay Buddhists in Ulaanbaatar. *Inner Asia* 14 (2): 279–297.

———. 2015. The Blossoming of Ignorance: Uncertainty, Power and Syncretism Amongst Mongolian Buddhists. *Ethnos* 80 (3): 346–363.

Ádám, Zoltán and András Bozóki. 2016. State and Faith: Right-wing Populism and Nationalized Religion in Hungary. *Intersections: East European Journal of Society and Politics* 2 (1): 98–122.

Apor, Péter. 2013. Autentikus közösség és autonóm személyiség: 1989 egyik előtörténete [Authentic Community and Autonomous Personality: A Prehistory of 1989]. *AETAS* 28 (4): 22–39.

Bakó, Boglárka. 1998. Az érdekességeket keresõ turisták és a turistákat keresõ érdekességek. In *A turizmus mint kulturális rendszer*, ed. Zoltán Fejős, 129–139. Budapest: Néprajzi Múzeum.

Barabás, Hajnal. 2016. Várják a diákokat az új csíkszeredai kollégiumba. *Krónika Online*, August 31. https://kronikaonline.ro/erdelyi-hirek/varjak-a-diakokat-az-uj-csikszeredai-kollegiumba. Accessed 16 Jan 2020.

Bárdi, Nándor. 1996. A Keleti Akció – A romániai magyar intézmények anyaországi támogatása az 1920-as években [The Eastern Action – Homeland State Support for Hungarian Institutions in Romania in the 1920s]. In

62   M. R. LOUSTAU

Magyarságkutatás 1995–96, ed. László Diószegi, 143–190. Budapest: Teleki László Alapítvány.

———. 2013. *Otthon és haza: Tanulmányok a romániai Magyar kisebbség történetéről* [At Home, There and Here. Research on the History of the Hungarian Minority in Romania]. Miercurea Ciuc: Pro-Print.

———. 2015. A népszolgálat genezise és tartalomváltozása. In *Népszolgálat: A közösségi elkötelezettség alakváltozatai a magyar kisebbségek történetében* [Service to the People: The Elementary Forms of Community Commitment in the History of the Hungarian Minority], eds. Nándor Bárdi, Tamás Gusztáv Filep, and József D. Lőrincz, 11–48. Pozsony: Kalligram Kiadó.

Bárdi, Nándor, Tamás Gusztáv Filep, and József D. Lőrincz. 2015. Bevezető [Introduction]. In *Népszolgálat: A Közösségi Elkötelezettség Alakváltozatai A Magyar Kisebbségek Történetében* [Service to the People: The Elementary Forms of Community Commitment in the History of the Hungarian Minority], 2–10. Pozsony: Kalligram Kiadó.

Bártok, Béla. 1947. Gypsy Music or Hungarian Music? *The Musical Quarterly* 33 (2): 240–257.

Bauman, Zygmunt. 1987a. Intellectuals in East-Central Europe: Continuity and Change. *East European Politics and Societies and Cultures* 1 (2): 162–186.

———. 1987b. *Legislators and Interpreters: On Modernity, Post-Modernity and Intellectuals*. Cambridge: Polity Press.

Bell, Daniel. 1973. *The Coming of Post-Industrial Society: A Venture in Social Forecasting*. New York: Basic Books.

Bialecki, Jon. 2017. Eschatology, Ethics, and Ēthnos: Ressentiment and Christian Nationalism in the Anthropology of Christianity. *Religion and Society* 8 (1): 42–61.

Biró, Zoltán, and Bodó Julianna. 1992. A "hargitaiság" – egy régió identitásépítési gyakorlatáról. Átmenetek – a mindennapi élet antropológiája. *Kommunikációs Antropológia Munkacsoport* 1: 14–29.

Bodó, Julianna. 1996. *Elvándorlók? Vendégmunka és életforma a Székelyföldön.* Miercurea Ciuc: Pro-Print Könyvkiadó.

———. 2008. *Migrációs folyamatok – közösségi megjelenítések.* Miercurea Ciuc: Státus Kiadó.

Bögre, Zsuzsanna. 2016. Individual Religiosity, Secularization and Seekers Among Hungarian Youth. In *Seekers or Dwellers? Social Character of Religion in Hungary*, ed. Zsuzsanna Bögre, 195–212. Washington, DC: The Council for Research in Values and Philosophy.

Böröcz, József. 1993. Simulating the Great Transformation: Property Change Under Prolonged Informality in Hungary. *European Journal of Sociology* 34 (1): 81–107.

Bottoni, Stefano. 2013. National Projects, Regional Identities, Everyday Compromises Szeklerland in Greater Romania (1919–1940). *Hungarian Historical Review* 2 (3): 477–511.

Boyer, Dominic. 2005. *Spirit and System: Media, Intellectuals, and the Dialectic in Modern German Culture*. Chicago: University of Chicago Press.

Boylston, Tom. 2018. *The Stranger at the Feast: Prohibition and Mediation in an Ethiopian Orthodox Christian Community*. Berkeley: University of California Press.

Brubaker, Rogers, Margit Feischmidt, Jon Fox, and Liana Grancea. 2007. *Nationalist Politics and Everyday Ethnicity in a Transylvanian Town*. Princeton: Princeton University Press.

Case, Holly. 2009. *Between States: The Transylvanian Question and the European Idea During World War II*. Stanford: Stanford University Press.

Chelcea, Liviu. 2002. The Culture of Shortage During State-Socialism: Consumption Practices in a Romanian Village in the 1980s. *Cultural Studies* 16 (1): 16–43.

Dezső, László. 1997. *A kisebbségi élet ajándékai*. Cluj-Napoca: Minerva Kiadó.

Domokos, Pál Péter. 1938. A magyar népzene és énekkari műveltségünk [Hungarian Folk Music and Our Choral Cultivation]. *Erdélyi Iskola* 2: 135–143.

Fehérváry, Krisztina. 2013. *Politics in Color and Concrete: Socialist Materialities and the Middle Class in Hungary*. Bloomington: University of Indiana Press.

Feischmidt, Margit. 2005. A magyar nacionalizmus autenticitás-diskurzusainak szimbolikus térfoglalása Erdélyben. In *Erdély – (de)konstrukciók*, ed. Margit Feischidt, 7–35. Budapest/Pécs: Néprajzi Múzeum – PTE Kommunikáció- és Médiatudományi Tanszék.

Fejérdi, András. 2016. *Pressed by a Double Loyalty: Hungarian Attendance at the Second Vatican Council, 1959–1965*. Budapest: Central University Press.

Fox, Jon. 2009. From National Inclusion to Economic Exclusion: Transylvanian Hungarian Ethnic Return Migration to Hungary. In *Diasporic Homecomings: Ethnic Return Migration in Comparative Perspective*, ed. Tsuda Takeyuki, 186–207. Stanford: Stanford University Press.

Gella, Aleksander. 1976. *The Intelligentsia and the Intellectuals: Theory, Method, and Case Study*. Beverly Hills: Sage.

Giesen, Bernhard. 1998. *Intellectuals and the Nation: Collective Identity in a German Axial Age*. Cambridge: Cambridge University Press.

Gouldner, Alvin. 1979. *The Future of Intellectuals and the Rise of the New Class*. New York: Seabury.

Hallam, Elizabeth, and Tim Ingold, eds. 2007. *Creativity and Cultural Improvisation*. London: Routledge.

Hanebrink, Paul. 2006. *In Defense of Christian Hungary: Religion, Nationalism, and Antisemitism, 1890–1944*. Ithaca: Cornell University Press.

Hann, Chris. 2011. Moral Dispossession. *InterDisciplines* 2 (2): 11–37.

64   M. R. LOUSTAU

Hegedűs, Rita, and Gergely Rosta. 2016. Seekers and Dwellers in the Light of Empirical Social Research. In *Seekers or Dwellers? Social Character of Religion in Hungary*, ed. Zsuzsanna Bögre, 213–235. Washington, DC: The Council for Research in Values and Philosophy.

Herzfeld, Michael. 1985. *The Poetics of Manhood: Contest and Identity in a Cretan Mountain Village*. Princeton: Princeton University Press.

———. 1987. *Anthropology Through the Looking-Glass: Critical Ethnography in the Margins of Europe*. New York: Cambridge University Press.

Hitchins, Keith. 2007. Erdelyi Fiatalok: The Hungarian Village and Hungarian Identity in Transylvania in the 1930s. *Journal of Hungarian Studies* 21 (2): 85–99.

Huseby-Darvas, Éva. 2001. Hungarian Village Women in the Marketplace During the Late Socialist Period. In *Women Traders in Cross Cultural Perspective: Mediating Identities, Marketing Wares*, ed. L. Seligmann, 185–209. Palo Alto: Stanford University Press.

Imre, Lajos. 1938. *Hivatás és Élet: Elmélkedések, Prédikációk, Előadások* [Calling and Life: Reflections, Sermons, and Lectures]. Cluj: Minerva.

Kaell, Hillary. 2014. *Walking Where Jesus Walked: American Christians and Holy Land Pilgrimage*. New York: New York University Press.

Keane, Webb. 2007. *Christian Moderns: Freedom and Fetish in the Mission Encounter*. Los Angeles: University of California Press.

Köllner, Tobias. 2016. Patriotism, orthodox religion and education: Empirical findings from contemporary Russia. *Religion, State and Society* 44 (4): 366–386.

Kürti, László. 2000. *The Remote Borderland: Transylvania in the Hungarian Imagination*. Albany: State University of New York Press.

———. 2015. Neoshamanism, National Identity, and the Holy Crown of Hungary. *Journal of Religion in Europe* 8 (2): 235–260.

Lampland, Martha. 1995. *The Object of Labor: Commodification in Socialist Hungary*. Chicago: University of Chicago Press.

Lange, Barbara Rose. 2014. "Good Old Days:" Critiques of Masculinity in the Hungarian Folk Revival. *The World of Music* 3 (2): 39–58.

Lindquist, Galena. 2006. *Conjuring Hope: Magic and Healing in Contemporary Russia*. New York: Berghahn Books.

Livezeanu, Irina. 1995. *Cultural Politics in Greater Romania: Regionalism, Nation Building & Ethnic Struggle, 1918–1930*. Ithaca: Cornell University Press.

Losonczy, Anne-Marie. 2009. Pilgrims of the "Fatherland": Emblems and Religious Rituals in the Construction of an Inter-Patriotic Space Between Hungary and Transylvania. *History and Anthropology* 20 (3): 265–280.

Makkai, Sándor. 1931. *Magunk revíziója* [A Revision of Our Own]. Miercurea Ciuc: Pro-Print Könyvkiadó. Available online at http://mek.oszk.hu/10900/10935/10935.htm

Márton, Áron. 1933. A kiszélesített iskola [The Expanded School]. *Erdélyi Iskola* (1): 5–8. Available online at https://ersekseg.ro/hu/node/3363
———. 1935. Az eszmény nyomán [On the Path of an Ideal]. *Erdélyi Iskola* 3 (5): 134–135. Available online at https://ispmn.gov.ro/uploads/014Marton_Aron_Az_eszmeny_nyoman.pdf
Meyer, Birgit. 2015. *Sensational Movies: Video, Vision, and Christianity in Ghana.* Berkeley: University of California Press.
McKenny, Gerald. 2021. *Karl Barth's Moral Thought.* Oxford: Oxford University Press.
Mohay, Tamás. 2009. A Csíksomlyói Pünkösdi Búcsújárás: Történet, Eredet, Hagyomány [The Csíksomlyó Pentecost Pilgrimage: History, Origin, Tradition]. Budapest: L'Harmattan.
Muehlebach, Andrea. 2012. *The Moral Neoliberal: Welfare and Citizenship in Italy.* Chicago: The University of Chicago Press.
Mutschlechner, Martin. 2022. A Diversity of Confessions. *www.habsburger.net.* https://ww1.habsburger.net/en/chapters/diversity-confessions. Accessed 28 Nov 2020.
O'Sullivan, Michael. 2018. *Patrick Leigh Fermor: Noble Encounters Between Budapest and Transylvania.* Budapest: Central European University Press.
Ozsváth Judit. 2012. Az Erdélyi Iskola című oktatásügyi és népnevelő folyóirat. *Magiszter* 10 (3): 68–83.
———. 2017. Márton Áron és Domokos Pál Péter népnevelői munkássága a két világháború közötti időben [Márton Áron and Domokos Pál Péter Educational Work in the Interwar Period]. *HUCER:* 370–381.
Pius XI. 1939. Pope Pius XI and Education. *Christian Education* 22 (4): 249–254.
Pusztai, Bertalan. 2004. *Religious Tourists: Constructing Authentic Experiences in Late Modern Hungarian Catholicism.* Jyväskylä: University of Jyväskylä.
Rada, János. 2020. Antiklerikális röpiratok vallással kapcsolatos attitűdjei a dualizmus idején: 1867-től 1895-ig. *Aetas* 35 (1): 18–39.
Scherz, China. 2014. *Having People, Having Heart: Charity, Sustainable Development, and Problems of Dependence in Central Uganda.* Chicago: University of Chicago Press.
Sutcliffe, Steven J. 2008. The Dynamics of Alternative Spirituality: Seekers, Networks, and 'New Age'. In *The Oxford Handbook of New Religious Movements,* ed. James Lewis. Oxford: Oxford University Press.
Szilágyi, Eszter. 2007. "Gyimes kevésbé devalvált vidék…" A gyimesi turizmus antropológiai megközelítése. In *A Miskolci Egyetem Bölcsészettudományi Kara tudományos diákköri közleményei,* ed. Csaba Fazekas, 271–289. Miskolc: Miskolci Egyetem.
Tavaszy, Sándor. 1936. Nemzeti léttünk kérdései: A prófétai nemzetszemlélet [The Questions of Our National Existence: The Prophetic National Perspective]. *Pásztortűz* 21.

Trencsényi, Balázs. 2010. Imposed Authenticity: Approaching Eastern European National Characterologies in the Inter-War Period. *Central Europe* 8 (1): 20–47.

Venczel, József. 1935. Collegium Transilvanicum. *Erdélyi Iskola* 5 (6): 180–184.

———. 1938. Márton Áron Püspök Népnevelő Rendszere [Bishop Áron Márton's Educational System]. *Erdélyi Iskola* 6 (6): 361–371.

———. 1991. "Metamorphosis Transylvaniae." In Albert T. (ed.) *Hitel, Cluj 1935–1944. Studii*, pp. 65–72. Budapest: Bethlen Gábor.

Verdery, Katherine. 2000. The Political Lives of Dead Bodies: Reburial and Postsocialist Change. New York: Columbia University Press.

von Klimo, Arpad. 2003. *Nation, Konfession, Geschichte. Zur nationalen Geschichtskultur Ungarns im europaischen Kontext (1860–1948)*. Munich: R. Oldenbourg Verlag.

Wessely, Anna. 2002. Travelling People, Travelling Objects. *Cultural Studies* 16 (1): 3–15.

CHAPTER 3

Love

SEEKER SERVANTS

This book's Introduction began with a speech by Brother Csaba Böjte, the founder of a network of Transylvanian Hungarian orphanages, to reporters in front of the Hungarian parliament. By 2010, Böjte had already spent years appearing regularly in newspapers, documentaries, book series, and radio and television programs. The 2005 film *Travels with a Monk* [*Utazások egy szerzetessel*], widely praised in the Hungarian media, portrayed him overseeing the construction of new schools and orphanages and generally as an influential reformer of the Transylvanian Hungarian educational system. Just as Áron Márton used his pastoral duties to reorganize institutions for students who had relocated to Cluj from Transylvanian Hungarian villages, the main action of *Travels with a Monk* features Böjte driving his van into impoverished areas and transporting young children to his urban orphanages so that they might receive an education, before they ultimately return home to serve their communities.

Since the election of a conservative government in Hungary in 2010, Böjte has continued his outreach to the right-wing Hungarian state and electorate, which had previously expressed concern for the fate of the ethnic minority population by attending "dance house" (*táncház*) concerts in Hungary as well as other events where they could consume authentic Transylvanian Hungarian culture. As he had in several key scenes in *Travels*

M. R. Loustau, *Hungarian Catholic Intellectuals in Contemporary Romania*, Contemporary Anthropology of Religion, https://doi.org/10.1007/978-3-030-99221-7_3

Brother Csaba Böjte. (Credit: Kriszta Lettner)

with a Monk, Böjte continued to address Hungary's growing right-wing by dramatizing how his orphanages were saving Transylvanian Hungarian children from forgetting their native language and culture, from ethnic and cultural assimilation into Romanian society.[1]

Emboldened by this success, Böjte also expanded his efforts to attract volunteers. He began reaching out to Hungarians from Hungary who had not been to Transylvania but whose growing nationalist sympathies were making them willing to support the Transylvanian Hungarian minority. A passage from a 2012 book of interviews, co-authored with Budapest journalist Éva Karikó and marketed to readers in Hungary, features Brother Csaba appealing to this population. Echoing these readers' disdain for mass-produced, cookie-cutter vacations, Böjte declares that he has never gone on holiday, "at least not the resort-style trip that most people think of" (*Signpost*, 65). Still, he's always up for a spur-of-the-moment lark: "If you come with me, especially in the summer, you should bring your swimming trunks, because I'm always likely to pull over to take a dip in a lake" (*Signpost*, 65). With this invitation, Böjte sent the message that helping the Saint Francis Foundation (SFF) not only shows one's political views but also a penchant for spontaneous fun and leisure.

I present two interrelated arguments in this chapter. My first is that Brother Csaba has risen to prominence through creatively adapting interwar

Transylvanian Hungarian Catholic intellectuals' educational reform program to address contemporary Hungarians' anxieties about the materialism
of post-socialist society. Like Márton and Venczel called on traveling busi-
nessmen to donate their time and expertise to rural students in the urban
Collegium Transylvanicum, Böjte reaches out to middle-class Hungarian
volunteers to serve in his orphanages. Böjte takes messages about adopting
vocational virtues and reframes them in media texts that appeal to contemporary Hungarian post-materialist seekers with "guided meditation"-style
modes of address. Brother Csaba's intellectual creativity lies, therefore, in
his ability to synthesize the Transylvanian Hungarian intellectual tradition
with Hungary's culture of experience tourism and religious seeking.

Böjte's media outreach succeeded in tapping into new resources. He
attracted visitors from Hungary who wanted something in addition to
what Hungarians from Hungary typically seek in Transylvania: the politicized leisure activity of consuming traditional Hungarian culture. These
travelers came also to donate their labor to his orphanages, to contribute
to the Böjte's educational mission to rural Transylvanian Hungarians. But
this influx also posed new challenges, which leads me to my second claim.
In 2010, I joined Böjte and a group of forty volunteers for the third year
of his popular volunteer program for Hungarians, during which we
restored the Csíksomlyó orphanage's backyard.[2] I was grouped with several first-time visitors to Transylvania from urban Budapest. On our team
was also Ambrus, in his late teens and a former orphanage resident. Ambrus
used his extensive local knowledge to lead us to a hidden swimming hole
where we temporarily escaped the dust and heat. Some were not pleased
by this; I overheard volunteers grumble as Ambrus led us back. Later
Brother Csaba took Ambrus aside, after which our swimming excursions
stopped. Although the trips were a gratifying indulgence, it seemed that
Böjte had counseled Ambrus to avoid further spontaneous excursions and
to set a better example of a hardworking and responsible servant.

While Brother Csaba felt he could grow the SFF by turning seekers into
volunteers, accessing these resources left the priest with a choice between
responsibility and enjoyment. On the one hand, Brother Csaba presented
himself as a paragon of service, a virtuous hard-worker, while on the other
he touted his own penchant for leisure and encouraged his readers to take
time to enjoy Transylvania's natural beauty. Brother Csaba also uses the
revelation of God's collaborative presence to mediate this conflict. I examine two cases from his collection of interviews with Éva Karikó in which he
guides her to discover that God is at work beside them. In Böjte's words,
he shows her that God is eternally continuing to create the world;

revealing God's labor allows him to put aside his orphanage work to address the questions and doubts that, in Karikó's words, exemplify the seeker attitude. By updating this Catholic ethical concept, Böjte also performs an act of ethical creativity that mediates responsibility and the enjoyment of pleasure.

This chapter is organized into three broad sections. Throughout, I weave material from Brother Csaba's publications together with ethnographic data from my participation in the 2010 Saint Francis Foundation volunteer building project. I use not only the 2005 documentary, *Travels with a Monk*, but also four collections of Karikó's interviews with Brother Csaba published between 2009 and 2012: *Window onto the Infinite*, *Path into the Infinite*, *Signpost toward the Infinite*, and *Dialogue with the Infinite*. I begin by analyzing these documents, finding in them calming and intimately direct appeals for seekers to combine the search for enlightenment with volunteerism in order to help poor Transylvanian Hungarians. I go on to analyze Böjte's use of allegorical storytelling to grapple with the contradictions that plague right-wing Hungarian public discourse. Although he plays into this demographic's concerns over ethnic assimilation, in his stories Brother Csaba advocates for conciliation regarding EU laws affecting his orphanages, albeit without naming the European context for this argument.

Finally, I give an ethnographic account of the SFF's garden restoration project, in which I focus on how Ambrus reappropriated the touristic and leisure cultural discourse of spontaneity to reassert a threatened sense of local belonging. Nevertheless, vocational culture's identification with virtuous hard work ultimately destabilized this effort. A muted conflict erupted over Ambrus's unplanned swimming excursions, a clash of ethical values that endangered the SFF's garden reconstruction project. More importantly, though, it was Brother Csaba who felt obliged to intervene with Ambrus, to ease the tensions that threatened to destabilize the volunteer group's sense of shared purpose and solidarity.

Ethical Enlightenment

During the late 2000s, as Brother Csaba began addressing Hungarian audiences through his media collaborations, he developed a message about the middle-class seeker's psycho-spiritual fragility in the face of post-industrial poverty. That the post-socialist state has effectively abandoned the rural population—at least the villagers who had moved to

Still image from "Travels with a Monk" (2005, Ibolya Fekete, dir.)

model socialist factory towns—is a major theme of Fekete's 2005 documentary film, *Travels with a Monk*. Fekete stages their conversations with herself as the passenger in Böjte's car while the latter drives to collect the orphanages' newest residents. In an early scene, her camera pans over dilapidated government-built apartment buildings, captioned "phantom blocks" (*fantomblokk*); what remains are mostly concrete shells that unemployed workers picked clean of their steel rebar, which they then sold on the black market. The buildings speed by while Brother Csaba plays the part of interpreter for this post-industrial landscape and way of life. He explains to Fekete's middle-class audience the haunted buildings' meaning. This foreign milieu, he says, "is a world outside the law. There are no rights guaranteed by the state, and in truth there is no obligation, either. Anything can happen here."

When filtered through Brother Csaba's appeals to potential donors in Hungary, the process of producing a withdrawn neoliberal state in Eastern Europe is shifted out of the context of the nation-state's subservience to international economic organizations. In the wake of IMF and World Bank "structural adjustment measures," anthropologists of Eastern Europe blamed these organizations for imposing neoliberalism in a top-down process that primarily involved changing state-level social welfare and economic policy (see Verdery 1996). However, Brother Csaba describes the state's cruel abandonment to provoke the Hungarian state to demonstrate its superior concern. His appeal produces charitable attention in the Hungarian middle classes and spurs the Hungarian state to competitively perform its care for the members of the ethnic Hungarian minority that the Romanian state has abandoned not only economically and legally but morally as well.

In his other major journalistic collaboration, Karikó's volume of theological dialogues, he describes one of the post-industrial sites that he had visited with Fekete, a neglected mining town called Muncelu Mic, or Kismuncsel in Hungarian (*Path*, 7). Böjte frames his portrait of Muncelu Mic's post-industrial abandonment within a story about a friend's recent ordeal: "I would like to share some thoughts I originally offered to a friend whose world was falling apart after one body-blow too many" (*Path*, 7). Böjte sketches the outline of a typical middle-class individual concerned with balance, stability, and happiness in his personal life; an orientation to everyday life that, according to Hungarian sociologist Péter Apor, emerged in the late socialist period out of the Hungarian state's effort to align material comfort with the triumph of centrally planned economies over Western society (Apor 2013: 30).

The friend remains fixated on his everyday life, only now it is falling apart; he wants to run away. The international destination Böjte's friend contemplates, a Nicaraguan village "in the mountains where there are trees and fresh air" (*Path*, 8), adds to the image of an urbanite trying to restore his spiritual centeredness in an exotic, distant, and natural locale. Böjte recommends instead Muncelu Mic, which offers his friend Transylvania's beautiful scenery and peasant-style entertainments. There, he can get to know a local family that will teach him to weave straw baskets and take him raspberry picking. Eventually, the family's poverty comes to light. "At first everything you see makes you embarrassed. It's possible you will start crying, and cursing this world in which the well-kempt spend three hundred Euros for a dog but an impoverished child has to live on state assistance of less than ten Euros" (*Path*, 8).

As Böjte continues his narrative, his friend comes to another low point. The man steps away into the forest, weeping at the injustice and vowing angrily to fight. He is suffering a combined psycho-spiritual and ethical crisis, a building-block experience of the genre of "ethical entertainment." Media theorist Kaarina Nikunen notes that today's ethical entertainment has become a widespread tool for fostering "media solidarities," efforts to increase charitable giving with reality-television-style dramas about volunteers' personal transformations (Nikunen 2018; see also Malkki 2015). When Nikunen writes, "care, help, and charity become commodified as something that educates on how to have a good life," she anticipates the denouement of Brother Csaba's story about his embattled friend. Böjte appeals to the man on an intimate level, reaching deep into the man's subjective experience with his comforting voice: "Slowly you will calm down and relax," he intones. "Your thoughts and desires will ease, and you will be filled with a great peace. You will become enlightened, and everything will become simple and clear" (*Path*, 8). Böjte's manner is soothing, as if he were a voice on a recorded guided meditation that the average Hungarian seeker might have used to calm down after an especially hectic or tense day. He guides his friend to an enlightenment of inner calmness and balance.

Böjte does not stop at healing his friend's troubled state. While on his way to feeling relaxed and at ease, the friend also senses God's presence. "You believe that you are not just a part of the world," Böjte writes, "but a partner of the God who, out of infinite love, eternally continues to create the world….You are God's coworker, and you have realized that you are already there in Nicaragua" (*Path*, 9). In the process, Böjte harkens back to a key theological motif of interwar Catholic thought. The man feels the presence of God, the creative laborer. God as collaborator was the theological centerpiece of Pope Pius XI's interwar encyclicals about education and social reform, *Divini Illius Magistri* (1929) and *Quadragesimo anno* (1931).

Divini Illius Magistri had inspired interwar Transylvanian Hungarian Catholic intellectuals—most notably Áron Márton—to develop a pedagogical tradition of "our own" rooted in the call to serve. Like Márton before him, Böjte highlights the collaborative version of grace, God's presence in the world. Böjte harkens back to the Transylvanian Hungarian intellectual tradition, but he does so through volunteerism appeals to urban Hungarians. The notion of God-as-collaborator emerges through Böjte's intimate address to his friend who has encountered Transylvania's post-industrial poverty as one more body blow to his personal stability, bringing him to the point of psychological collapse under the weight of his guilt. Böjte then reveals God's collaborative grace at work in the narrative styles of a seeker-type spirituality to people who have been disciplined to desire enlightenment and view their personal lives as the field of a divine drama.

This guided meditation-style narrative journey to enlightenment also dramatizes one of Brother Csaba's oft-repeated messages: God wants vocational servants to have a rich and pleasurable life. In a passage from *Window onto the Infinite*, Brother Csaba declares that "Jesus Christ wants His joy to be our joy, and for our joy to be full" (*Window*, 68). With this motif, Böjte departs from interwar Transylvanian Hungarian advocates of vocational service who insisted that a calling requires self-denial and asceticism. Böjte manages to have it both ways by praising the kinds of pleasures one might find on a Transylvanian Hungarian vacation, especially the post-materialistic practice of enjoying nature. For example, Böjte describes jumping into a lake on a hot day and his friend strolling for wild raspberries. But in *Window onto the Infinite*, Böjte is challenged by his interviewer to provide a theological basis for affirming Hungarians' desires. Karikó's worry is that moderating the obligation to asceticism and affirming pleasure-seeking could lead to narcissism; and she points out that Jesus often says one should not do good with the expectation of reward, a typical interpretation of the famous biblical maxim, "But when you give alms, do not let your left hand know what your right hand is doing" (Matthew 6:3, NRSV).

Böjte disagrees with her interpretation; God's love is overabundant, he tells her. "But, in his overflowing love, God does not stop here," he insists, "He sees our good deeds even when they are secret, and rewards us lavishly for them" (*Window*, 220). The theological notion underlying this declaration emerges from a logical syllogism about God's being: Because love is God's essence, and because the fact that God created the world shows that God necessarily goes beyond God's self, then God's love overflows by necessity. In contrast to interwar theologians who advocated asceticism, Böjte affirms his readers' desire for overabundance. In the 1920s and 1930s, Transylvanian Hungarian Reformed (Calvinist) theologians warned future village teachers away from expecting any immediate return for their work, but Böjte counsels his readers that it is acceptable—and even a way of recognizing God's love in the world—to expect rewards.

While historians have argued the asceticism of interwar Transylvanian Hungarian intellectuals and that the intellectual tradition they crafted is post-Protestant, being deeply influenced by Reformed (Calvinist) ethical beliefs (Bárdi et al. 2015; Bárdi 2015: 22), anthropologists like China Scherz have used Jesus' view on alms-giving to theorize that the essence of Christian ethical culture is a refusal to count the benefits of one's ethical actions, a version of the classic Weberian "Ethic of Conviction" that Christians should do what is right and leave the outcome to God (Scherz

2014: 114).[3] Certainly, like the Catholic nuns in the Ugandan orphanage where Scherz did fieldwork, Böjte does not like bookkeeping, which he associates with the external interventions of the European Union in accord with his readers' right-wing, Euro-skeptic views (*Window*, 186–8).[4]

At the same time, Böjte encourages any potential Hungarian seeker-volunteer to expect rewards from doing good and that one can expect to enjoy serving in his orphanages. The difference lies in Böjte's reinterpretation of counting an ethical act's benefits, recasting the external bureaucratic demand to show programmatic effectiveness as a middle-class Hungarian visitor's anticipation of the non-materialist "simple pleasures" of traditional rural culture. What this really amounts to is redirecting his readers' inclination to take the bureaucratic audit culture of the EU as authoritative by replacing readers' interpretative context with the project of building an ethical nation, whereby Böjte is able to suggest that goodness is born of doing good. He refuses to stop working when faced with two seemingly conflicting and opposed ethical cultures: the Ethic of Conviction and a bureaucratic Ethic of Responsibility that intends to calculate the benefits of virtuous behavior. Attending to the way Böjte updates the Transylvanian Hungarian intellectual tradition, developing it within a familiar yet authoritative consumer cultural context, makes anthropological accounts of intractable conflicts between these cultures look like artificial abstractions.

Although Karikó is now a Catholic, in the introduction to *Pathway into the Infinite* she writes about converting after a secular upbringing that included seeking in diverse religious traditions.[5] Moreover, Karikó reveals that she designed the book's question-and-answer interview format to appeal to religious seekers. "While preparing for the interviews," Karikó writes, "I tried to excavate out from within myself that former 'I' of mine, the one who was so skeptical, inquisitive, and investigated everything" (*Dialogue*, 11).

In the Introduction to their final volume of interviews, Karikó confesses that her seeker mentality sometimes interfered with Böjte's work. Her questions got in the way when Böjte was trying to solve problems in his orphanages. Like the documentarian Fekete, Karikó recorded her discussions with Böjte while riding in his van. It was normal for Böjte to address questions as he drove, fielded calls, or tended to the orphans who rode along with them: "The car was often packed full of children and coworkers. Every few seconds, his phone would ring with another problem to solve, another request for help" (*Dialogue*, 10). She was deeply impressed by the mental agility that allowed him to reply amid constant interruptions. "Without extensive thought," Karikó gushes, "he answered almost immediately while his brain was working on all that we experienced throughout the day" (*Dialogue*, 10).

When seeking interfered with service, Karikó experienced these conflicts at the same psychosomatic level as Böjte's unnamed acquaintance—as body blows to her personal life. In *Dialogue with the Infinite*, Karikó narrates a time when a volunteer called to rescind an offer to oversee a newly established orphanage. She recalls her sudden uneasiness: "Overwhelmed by the news, we got into the car and continued our trip. I didn't dare speak, since most people would have become irritated in such circumstances." Fearfully, she whispered her next question.

But Brother Csaba had remained cheerful. He was smiling as he explained that although his mind was spinning its wheels over the unexpected problem, God's mind was working on it even harder (*Dialogue*, 10). At Brother Csaba's suggestion, they resumed the interview, with the further remark, "Let's give him the task so that He might care for us" (*Dialogue*, 10). Böjte uses this interaction to reveal that God is always working alongside us. The manner Böjte imagines for God's presence is shaped by Pius XI's image of God the collaborator—the theological motif that inspired Transylvanian Hungarian Catholic interwar advocates of vocational service.

Like Böjte's seeker acquaintance, the one who considered fleeing to Nicaragua, had combined enlightenment with a rural getaway, Karikó's subsequent comment evokes the pleasures of rural vacationing as tantamount to the search for enlightenment. After the phone call, Karikó and Böjte got back on the road. She remarks, "We drove on and gazed dreamily at the Gyimes [Ghimeş] countryside, so beautiful it's like out of a folk tale, just chatting and joking as if nothing had happened" (*Dialogue*, 10).[6]

The story Böjte relates concerning his seeker friend defined crisis and the revelation that God is at work as the two central events on the path from seeker to servant. Introducing Karikó to a passing view of postindustrial poverty, Böjte then gives shape to her crisis, by which he attests to God's collaborative presence. After the inopportune phone call, the employee's resignation has made Karikó acutely aware that Böjte's orphans will continue to deal with lack of care, and perhaps even disappointed in or bitter about the erstwhile volunteer's weak sense of dedication and responsibility. As a seeker, she is also driven to ask questions, such that she wonders if these questions will distract Brother Csaba from tending to the needs of the poor children in his care and alleviating their suffering. Karikó is first struck silent by fear that he might get angry, but she then gives in to the seeker's desire to ask, though shyly, as all she produces is a whispered question.

Böjte once more acts like the personal coach. While relating the story of his friend, Böjte offered the enraged, weeping man language like "relax" and "calm." God-as-collaborator becomes active in this personal situation when the man then senses, in Böjte's words, that he is partnered with the God who continues to create the world. To Karikó, Böjte also suggests the two of them take a break, this time handing off a troubling task to God. Once again, Böjte speaks calmly and kindly, restoring Karikó to a relaxed state personal that she enacts as by gazing upon Transylvania's dreamy landscape.

In both cases, Böjte plays a necessary role to the revelation of God's presence. Although Böjte portrays God's collaborative presence as emerging in a *one-on-one* and *intimate* exchange, this revelation also requires the seeker's physical proximity to and sensory awareness of the orphans' suffering. Seekers come to an emotional crossroads of bitterness and joy, responsibility and pleasure, concern and relief, by traveling to places like Muncelu Mic or Ghimeş and following Böjte as he meets each region's inhabitants. That is to say, a seeker's personal crisis, in which Böjte intervenes, wholly depends on an invitation to join him on the road as he cares for his ward's needs.

Regressive Pleasures

Even beyond Böjte's theological publications for Hungarians, for instance in the itinerary guiding the Saint Francis Foundation's volunteer projects, we can see how Brother Csaba did not accept the assumption that charity and pleasure should necessarily conflict. Each day after digging and planting, the other volunteers and I gathered in the orphanage's meeting room to enjoy a performance of Transylvanian Hungarian folk music and culture. The SFF offered arts programs based on Marian devotionalism, including presentations by the Hungarian priest and ethnomusicologist, Sándor Teodóz Jáki.

Father Jáki lectured about and taught us to sing Transylvanian Hungarian folk songs on the second and third days of our stay, and he began by proudly reviewing his lifetime of ethnomusicological research. But he was equally adept at developing a bond with visitors based on memories of life in socialist-era Hungary. Father Jáki regaled us with attention-grabbing stories, including one about an elderly female acquaintance whom the Hungarian state socialist-era secret police had interrogated after she asked the Virgin Mary to expel occupying Soviet forces.

A lexical signal helped him create a bond of shared historical knowledge with his audience: for the secret police, he used the nickname "Ávosok," which derives from the acronym for socialist-era Hungarian secret police. (Transylvanian Hungarians use a different name for the Romanian secret police.) Moreover, the issue of Soviet occupation was particular to Hungary; Soviet soldiers had left Romania in the early 1960s. In contrast, they remained in Hungary until 1989, and their presence remained a charged issue in Hungarian politics throughout the socialist period.

In the anecdote, Father Jáki described both familial and national spaces as fragile refuges that had been threatened by a foreign state. The Hungarian socialist state, because it was dependent on the Soviet military, came across as a foreign invader of the homeland, just as the secret police were foreign invaders of the elderly woman's house. Father Jáki gave this post-socialist trope a Catholic devotional twist by adding that the socialist state, by intervening in the woman's petitionary prayer, also helped constitute the woman's intimate face-to-face relationship with the Virgin Mary.

This strategy also played to the anti-EU and right-wing sympathies of Father Jáki's audience. The right-wing often critically compared joining the EU to Hungary's socialist-era loss of sovereignty to the Soviet Union (Fehérváry 2013: 243). By mentioning secret police abuses, Father Jáki signaled his sympathy with the argument that in Hungary the Soviet-backed Communists had never really been ousted from power and that the country's left-wing parties were led by holdovers from the discredited pre-1989 regime (Fehérváry 2013: 242). The priest and ethnomusicologist nested subtle post-socialist right-wing political signaling within the arc of a Catholic narrative about intercessory prayer; and in the process he described how the Virgin Mary's protective embrace, renewed in the old woman's act of prayer, constitutes a powerful sense of maternal intimacy and safety between saint and devotee, an intimacy that was itself dependent on the existence of a foreign state as a looming external threat.

At his first afternoon session, Father Jáki explained that he was going to teach us a special type of folk song. He had spent most of his life visiting and conducting research in a region populated by a sub-ethnic group known in Romanian as "Ceangău" (in Hungarian, "Csángó," and in international anthropological and historical research, "Csango"). This ethnonym is a catchall term for a group living in the Romanian region of Moldavia, across the Carpathian Mountains to Csíksomlyó's southeast, who speak a dialect of Hungarian (Davis 2019: 11). Many Csango have converted to Charismatic/Pentecostalism, but others are Catholic, a fact that many Hungarians use to claim them for the Hungarian nation (Peti 2020). The Csango exemplify Rogers Brubaker's concept of "nationally mismatched persons" with "structurally ambivalent membership status, belonging by residence to one state and by putative ethnonational affinity to another" (Brubaker 1996: 55–6). In the Hungarian ethnological imagination, which Father Jáki ably represented during his lectures, the Csango are a diasporic population of Catholic Szeklers who supposedly fled from Habsburg persecution to the Romanian Kingdom in the late eighteenth century.

Hungarian ethnological representations of Csango culture are destabilized, however, by a contradiction at the level of cultural identification: "While on the one hand Hungarian intellectuals believe that the Csángó diaspora is different in many ways from the surrounding populations," anthropologist László Kürti writes, "this difference actually reinforces their attachment to the Hungarian nation on the other hand" (Kürti 2000: 112). Insofar as performances of Transylvanian Hungarian folk culture revolve around such contradictory statements about Csango identity, these representations are part of what anthropologist Michal Buchowski calls a newly emerging form of "internal orientalism" (Buchowski 2006). The rise of state-transcending ethnocultural national imaginaries and the increasing freedom to move across political borders means that today's Eastern European "diasporic orientals," including the Csango, are no longer outside the borders of a polity but neighbors who "live side by side with 'us', occupy the same place, speak the same language and believe in the same god" (2006: 466).

In his lecture-performance featuring traditional Transylvanian Hungarian Marian devotional music, Father Jáki continued to play to the tastes and expectations his audience members had developed in their urban Hungarian milieu, especially by evoking the pedagogical orientation of a dance house emcee. He indicated that by learning these songs, we would be embodying the sentimental and regressive attitude that Csango devotees adopt when they sing to the Virgin Mary. The songs, he said, are lullabies that express the Csangos' belief that they are innocent, content, and at peace, like infants safe in their mother Mary's arms. In fact, Csango mothers use these songs to lull babies to sleep.

Father Jáki took several minutes to recall how once during Mass an infant was crying so loudly that he wondered if he would even be able to continue the rite, but then he began singing a Csango lullaby.

By the end of the song, the baby was snoring. There was a Csángó man behind me who said, 'Father, that must have been a Csángó baby because before you started singing, I didn't think he was ever going to stop. He was wailing so badly they must have been hearing him three streets away.'

While teaching us to sing, he repeatedly told us to open our throats and expand our diaphragms so that we would sing like Csango mothers and, in his words, "in the proper Csángó manner." Father Jáki urged us to pay close attention to each song's rhythm and meter. He treated us as if we were dance house learners bending our bodies to a series of steps and gestures organized according to an unfamiliar rhythm that we nevertheless could rediscover as our own. Father Jáki implied that song might bridge the gap of otherness between Csangos and other Hungarians: with the persistent disciplining of our bodies, we could learn to sing like the Csango and maybe even rediscover their profound childlike intimacy with the Virgin Mary.

American immigrant communities often enter Catholic devotional festivals to the Virgin Mary in a mood of atavistic regression, historian Robert Orsi argues, seeking to temporarily overcome the sensory anomie of living in a foreign land. While the urban Hungarian volunteers were not permanent residents of Transylvania, Father Jáki was drawing on a similar trope, popular in right-wing Hungarian culture, that describes Hungarians as an exilic people, given that after World War I they lost control of Transylvania, the home of authentic Hungarian culture. By returning to Transylvania, these urban Hungarians were supposed to be like the immigrant stepping into an annual festa, "able temporarily to reexperience the smells, tastes, and sounds of the lost world of his or her past" (Orsi 1985: 169). In this case, though, our group was supposed to regress even further back to the earliest days of infancy, picturing ourselves under the gaze of the Virgin Mary while being rocked to sleep in maternal arms.

STAYING ON THE PATH OF LOVE

When he spoke to us during the garden rehabilitation project, Brother Csaba largely avoided portraying parenthood in Father Jáki's terms: a soothing maternal embrace that safeguards the contented innocence of infancy, with the infant in this case an allegorical figure of rural Transylvanian Hungarian culture. While Brother Csaba often spoke about parenting, he encouraged his audience to cultivate the activist ethical values of the Transylvanian Hungarian tradition of intellectual vocational service: maturity, hard work, discipline, and responsibility.

These virtues run counter to the romantic picture of a maternal figure providing a protective mantle to preserve rural culture in a state of infantile purity and stability that appeared in Father Jáki's lectures, though Brother Csaba never denigrated this idealized image outright. He did not tell us explicitly that a protective stance, simply preserving the Transylvanian Hungarian minority's culture in a state of somnolescent purity, would do little to help them improve a faltering educational system and, in his view, modernize rural Transylvanian Hungarians' economic, religious, and social life. Rather than use his lectures to mount an explicit critique on this basis, he praised Father Jáki's performance, thanked him, and showed him the respect due to a fellow Catholic priest.

Yet a starkly different interpretation of parenthood emerged from Brother Csaba's lectures, one that departed radically from Father Jáki's message that, by providing a protective embrace for Transylvanian Hungarian culture, we might also experience their state of primal innocence ourselves. Brother Csaba called his talks not performances (*előadások*) but "spiritual practice sessions" (*lelkigyakorlat*). He stood behind a folding table with a microphone stand. To his right was a staffperson from the Catholic radio station, Radio Mária Transylvania, which was broadcasting the lectures. From behind this setup, Brother Csaba spoke directly to us sitting on a ring of chairs to either side and against the facing wall.

Brother Csaba urged the volunteers to realize that rural service—in the guise of teaching and raising children—is exhausting, lonely, frustrating, and demoralizing, and to take seriously these experiences as sin that can distort one's pedagogical relationships. Historian Hillary Kaell writes that problematic parental love was likewise a preoccupation of nineteenth-century North American missionaries writing articles about their work in foreign orphanages. They had a clear sense that sin was "out there"; it was far from white middle-class Protestant parents, and present instead in foreign cultures and unconverted "natives" and "heathens" (Kaell 2020: 35).

In contrast, Böjte told us that sin was as close as his own shame and insecure masculinity. Both, he admitted, have the power to tempt him to violence. Later on in the week, he summarized a story that I recognized later in *Window onto the Infinite*, featuring an encounter with a group of boys who have run away from an orphanage. An orphanage caretaker calls to report that they are somewhere on the roadside walking to the nearest city. Böjte gets the call while at a clergy meeting. As he gets up to go, his colleagues compare him to a mother hen running after his little chicks (*Window*, 74–78). Böjte feels deeply ashamed as he sets out in his car. So much so, he begins fantasizing about giving them a beating.

"Just then," he writes, "it was as if Jesus sat down next to me and said, 'Brother Csaba, no matter what these children did, it doesn't give you the right to turn away from the way of love'" (*Window*, 75). Although Böjte doesn't say as much, the car becomes a mobile confessional booth. The analogy with confession is clear not only because Jesus was confronting Böjte about being tempted to sin, but also because, in confession, the priest sits *in persona Christi*, in the person of Christ. Böjte ends up confessing to the actual Christ while speeding down the road after his lost charges.

After describing his predicament, Brother Csaba tries bargaining with his confessor.

"Well, fine," he tells Jesus, "What if I just box their ears a little? That's not such a big deal, right?"

Jesus's answer is informal but curt.

"Listen," Jesus says, "you didn't see me reach down from the cross to give Herod's ears a good boxing, did you" (*Window*, 76)?

On one level, Brother Csaba is breaking open the space of the confessional booth and reconstructing this sacrament by placing it in a car, one of the banal spaces of everyday middle-class life. On another, he is reimagining the source of clerical authority in confession for a Hungarian Catholic public that, according to anthropologist Bertalan Pusztai, has grown increasingly wary of confessing individual sins to priests (Pusztai 2004: 77). In his improvised car-confessional booth, Böjte does not encounter a priest who listens and then tells him to say ten decades of the Rosary. In this model, the priest acts like a judge extracting the believer's penitential labor in return for sin. Instead, Brother Csaba engages in informal banter with an intimate friend.

Yet this is a hard-nosed intimacy, a pragmatic and let's-get-to-work togetherness, which puts a spin on the feminized form of ethical citizenship that, among Italian eldercare volunteers (Muehlebach 2012: 84–5) and Catholic immigrant domestic workers (Napolitano 2015), manifests itself in providing empathetic presence to the lonely. Jesus tells Böjte he has been in exactly the same position and knows what he's going through.

He understands Böjte's shame and knows his inner feelings. Jesus speaks to the priest and volunteer educator in the midst of his everyday activities. However, Jesus has no tolerance for Böjte's temptation to sin.

Böjte's dialogue about corporal punishment demonstrates a sensitivity to how Hungarians today are sometimes an ethically denigrated "other" to universalizing discourses about parental love. As part of Hungary and Romania's post-socialist transition and accession to the European Union, these countries were forced to change their child welfare laws into conformity with international human rights standards. Hungary, for example, first ratified the UN Convention for the Rights of the Child in 1991 and later in the 1990s integrated it into a national legal framework that included a stipulation forbidding corporal punishment. (Anghel et al. 2013). While citizens in the EU's new member states voted on referenda whether or not to join the international bloc, they had no say in negotiating the terms of accession that featured the wholesale adoption of voluminous family policy regulations (see Kereki 2011).

Through this period, sensationalist media reports about rampant corporal punishment among Eastern European parents living in Western European countries fueled complaints that new member states needed to work harder to fully live up to international standards.[7] In 2016, after Finnish authorities removed five children from a family with a Romanian father over claims that he used corporal punishment, child welfare took a place alongside privatization (Dunn 2004), industrial pollution (Gille 2007), and labor migration (Georgescu 2011) in shaping a condescending political discourse about the newest EU member states still "transitioning" into Europe's universal regime of human rights.

One way of interpreting a recent "retraditionalization" of family norms in Poland, Romania, and Hungary is that the Church has substituted its own competing universalizing discourse for the EU's system of human rights. And yet Böjte's story shows that he is no less aware of the ethical ambiguities entailed in many post-socialist nations' institutionalization of "traditional" and "Christian" family norms. Although the Catholic Church has enjoyed significant state support following the Hungarian right wing's victory in the 2010 elections, the Church's ambition often outpaces its labor resources. Brother Csaba's Saint Francis Foundation has struggled to retain employees, as Karikó's earlier story about the couple who backed out of staffing his orphanage demonstrated.

In the case of the runaway orphans, Böjte might be describing another problem resulting from short-staffing: If the SFF's house had had enough employees to supervise the children, maybe they would have caught the children before they snuck out. Catholic Church leaders, like post-socialist elites in many European countries formerly governed by officially atheist socialist regimes, have argued that involving ecclesiastical officials in teaching and raising children will help heal socialism's moral wounds (Dunn 2004: 130–141; Zubrzycki 2006).[8]

Yet Böjte also struggles with Church representatives' demeaning enforcement of complementary and hierarchically ordered gender roles. He is mocked by his fellow priests, who disparagingly compare him to a female hen running after her baby chicks. The mockery reveals the priests' belief that childrearing is "women's work" and beneath a man's proper social role.

There may also be a competitive instrumental rationale to Böjte's dramatization of moral ambiguity. While the stories show how his foundation is frustrated by limited resources and his own work is misunderstood, he may just be trying to win the favor of a right-wing Hungarian government that seeks needy institutions on which to lavish money, thereby following through on its dual promise to "rescue" a struggling Transylvanian Hungarian community and bolster Hungarian Christian schools.

The answer to this critique is, simply, yes. The Hungarian state may be using Böjte to legitimize its rule, but this does not make Brother Csaba any less creative. In fact, what from one angle is a crassly expedient tool could just as easily be a redirection of the new right-wing government's effort to justify its economic and political policies under the guise of bolstering Hungarian Christendom. After all, Böjte also uses this appeal to a potential state patron to reimagine the Catholic sacramental ritual of confession for a population of readers who had grown unfamiliar with it.

When Böjte eventually finds the boys walking on the side of the road, they choose to get in his car, and he writes, "There was a true joy and gratitude in my heart because God had not let me turn away from path of love" (*Window*, 76). Böjte himself comes close to being a morally offensive allegorical figure. He is tempted, but he does not actually engage in corporal punishment. As he struggles with the desire to lash out, he directs at himself the same doubts that the European Union's family-policy gatekeepers have about post-socialist countries: that despite adopting EU human rights laws these societies still (perhaps secretly) tolerate corporal punishment, are not quite European, and require further "transition."

Within Hungarian right-wing public discourse about the family, Christian love is an ambiguously, surreptitiously European value. Böjte's "path of love" is a post-socialist journey, a "transition" into the familial emotional and social relations demanded by the EU's universalizing human rights regime. His commitment to this transition is as emphatic as it is rueful, since the model of family love he embraces takes shape against a backdrop formed by Hungarian society's process of moral and legal adjustment within an expanding Europe. Böjte's self-critique shows an awareness that the involvement of Catholic priests in family life has not necessarily healed Hungarian society, but rather produced opportunities to sin that he uses to reimagine the sacrament of confession and the priest's authority in this ritual.

Böjte's approach is no less allegorical when he portrays characters from the Bible who are likewise ethically tempted. Böjte and Karikó begin their conversation about the Bible with the observation that its readers usually shrink in horror at what they find in the text. The greatest challenge to interpreting the Bible, it seems, is that its main figures are so often *un*ethical. Over the course of the next 120 pages in *Dialogue with the Infinite*, Böjte and Karikó move from one biblical story to another, piling up example after example of acts and advice they contend one would be unwise to imitate and heed.[9] But before all this, Böjte's first move is to surreptitiously claim a classical pedigree for his allegorical approach to biblical interpretation.

At the start of *Dialogue*'s section about the Bible, he tells a personal version of ancient Greek philosopher Plato's allegory of the cave. "When I was a spelunker [*barlangász*]," he writes, "it happened that we got lost deep underground." They stumbled around in the dark for twelve hours. They searched around knowing there had to be a way out somewhere, and eventually they found it. Plato explains that the philosopher is like a prisoner who has been freed from a cave and, and as he is rising toward the light, perceives the true form of reality.

For Böjte, the Bible is the tunnel that leads from finitude to God's eternal embrace: "God's Word is the light at the end of the tunnel. So have the courage to get started, because it won't betray your hope on the earthly journey to the light and into the arms of the living God" (*Dialogue*, 154)! Böjte's allusion to Plato's allegory of the cave suggests that he is allying himself with an ancient Greek hermeneutic tradition.

In her study of philosopher Walter Benjamin's writings on allegory, historian Susan Buck-Morss notes that European intellectuals, going back to the Italian Renaissance, have responded to periods of social transformation by renewing their interest in ancient Greek philosophers' use of allegory and rooting their intellectual authority in this supposedly authentic European tradition.[10] Böjte the Catholic allegorical interpreter is not simply imitating the past, a point that philosopher Samuel Weber makes in reference to Walter Benjamin's 1928 book, *Origins of the German Trauerspiel.* Weber suggests Benjamin found German Baroque playwrights appealing because these authors simultaneously enacted and played with modernity's normative historical consciousness.

Through allegory, Baroque playwrights encouraged later European critics to evaluate their work according to the criteria used to judge ancient Greek sources, even though the authors could never hope to conform to these standards (Weber 2008: 142–4). Baroque theater enacts a strategically misleading attitude toward tradition: The legacies of the past should be both visible and hidden, apparently unknown to the public but actually known in secret.

Reading Benjamin in relation to contemporary Hungarian Catholic authors reveals something startling about allegorical interpretation as well as Benjamin's attraction to the form: Allegorical interpretation is a distinctively Catholic practice, and it took on this meaning through Baroque-era Protestant polemics against Catholicism. Buck-Morss, Weber, and other interpreters of Benjamin often assume that Benjamin's book is a study only of German Baroque theater. It can also be read as a *comparative* study of German and Spanish theater of this period. Early on, Benjamin writes that, "Spain's drama [is] the supreme form of European theater, in which Baroque features develop so much more brilliantly, so much more sharply and successfully, in the land of Catholic culture" (2019: 68).

When viewed as a comparative analysis, Benjamin's *Origins of the German Trauerspiel* also doubles as a comparative study of Protestant and Catholic literary cultures and their relationship to modern historical consciousness. His subsequent analysis of allegory's use of secrecy and misdirection should read as an interpretation of the form that literary interpretation takes in post-Protestant Catholic culture: The German Baroque theater, Benjamin insists, "was never able to arrange the traits of character in the myriad folds of an allegorical argument as secretively as [the Spanish writer] Calderon could do it" (2019: 210). Arguably, what can be said about Baroque allegory also goes for Catholics' allegorical interpretation. Catholics obliterate the historical, and thereby they help constitute Europe's historical consciousness even as they make this intention inaccessible to later readers.

When discussing the story of Cain and Abel, one of the earliest passages in Genesis, Böjte treats the text as a just-so parable about sincerity while integrating this distinctively Reformed (Calvinist) virtue into what is his overriding project: to renew, expand, and adapt the Transylvanian Hungarian intellectual tradition by converting seekers into servant educators called to serve Transylvanian Hungarian villages. He sets out to prepare these volunteer intellectuals for their foremost challenge: encountering peasant otherness, especially the peasantry's unfamiliar rural culture and ethical attitude.

"How many times," Böjte asks rhetorically, "does it happen that someone approaches us with a honey-sweet smile, but you get the feeling that you just can't trust this person" (*Dialogue*, 174)? Böjte speculates that maybe God rejected Cain's offering because he approached God with an insincere heart; God saw the intentions behind his actions and that he was jealous. In this allegory, Böjte's readers are in God's position. The readers encounter peasants whose actions they do not understand, and whose intentions are unclear. In this encounter with otherness, the volunteers disbelieve the peasants' sincerity.

In his study of Reformed (Calvinist) missionaries in the Dutch East Indies of the early-twentieth century, Webb Keane identifies this belief in the value of sincerity as a key part of Protestant culture's individualistic ethical commonsense knowledge (Keane 2007: 184). Reformed (Calvinist) Christianity demotes the labor instantiating God's collaborative presence to a secondary position relative to the inner state of sincerity, since in this tradition the latter is the sign that an individual is one of the saved elect. Human beings' ethical responsibility is of secondary importance to their salvation and a primary reason that, in Courtney Handman's assessment of the anthropological view, "the refusal of sociality has become a central predicate of contemporary views of the Christian subject" (Handman 2015: 15). However, Böjte's allegory was intended to teach his readers to persist in their pedagogical service, not to walk away muttering recriminations about peasants' insincerity.

On a deeper theological level, Böjte affirms the value of this element of the Reformed (Calvinist) worldview, except he does so by making it a hallmark of his own concept of collaborative presence. Böjte finds an even deeper social meaning beneath the events of the Cain and Abel story: "The essence of love is also that we should not leave others to walk the path of lies and insincerity. This is an important lesson that speaks to us all" (*Dialogue*, 174). This is a Catholic ethical appropriation of a Protestant value, a creative reinterpretation to turn Keane's sincerity of salvation into the sincerity of service.

An Orphan Between Love and Tradition

Böjte kicked off the third day's spiritual practice session of the garden restoration project by pointing to his left, at Ambrus sitting against the wall: "It's so interesting that Ambrus is here, you know, because I feel like I might burst if I don't tell you one of my favorite old stories." Böjte's voice piped impishly as he pointed to this wiry young man, one of the Csíksomlyó orphanage's graduates. Although he was alone as the only former ward helping out, Brother Csaba had personally invited him.

This was not the only time that Ambrus was the focus of attention during the project's recreation sessions. The previous day Father Jáki asked if anyone among the volunteers had ever visited the Csango region where he had conducted ethnomusicological research. The inquiry was really an excuse to establish his own expertise. Before anyone could reply, Father Jáki reported, "I've been there 150 times."

He then asked if there were any Csango individuals in the room. After raising his hand, Ambrus said he was born there. But he qualified his identification with the Csango culture Father Jáki had been teaching us about, explaining how he had relocated to the orphanage as a child and in fact had not returned in three years. Now Brother Csaba launched into one of his signature ethical allegories featuring Ambrus as the main character:

> This lad was in fifth or sixth grade, I think, when a man came up to the door here and knocked. He said that one of my boys had broken his car window with a rock. And in fact it was a very expensive sportscar. And every sign suggested, at least according to the driver who had experienced the harm, that Ambrus was guilty of the thing. Did I become angry or feel embittered? No, I talked with Ambrus: "Why did you need to break the window?" And Ambrus explained that it's always girls' fault. [Laughter] Now about this in particular we're in agreement. [Laughter] And so I said, but why is it precisely that a woman made you break the window? And it turned out that a girl made fun of him so much, bothered him so much that, that this rock was waiting just for her. I just didn't count on the fact that she would roll up the window. [Laughter] And it's so good that Ambrus is right here and I can say this right to his face. And Ambrus said that he really liked working with me; a serious young man. I said to him, I will look for a job for him somewhere around here and we'll build God's kingdom together.

Telling the story helped Böjte ally himself with his Hungarian audience's post-materialistic mentality—like them, he enjoys spontaneity.
Indeed, Böjte introduced the tale by highlighting that he had not *planned*
to tell it. So with his impish grin he conveyed the pleasure of acting on an
impulse, telling the story against the possibility that he would "burst"
(*kikivánkozni*).

The story's message is the same as in Böjte's other allegories about
parenting behavior and pedagogical conduct. While children can exhibit
transgressive behavior, one should not lapse into anger but remain on the
path of love. As in the tale about the hitchhiking boys, Böjte addresses his
audience as a group of parents and educators; that anecdote had taken
shape against the backdrop of the European Union's universalizing child
welfare and human rights discourse.

This time Böjte returned to a theme from the story about his anony-
mous friend who raged at drastic wealth disparities. The expensive sportscar stood in for the middle-class identity of Hungarians from Hungary. As
I noted in Chap. 2, they were the envy of Transylvanian Hungarians
because they enjoyed the benefits of Hungary's quasi-private system of
production, known as "goulash communism," which made the country
into Eastern Europe's most consumerist and "Western" society (Fehérváry
2013; Lampland 1995). In the story, at least judging by the sportscar
Ambrus damaged, it still is. Perhaps Böjte meant to provoke our shame
and anger, like the friend experienced in Muncelu Mic, at the thought that
someone might own a luxury automobile while young adults struggle to
get by on state assistance.

Against this backdrop, Böjte raised what may very well have presented
my volunteer group with a crisis-inducing question: Did Ambrus throw
that rock due to some undisclosed resentment, a poor person's rebellious
anger at another's ostentatious display of wealth? The very structure of
the spiritual practice sessions—which put Brother Csaba in the position
of helping a group of middle-class Hungarians from Hungary make sense
of their experience helping a group of impoverished children—made this
potentially disturbing awareness of class differences into an especially
pressing problem in need of addressing. After all, the majority of Brother
Csaba's audience were middle-class Hungarians, people with enough
money to drive twelve hours for a week's working vacation at Csíksomlyó.

In the story, Ambrus the child seems to resent the wealthy sportscar
driver. But Böjte closed the story with Ambrus as a young man and paragon of the vocational servant. He is serious and hard-working, faithful

and community-oriented. Böjte said he is ready to build God's kingdom. Böjte accomplished in this live "spiritual practice" lecture what he did in one of his dialogues with Éva Karikó in *Path into the Infinite*. In that book, he had described seeing "little Noémi, Magdi, and so many others" turn into "serious" (*komoly*) and "trustworthy" (*megbízható*) adults. Böjte tells his readers, "If we place our shoulders besides His shoulder, then for sure miracles await both us and our children" (*Path*, 42). On a deeper level, the story about Ambrus thus recreated the social dynamic that had animated his practice of ethical pedagogy and helped make God's collaborative labor real to readers.

Brother Csaba's closing statement, about finding Ambrus a job "around here" in his adopted home of Csíksomlyó, came across as a counterpoint to one of Father Jáki's claims about the Csango sense of place and home. The Csango even have a different habit for referring to their homeland, he told us. He said that in Hungarian, ethnonyms can be joined to the word for "land." This is common among European nations, "but the Csángó are different from Hungarians because they do not talk about the 'Csángoland.'"

He started to translate the Csango word into Hungarian but paused dramatically. "It can't be translated into Hungarian. The Csango have a special attachment to their land that they are born with, it comes with their mothers' milk." Father Jáki seemed to imply that Ambrus, since he was born in the Csango region, should have this same sense of attachment. He implied that persons like Ambrus naturally belonged among the Csango villages where they were born and spent their childhood. He did not make the purpose of this comment explicit, but he seemed to question Ambrus's desire to stay near Csíksomlyó.

Did such statements humiliate Ambrus, leaving him embittered toward these powerful priests who were exploiting a young man's presence to benefit themselves—either to establish their own authority to represent Transylvanian Hungarian culture or to deepen these visitors' calling to serve? This question is quick to come to mind in the wake of prolific anthropological research showing that while charity benefits givers like Böjte, Jáki, and the Hungarian volunteers, it necessarily harms the stand-ing of receivers like Ambrus. Andrea Muehlebach, in her study of Italian NGOs and neoliberal volunteerism, has recently revived the critique prof-fered by Marcel Mauss, Mary Douglas, and Pierre Bourdieu that the free charitable gift is a mystifying fantasy (Muehlebach 2012: 6–7; see Douglas 1990; Bourdieu 1977; Mauss 1990). Donors' rhetoric masks a brutal competition for prestige, and the wealthy humiliate recipients who find themselves unable to make a return gift.

While anthropologist China Scherz (2014: 93–6) has questioned whether charity is necessarily and universally harmful, calling for closer attention to the role that particular sociohistorical junctures play in shaping how givers and receivers understand the acts of charitable giving, I want to elaborate a concomitant methodological dispute with the structural critique of charitable giving. Often the desire to discover that charitable recipients secretly resist the domination of donors presumes that the anthropologist will convince the recipients, through some combination of persuasion and action, that they have common cause or solidarity on the basis of which the recipients will then reveal their actual resentment.

Not only does this imaginary recreate a problematic "first contact" dynamic in which the anthropologist is the agent of liberatory modernity impinging on a native culture, it also ascribes to the anthropologist the agency to overcome, break through, or undermine the charitable system's violent structural dynamic, leaving unanswered how orphans like Ambrus, through the agency ascribed to them within the charitable dynamic, might ironize the anthropologist's efforts at creating common ground. Scherz's call for more interest in local cultural interpretations of charity that destabilize presumptions about its violence should also include how receivers take up and frame the process of anthropological participant observational research itself.

Even if Ambrus had been mortified at Brother Csaba's story or resented Father Jáki's implication that he did not belong in the Ciuc Valley, I had given him no concrete reason to expect that he would have benefited from complaining about them had I decided to start asking him to reflect on how these men exploited his presence during the volunteer project. On other occasions, one of which I describe in Chap. 6, I observed former orphanage residents complaining about Brother Csaba; however, they did so to the directors of a competing Transylvanian orphanage network from whom they were seeking a job, thus using slander to play one patron against another in the hope of winning favor. I had given no sign that I could be such a patron to Ambrus.

However, the dust and heat during our project nonetheless offered Ambrus occasion to make an implicit claim to useful local knowledge, which was based on his Ciuc Valley upbringing. It was a dry August. Our pickaxes kicked up a lot of dirt, and we quickly emptied the water bottles provided by the orphanage. On the volunteers' third afternoon, Ambrus and I offered to get more. The area's tap water is not the best and paying for bottled water strikes penurious locals as wasteful when the Ciuc Valley is home to many natural springs. Csíksomlyó has an especially famous one. So once Ambrus and I had collected the used plastic bottles under our arms we turned left out the orphanage's front gate. Fifty paces down the paved road, we came upon another volunteer. Ambrus asked in passing if he had seen a line at the spring.

"Quite long," the volunteer told us.

But Ambrus was unfazed. "No problem," he explained, "we'll each take up three bottles and ask for a space in line. That way we'll get water and come back quick."

Csíksomlyó's spring lay ahead on our right and it was decorated with the architectural design hallmarks of the Szekler cultural revival with additional symbolism that identified Szekler-ness with Hungarian culture. One hand-crafted wooden sign pointed the way with flowing natural script framed by the Szekler national flag's moon-and-star motif. I caught sight of the line leading away from the spouts, which were affixed to a short stone column sheltered over by a top piece of local softwood pine. Benches on either side were decorated with carvings of nineteenth-century Hungarian Secessionist-style tulips and vines, all imagery associated with the Hungarian tourism market (see Losonczy 2009: 6–8).

As I counted the groups waiting there, I noticed the nylon bags at their feet, each one with tops of five, six, and seven empty bottles peeking out. But Ambrus had given me further instructions on the way over. He pointed out a woman bending at one of the spouts and I went to squat next to the line of green bottles she had set up to fill. When she turned and saw me, she said to hand over her bottles.

"All of them?" I asked.

"Yes," she said, "if you want to be next in line." Meanwhile, Ambrus had crossed to the other side.

"I just have these three," he pointed out after asking to cut in. By the time I had filled my first bottle, Ambrus was nearly done.

The Hungarian volunteer we passed on the way over, thinking we would have to start from the back of the line, had estimated that the task would take a long time. But thanks to Ambrus's savvy about the queuing etiquette, born of his many trips to the Csíksomlyó spring during time spent at the orphanage, we finished refilling in fifteen minutes and were back to the work site in twenty.

The next afternoon was just as hot. This time when Ambrus and I left for water two others tagged along. Laci and Sanyi were two young men in their twenties who lived in Budapest. They came across as stylish and had a confident, relaxed demeanor. They were not Catholic, but even so felt comfortable addressing the group. The night before at the spiritual practice session Böjte had invited them to the microphone, saying that they wanted to give a personal testimony.

Laci and Sanyi spoke about a personal crisis, heroin addiction, and their subsequent recovery. They were seekers, or at least Laci explained during his testimony, "I believe in God in my own way." They were the only non-priests to address the group that week, and I was struck by Brother Csaba's deference to their desire to speak as well as their confidence in making the request. For example, neither Ambrus nor the orphanage's Transylvanian Hungarian employees, who occasionally sat in on the spiritual practice sessions, had thought to ask for the microphone to share their stories.

After we were done at the spring, I was ready to return. On a whim, Ambrus asked if we wanted to see what he called the "well" (kút), and Laci and Sanyi both said yes. So Ambrus led us in a line across a narrow path of wooden planks, which zigzagged away from the spring toward a field. The path led to a circular wooden structure, open to the sky but had low walls that hid it from the road. In the center lay a hexagonal pool—Ambrus's "well"—bubbling with water the color of rust.

Around the corner, we surprised two teenage girls sitting on the far end of a bench. Ambrus waived us over to the opposite side and there we set our bottles down to wait. When the girls left, Ambrus grinned and announced, "Good, now we can go in." I wondered to myself if single-gendered swimming was the rule here, but there was no time to ask because Ambrus was already pulling off his shirt. Laci stopped to unbutton his shorts, but Sanyi simply walked up to the spring and half slipped, half stepped in; he let out a low squeal that Ambrus shushed. Next in, I exhaled, "oof," at the water's shocking cold.

After we each had a first dip, Ambrus explained the local custom. "You are supposed to cross yourself before you get in, and go underwater for as long as a full Rosary." On the other side, after pulling himself out on his stomach, he crossed himself again. "That's how you do it," he finished. The second time around, Laci, Sanyi, and I all managed to cross ourselves getting in and out, although I don't know if they prayed while they were underneath. Unlike the girls, we had no towels, so we laid out in the shad-owless afternoon sun. As my gaze slipped across Csíksomlyó's pine-green hills, it occurred to me that Éva Karikó would have recognized my feeling—that the Ciuc Valley is so beautiful it's like a folk tale. Laci lay prone at my feet, with his chin on his crossed arms. I closed my eyes. It took so long for someone to speak that, by the time I opened them, Sanyi's sleeves were nearly dry.

Lying there, we were an image of restful pleasure in a natural setting that seemed in keeping with what Brother Csaba had promised to his Hungarian readers in *Signpost toward the Infinite*. Discussing his views about vacations, he said his volunteers always knew to pack a pair of swimming trunks when they came to help out. He never went to resorts, but was always willing to take a break beside one of Transylvania's lakes. Until that point in the volunteer project, there had been opportunities to be present as God's collaborators. We had been rebuilding the garden, like God labors slowly to build God's kingdom. Now Ambrus had offered us an opportunity to heed Brother Csaba's invitation to spontaneous plea-sure. For me at least, as I took in Csíksomlyó's hillsides, this pleasure also evoked Karikó's description of chatting and laughing and dreamily gazing out the window of Brother Csaba's car at the local scenery.

One could also say that, by taking us to the well, Ambrus had simply met the volunteers' expectations; that is, he provided Hungarians with an experience that Brother Csaba's books had primed them to have. In the process, however, he also seized an opportunity to demonstrate his knowl-edge of Csíksomlyó, to show a sense of place that Father Jáki undermined during his talk about Csango culture. Father Jáki's implicit message was that Ambrus, by virtue of being born and raised through infancy in the Csango region, was culturally set apart from the Szekler community around the Csíksomlyó orphanage.

But Ambrus showed off his knowledge of the local etiquette of lining up for water, when and how it was acceptable to ask to cut in at the front, and when one should actually start at the back. At the well, Ambrus again radiated subtle indications as to his deep local experience, first by telling us we should wait for the girls to leave and then by shushing Sanyi. And finally, his oversight of our behavior even resembled Catholic evangelism, insofar as Ambrus encouraged two non-Catholic seekers to cross them-selves and pray to the Virgin Mary. Whereas Father Jáki had taught us to sing to Mary in a way that might have reinforced our sense that Ambrus should feel out of place in the Szekler region, the latter taught us a Catholic practice of prayer tailored to the well's specific dimensions: how long it took to get from one side to the other.

CONCLUSION

More than the blisters many of us developed during the week spent pickaxing the earth behind the Saint Francis Foundation's Csíksomlyó orphanage, I also developed a sense for the challenges Brother Csaba faces as a Transylvanian Hungarian and Catholic intellectual addressing Hungarians from Hungary. Events during the volunteer project exemplified the shift that Brother Csaba claimed for himself in the opening vignette: Until the mid-2000s, he had used his intellectual production to conduct outreach to other Transylvanian Hungarians. In his words from his speech to reporters in front of the Hungarian parliament, before he believed that, "this work is mine as a Transylvanian Hungarian." His success in persuading Hungarians from Hungary to give aid showed that expanding his outreach meant he was the right path. On a deeper level, he struggled with Transylvanian Hungarians' deference to Hungarians' post-materialistic desires.

The motif running threadlike through this chapter is the extent to which Brother Csaba draws on the interwar culture of vocational service to help Hungarians from Hungary recast their desire for spiritual enlightenment in ethical terms. While Brother Csaba felt he was heading in the right direction by giving Hungarian seeker-tourists opportunities to cultivate vocational virtues, his intervention in Ambrus's trips to the swimming hole suggests that love does not conquer all. Rather, the programs Brother Csaba invented to teach Hungarians how to be loving servants actually created opportunities for us to become aware of specific ethical contradictions that Brother Csaba himself stands astride, as he encourages middle-class Hungarians to hear a calling to serve the children of Transylvania's post-industrial poverty. Ultimately, Transylvanian Hungarians' regard for their ethnic kin's post-materialistic desires destabilized Brother Csaba's efforts to cultivate an ethical nation.

In Chap. 4, I further develop this account of intellectuals cultivating an ethical nation. On the one hand, contemporary educators look in two directions to conduct this work. Brother Csaba exemplifies how Transylvanian Hungarians address urban, middle-class Hungarians from Hungary. On the other, the volunteer choir of the Csíksomlyó shrine church consists of Transylvanian Hungarian educators who address the rural "folk" or "people" (*nép*). But as I learned as a member of the bass section—I sang with them during the first year of my fieldwork—choir members themselves are not at all secure in their urbane status. They address themselves with their pedagogy of ethical cultivation as much they try to change rural others. Their own inclination toward peasant vices—especially toward a genre of rough, sloppy, maudlin soldier ballads—both animate and subvert their educational mission.

While in the next chapter I focus on Transylvanian Hungarians' pedagogy of rural Szeklers, Hungarians from Hungary are never far from the stage. In Chap. 4, I reverse the direction of travel that I portrayed in this chapter. Here, Brother Csaba's project brought tourist/volunteers to Transylvania. In the next, I give an account of my participation in the choir's performance tour to the Hungarian city of Székesfehérvár. Ultimately, I show that the appreciative gaze from abroad undermined but also confirmed choir members' confidence in their pedagogical mission at home.

NOTES

1. Böjte also takes over interwar Transylvanian Hungarian intellectuals' worries about ethnic assimilation and stokes his audience's fears about the Romanian state's nationalizing educational policies. In one scene, Böjte meets with Hungarian-speaking parents at one of his orphanages. To their child, however, Böjte says in Romanian, "How are you?" The director Ibolya Fekete reveals that the girl does not know Hungarian because she has only attended Romanian schools.
2. Böjte was reimagining the popular practice of contemplating the "Stations of the Cross," twelve sequential images of Jesus' arrest, trial, and execution.
3. For Scherz, Matthew 6:3 suggests that because goodness must be occluded from view, Catholic nuns who embrace this virtue forego international funding opportunities rather than audit their books. For Weber's Ethic of Conviction, see Weber 2004.
4. Strathern (2000) has delineated the ways in which the demand to audit signals not only the pragmatic restructuring of institutions but also the emergence of globally scaled cultural forms like the European Union.
5. Other Hungarian journalists have published book-length theological interviews with priests. See, for instance, Hungarian journalist Mónika Néráth's interviews with Fr. Ferenc Pál (Néráth 2008).
6. Throughout these volumes, Böjte celebrates but also calls out Hungarian tourists in Transylvania for what he sees as their landscape-gazing. He recommends a properly reverential attitude in a passage that uses an analogy to explain the Catholic doctrine of real presence: "If we gaze out the window of a car, the landscape that we are passing through right at this

moment is enormous. Still, we are able to take it in through these minis-cule organs, our eyes...If our eyes can take in the enormous Hargita Mountains [Harghita Mountains], why wouldn't it be possible to contain the entirety of Christ in a small wafer" (*Path*, 90)?

7. See, for instance, this comment from a study of child protection laws in Hungary and Romania: "Although Hungary had begun deinstitutionalisa-tion and reform before the fall of communism, after 1989, the approach to change in both countries appeared at times to focus on changing the image rather than the nature of care" (Anghel et al. 2013: 248).

8. Of course, the "re-traditionalization" of gender roles selectively rewrites history to give the impression that religion vanished under socialism; while many anthropologists of religion and gender would understand this point to be self-evident, anthropologists studying religion after socialism con-tinue to relitigate this moot debate as to whether the term affords a correct reading of history. See the debate between Irene Hilgers (2009) and Habiba Fathi (2006), summarized in Halemba (2015). A more fruitful approach lies in exploring the ethical and practical dilemmas that emerge from this discourse. For the latter, see Köllner (2016).

9. In other stories, the merciful God is bloodthirstily vindictive (*Dialogue*, 174) and the docile Jesus is violent (*Dialogue*, 199).

10. Benjamin argues that "modern allegory," meaning the self-conscious revival of the classical genre, began during the Renaissance (Buck-Morss 1989: 172).

REFERENCES

Anghel, Roxana, Maria Herczog, and Gabriela Dima. 2013. The Challenge of Reforming Child Protection in Eastern Europe: The Cases of Hungary and Romania. *Psychosocial Intervention* 22: 239–249.

Apor, Péter. 2013. Autentikus közösség és autonóm személyiség: 1989 egyik előtörténete [Authentic Community and Autonomous Personality: A Prehistory of 1989]. *AETAS* 28 (4): 22–39.

Bárdi, Nándor. 2015. A népszolgálat genezise és tartalomváltozása. In *Népszolgálat: A közösségi elkötelezettség alakváltozatai a magyar kisebbségek történetében* [Service to the People: The Elementary Forms of Community Commitment in the History of the Hungarian Minority], eds. Nándor Bárdi, Tamás Gusztáv Filep, and József D. Lőrincz, 11–48. Pozsony: Kalligram Kiadó.

Bárdi, Nándor, Tamás Gusztáv Filep, and József D. Lőrincz. 2015. Bevezető [Introduction]. In *Népszolgálat: A Közösségi Elkötelezettség Alakváltozatai A Magyar Kisebbségek Történetében* [Service to the People: The Elementary Forms of Community Commitment in the History of the Hungarian Minority], 2–10. Pozsony: Kalligram Kiadó.

Benjamin, Walter. 2019. *Origin of the German Trauerspiel*. Trans. Howard Eiland. Cambridge: Harvard University Press.

Bourdieu, Pierre. 1977. *Outline of a Theory of Practice*, translated by Richard Nice. Cambridge: Cambridge University Press.

Brubaker, Rogers. 1996. *Nationalism Reframed: Nationhood and the National Question in the New Europe*. Cambridge: Cambridge University Press.

Buchowski, Michal. 2006. The Specter of Orientalism in Europe: From Exotic Other to Stigmatized Brother. *Anthropological Quarterly* 79 (3): 463–482.

Buck-Morss, Susan. 1989. *The Dialectics of Seeing: Walter Benjamin and the Arcades Project*. Cambridge: MIT Press.

Davis, R. Chris. 2019. *Hungarian Religion, Romanian Blood: A Minority's Struggle for National Belonging, 1920–1945*. Madison: University of Wisconsin Press.

Douglas, Mary. 1990. Foreword: No Free Gifts to *The Gift: The Gift: The form and Reason for Exchange in Archaic Societies*, by Marcel Mauss. xi–xxiii. New York: Routledge.

Dunn, Elizabeth C. 2004. *Privatizing Poland: Baby Food, Big Business, and the Remaking of Labor*. Ithaca: Cornell University Press.

Fathi, Habiba. 2006. Gender, Islam, and Social Change in Uzbekistan. *Central Asian Survey* 25 (3): 303–317.

Fehérváry, Krisztina. 2013. *Politics in Color and Concrete: Socialist Materialities and the Middle Class in Hungary*. Bloomington: University of Indiana Press.

Georgescu, Diana. 2011. Marrying into the European Family of Nations: National Disorder and Upset Gender Roles in Post-Communist Romanian Film. *Journal of Women's History* 23 (4): 131–154.

Gille, Zsuzsa. 2007. *From the Cult of Waste to the Trash Heap of History: The Politics of Waste in Socialist and Postsocialist Hungary*. Bloomington: University of Indiana Press.

Halemba, Agnieszka. 2015. *Negotiating Marian Apparitions: The Politics of Religion in Transcarpathian Ukraine*. Budapest: Central European University Press.

Handman, Courtney. 2015. *Critical Christianity: Translation and Denominational Conflict in Papua New Guinea*. Berkeley: University of California Press.

Irene Hilgers. 2009. *Why Do Uzbeks have to be Muslims? Exploring Religiosity in the Ferghana Valley*. Münster: Lit Verlag.

Kaell, Hillary. 2020. *Christian Globalism at Home: Child Sponsorship in the United States*. Princeton: Princeton University Press.

Keane, Webb. 2007. *Christian Moderns: Freedom and Fetish in the Mission Encounter*. Los Angeles: University of California Press.

Kereki, Judit. 2011. Bántalmazás a családban: Lehet-e verni a gyerekeket? [Violence in the Family: Are You Allowed to Beat Children]. *Koloknet.hu*, January 7. https://www.koloknet.hu/csalad/tabu/eroszak/lehet-e-verni-a-gyerekeket/. Accessed 6 July 2021.

Köllner, Tobias. 2016. Patriotism, orthodox religion and education: Empirical findings from contemporary Russia. *Religion, State and Society* 44 (4): 366–386.

Kürti, László. 2000. *The Remote Borderland: Transylvania in the Hungarian Imagination*. Albany: State University of New York Press.

Lampland, Martha. 1995. *The Object of Labor: Commodification in Socialist Hungary*. Chicago: University of Chicago Press.

Losonczy, Anne-Marie. 2009. Pilgrims of the "Fatherland": Emblems and Religious Rituals in the Construction of an Inter-Patriotic Space Between Hungary and Transylvania. *History and Anthropology* 20 (3): 265–280.

Malkki, Liisa H. 2015. *The Need to Help: The Domestic Arts of International Humanitarianism*. Durham: Duke University Press.

Mauss, Marcel. 1990. *The Gift: The Form and Reason for Exchange in Archaic Societies*, translated by W.D.Halls. New York: Routledge.

Max Weber. 2004. *The Vocation Lectures*, edited with an introduction and notes by David S. Owen and Tracy B. Strong, translated by Rodney Livingstone. Indianapolis: Hackett.

Muehlebach, Andrea. 2012. *The Moral Neoliberal: Welfare and Citizenship in Italy*. Chicago: The University of Chicago Press.

Napolitano, Valentina. 2015. *Migrant Hearts and the Atlantic Return: Transnationalism and the Roman Catholic Church*. New York: Fordham University Press.

Nérath, Mónika. 2008. *A jelen lévő Isten: Pál Ferenccel beszélget Néráth Mónika* [The Presently Existing God: Mónika Néráth Talks with Ferenc Pál]. Budapest: Kairosz.

Nikunen, Kaarina. 2018. *Media Solidarities: Emotions, Power and Justice in the Digital Age*. London: SAGE Publications Ltd.

Orsi, Robert A. 1985. *The Madonna of 115th Street: Faith and Community in Italian Harlem, 1880–1950*. New Haven, Conn.; London: Yale University Press.

Peti, Lehel. 2020. *"Krisztus ajándéka van bennünk." Pünkösdizmus moldvai román, roma és csángó közösségekben* ["The Gift of Christ Is Within Us." Pentecostalism in Romanian, Roma, and Csángó Communities in Moldavia]. Budapest-Cluj-Napoca: Balassi Kiadó--Erdélyi Múzeum Egyesület.

Pius XI. "Divini Illius Magistri." The Holy See, December 31, 1929, https://www.vatican.va/content/pius-xi/en/encyclicals/documents/hf_p-xi_enc_31121929_divini-illiusmagistri.html

Pusztai, Bertalan. 2004. *Religious Tourists: Constructing Authentic Experiences in Late Modern Hungarian Catholicism*. Jyväskylä: Jyväskylä Studies in Humanities.

Scherz, China. 2014. *Having People, Having Heart: Charity, Sustainable Development, and Problems of Dependence in Central Uganda*. Chicago: University of Chicago Press.

Strathern, Marilyn. 2000. The Tyranny of Transparency. *British Educational Research Journal* 26 (3): 309–321.

Verdery, Katherine. 1996. *What Was Socialism, and What Comes Next?* Princeton: Princeton University Press.

Weber, Samuel. 2008. *Benjamin's -Abilities.* Cambridge: Harvard University Press.

Zubrzycki, Genevieve. 2006. *The Crosses of Auschwitz: Nationalism and Religion in Post-Communist Poland.* Chicago: University of Chicago Press.

CHAPTER 4

Composure

Civilized Szeklers

The summer I volunteered at Brother Csaba's orphanage, I was renting a bedroom in a ground-floor apartment in Harghita County's urban capital, Miercurea Ciuc. My landlady sang in the Csíksomlyó shrine's volunteer choir, which met weekly in a church across the street from the orphanage. When I asked if I could join, Gizella placed a call to the choir director, Lajos, and then to a woman she carpooled with to rehearsals. The next evening Gizella and I squeezed into the backseat beside a bass who lived on the fourth floor of the building next door; a soprano from the same city neighborhood already had the passenger seat. Over the next few months of weekly meetings, as I got to know the forty volunteer singers, I learned that nearly all of them lived in Miercurea Ciuc; but they had not been urban their whole lives.

During the 1970s, Romania's socialist government had drawn Gizella out of the village of her birth by housing her in a Miercurea Ciuc dormitory apartment and giving professional training, followed by an administrative job in the city's new textile factory. She was part of a generation that helmed as well as benefited from state financial investments to transform urban county seats like Miercurea Ciuc, which grew from a population of 7000 in 1968 to over 40,000 by 1989. In accord with a well-understood analysis among anthropologists, I view the state

M. R. Loustau, *Hungarian Catholic Intellectuals in Contemporary Romania*, Contemporary Anthropology of Religion, https://doi.org/10.1007/978-3-030-99221-7_4

bureaucracy, through the centralized political economic system it managed, to have acted like an institutional patron, bestowing on talented young people with political connections and the right proletarian background opportunities to become educated and leave their villages.

Yet on some ritual occasions and in front of particular audiences the choir members do not strike one as teachers of Szekler peasants but rather like the peasants whose behavior they sought to transform. In the summer of 2010, we sang the Szekler national anthem to conclude the final evening of our annual tour of Hungary, bringing concertgoers in the city of Székesfehérvár to their feet as choir members and audience alike began to weep. Afterward, Gizella made us laugh: "You know how it was after the change, how we sang it at every wedding reception. But now, this, when we sang the Szekler anthem, this was more civilized." She had reminded choir members of the early 1990s when bands of drunken men sang the anthem, seemingly whenever they could, since for decades Romania's increasingly nationalizing socialist government had discouraged such displays. In Székesfehérvár the choir members had also turned weepy. Gizella had made the group guffaw by comparing the two instances of emotional display, only to highlight how the latter was different; in her words somehow "more civilized."

In this chapter, by studying the Csíksomlyó choir's pedagogical work, I instead explore a second key pedagogical interface between rural teachers and peasants that interwar Catholic intellectuals described in their program for renewing and reforming the Transylvanian Hungarian educational system. Under the auspices of a project to emotionally reengage Catholic believers in worship, urban intellectuals performed a civilizing pedagogical mission to rural Transylvanian Hungarians. In the first section, I sketch out the training they received in the socialist-era urban educational system and how it shaped their understanding of civilization.

While choir members did not regularly use the virtue term "composure" that appears in my chapter title, I use it to draw attention to choir members' self-conscious reflection on a specific and valued style of embodiment. They referred to this embodiment in terms that harkened back to Pál Péter Domokos's writings for the journal *Transylvanian School* about the Romanian Hungarian Musical Association. In addition to the word for educated and cultivated (*művelt*), which appeared in the title of Domokos's article, "Hungarian Folk Music and Our Choral Cultivation," choir members spoke of a civilized (*civilizált*), refined, (*kifinomult*), and relaxed or tranquil (*nyugodt*) attitude.

However, the civilizing project that shaped this cohort's self-identity, sense of ambition, and belief in progress has come under critical scrutiny from some contemporary Transylvanian Hungarian intellectuals, who link urbanization with the Romanian state's effort to assimilate the ethnic minority by referring to government-imposed or "forced" urbanization (Demeter 2011). Adding to the body of research on how contemporary religious institutions take up and adapt the ideas, practices, and personnel of secular socialist education, I argue that choir members redeploy the now-tarnished civilizing mission of socialist-era urban cultural institutions within the Catholic Church's liturgical revival movement, finding new institutional means to enact the pedagogical mission that helped them move into the urban middle class in the first place.

I take this approach a step further through foregrounding the ambivalence of these singers toward their civilizing mission. Instead of asking how atheistic education helped religious teachers in their new pedagogical pursuits—a way of structuring inquiry into religion after socialism that over-represents institutional success and underappreciates instability in post-socialist religious intellectual movements—I explore the conditions under which the choir members came to feel uncivilized and how this affected their thinking about educational service. While the concept of civilization also circulates within Hungarian political discourse, informing right-wing nationalists' exhortations to defend Europe's Christian civilization, originally choir members learned to identify with civilizational virtues in socialist-era cultural institutions where the concept was more akin to moral refinement, discipline, hygiene, and decency (Rivkin-Fish 2005: 60–96; see also Zigon 2010; Trencsényi 2011).[1]

They have their doubts about the former project; they are not quite sure of their place in the effort to perform the European-level achievements of Hungarian Christendom, and wonder if it has really been designed to help them succeed at their own pedagogical mission. These doubts have the ability to destabilize village teachers' identification with their cross-border ethnic kin in Hungary. Much as in Domokos's time, when today's Transylvanian Hungarian musical pedagogues perform in cities, they struggle with the consequences of putting authoritative urban audiences in the position of determining folk teachers' success.

My argument works through material from my own ethnographic observation as well as from published documents. The former derives from my participation in weekly rehearsals, two county-funded parish choir festivals, and the choir's tour of Hungary. Since 2000, the

Csíksomlyó choir has been represented by its own non-governmental organization, the Csíksomlyó Shrine Choir Association, which receives funding from Harghita County's cultural program as well as the Hungarian government.

Although I cite material from a "Tenth Anniversary Booklet" that suggests the group was founded at this time, the booklet includes information on the choir's role in a late-socialist society that, based on my analysis, suggests its mission was in fact shaped by cultural projects associated with Romania's post-1968 urbanization process. I then go on to describe the Ciuc Valley's annual choir festival, which doubles as a celebration of Szekler identity. Finally, I describe the choir's summer performance tour in Hungary and choir members' subsequent conversations about how experiences on this trip might help them persist in and even expand their pedagogical mission.

STATE PATRONAGE AND SOCIALIST CIVILIZATION

In 1968 Romania's new Communist Party General Secretary, Nicolae Ceauşescu, in an effort to undermine potential rivals' existing bases of power, replaced the country's regional governments with a system of smaller county units. After the Romanian government created Harghita County, it made Miercurea Ciuc—then the Ciuc Valley's largest town— into the seat of county government (Demeter 2010). Through the 1970s, county-level government bureaucracies became the primary distributors of urban and industrial investment.

In a historical shift from bureaucratic impersonalism to patronage clientelism that Jowitt called the "traditionalization" of state socialist regimes, Party functionaries in industrial sectors like light industry, heavy industry, and urban housing and construction vied for resources and used personal connections in the county government bureaucracy to win investment (Jowitt 1983; Kligman and Verdery 2011: 61–2). Bureaucrats in county governments kept industrial funding close to where they lived in the county seats, ensuring they would be the primary beneficiaries of this investment, and the city's population began to grow rapidly with an influx of new workers. Miercurea Ciuc's new urbanites—from whom the choir drew its membership—grew up in this system and benefitted from it by securing state resources like educational opportunities, jobs, and apartments.

As detailed in an early-1970s edition of the official county newspaper, the government gave the Socialist Cultural and Educational Council the responsibility of "working toward securing the Romanian people's high level of intellectual civilization, [and] the unceasing enrichment of our society's ideological and cultural life" (quoted in Demeter 2011: 80, 150). The targets of this civilization project were not only the peasants who remained in the countryside but also Miercurea Ciuc's new urbanites. Csíksomlyó's singers represent an aging first-generation urban cohort that, during the 1970s and 1980s, joined government-sponsored cultural groups designed to prevent rural and uncivilized behaviors.

When Harghita County officials convened intellectuals for a roundtable discussion on preventing drunkenness among recent rural transplants, the report that followed stated, "it is necessary to work more with young people and already in their school-aged years we must strengthen health and cultural education" (Demeter 2011: 146). And when Miercurea Ciuc's young urbanites spoke via official government organs as propaganda mouthpieces, they echoed these same sentiments that allude to the value of personal civilization. A late 1970s survey of Miercurea Ciuc's young female factory workers reported that the majority wanted a spouse who was "good to his family, that is he should not drink, smoke, or work in a dangerous workplace" (quoted in Demeter 2011: 134). For this generation, civilizational values overlap with personal habits of consumption, cleanliness, sophistication, and education.

During the 1970s, the Csíksomlyó choir did not receive funding from county cultural programs, which after all were dedicated to creating an atheist socialist culture. However, in the choir's Tenth Anniversary Booklet, the priest who led Csíksomlyó's choir at this time, Father József Mark, recalls benefitting residually from the government's push to provide musical education to the city's growing population. He goes on to reveal the challenge he faced upon relocating to Csíksomlyó in the mid-1970s: "The remnant of a choir that had existed before my arrival had only sung the Palm Sunday Passion Play." Rural parish choirs typically perform only on this annual holiday, gathering for rehearsals a few weeks beforehand to refresh their memory of the parts they sing every year. While Father Mark implies that he discovered a typical rural choir at Csíksomlyó, he slighted the group for this reason, calling it a "remnant" that he immediately reorganized into a year-round institution.

The Csíksomlyó choir's "Tenth Anniversary Booklet"

This latter incarnation of the choir also attracted more singers, mostly young men from Miercurea Ciuc. By tapping into the demographic of new young urbanites, Father Mark wrote that the group achieved a "higher level" of artistry (*nívósabb*); and "more skilled" (*képzettebb*) members helped him cultivate the skills of the preexisting "simple choir members" (*egyszerű énekkari tagok*). The Csíksomlyó choir thus took on the folk educator's key pedagogical interface with the peasantry within its own membership.

The Tenth Anniversary Booklet's editor, Ferenc, who sang in the group and who was married to a soprano, asked the singers to elaborate on

Father Mark's comments regarding the folk educator's pedagogy. Ferenc wrote to them with the question, "What difference do you see between the two qualities, how you take/took part in the Mass as a 'simple' believer and how you took/take part as one of the liturgy's active participants?" Father Mark had imagined newer and younger members teaching older peasant performers, describing a pedagogical cleavage that divided and united factions within the group; but Ferenc's question shifts the vocational teacher's pedagogical encounter into a choir member's own self. He presumes that the transition from socialist-era to post-socialist choir was accomplished within the respondents' own embodied selfhood as they went from worshipping like simple peasants to active participants in the liturgy. Yet by inviting choir members to identify with the peasantry, at least in their own biographical pasts, he invited a destabilization of the typical image of postcolonial administrative urban intellectuals who, according to Rama (1994) and Schweizer (1988), deploy representations of civilization to justify the domination of the city over the rural hinterlands.

These newly urbane choir members narrated the change of embodied selfhood within the framework of personal biographies that centered around turning points when they felt called to sing and join the choir, echoing Elizabeth Dunn's argument that Polish factory workers came to see embracing the project of remaking subjectivity as the foremost sign they had succeeded to the post-socialist middle class (2004: 94–129; see also Gog 2020).[2] While singers said that the Mass was an opportunity to cultivate highly experiential and emotional encounters with characters like Jesus, Mary, and others who appear in the liturgy, choir members never lost sight of their overarching pedagogical mission. In soprano Emőke's statement, she called the encounters with divine figures during the Mass a kind of intimacy: "So that our singing should become high-quality, it's not enough just to work – everyone must create quiet around themselves, but mainly within themselves so that liturgical participation becomes intimate [*bensőséges*]."

Members often joined these descriptions of intimate encounters to the practice of teaching other Catholics to worship in this manner. According to an alto, Regina, "I feel that the choir does enough to accomplish the task it was created for: to lead believers to God by using song to make the liturgy more experiential [*átérezhető*]" Imola, a soprano, praised Lajos for explaining Catholic doctrinal beliefs about the Mass, but reframed truth as an experiential value that the choir tried to cultivate in others:

[Lajos] teaches us the correct interpretation of the lyrics, that is, to teach the people just simply sitting there in the pews to sense the agony of the crucifixion, the consoling love of the Holy Spirit, and the joyful celebration of birth.

A soprano named Zsófia concluded her personal statement for the anniversary booklet by adopting a poetic, imagistic tone that compares liturgical singing to the spiritual experience of self-transcendence in contemplative prayer. Instead of full sentences, Zsófia uses ellipses to string together phrases that convey the experience of rising: "For me, singing is an experience, joy, taking flight on the wings of sound…far away…high up…beyond All Existence…this is *my* prayer." Self-transcendence, according to anthropologist Sonja Luehrmann, is an essential aspect of Charismatic/Pentecostal traditions: these church groups use music "to transcend the bounds of natural emotions" and thus "thrive on the limits of what self and society can provide" (2011: 180, 175).

Indeed, this emphasis on live, direct, and personally immersive worship experiences might reflect the broad influence that Charismatic/Pentecostal traditions have had on multiple branches of Christianity, including the Catholic Church. Several choir members joined after years of enthusiastic involvement in the Transylvanian Catholic Church's branch of the global Catholic Charismatic Renewal, but notably they spoke about making the transition to the choir in a mood of repentance. In soprano Rita's words, while the choir was singing at the Pentecost pilgrimage—dressed in Szekler national costumes for event—her heart began beating along with Mary's heart. "I asked Mary to forgive me for neglecting her, and since then I've asked from the depths of my heart and soul for her intercession and protection."

Our Lady of Csíksomlyó is a Szekler and Hungarian national intercessor. Rita gestures obliquely toward the foreignness of the Catholic Charismatic Renewal by suggesting that her involvement in this movement had led her to neglect her duty to Mary. Yet Rita found she could still cultivate a Charismatic/Pentecostal-style mode of experiencing in the choir. Indeed, the effort to renew liturgical participation along Charismatic/Pentecostal lines might be a sign that this tradition's influence has become so pervasive in the Catholic Church that believers treat it simply as the way that Catholics should learn how to worship (see Csordas 1994).

But choir members also construe their singing as an extension of the Transylvanian Hungarian tradition of vocational service and therefore as pedagogy, or an expression of responsibility to rural or "simple" others. Indeed, in the same response, Zsófia emphasized the choir's pedagogical task to encourage others to embrace personal and intense worship:

> We are doing a kind of 'cultivation of the people' [*népnevelés*], since the choir's task is to lead the music that the faithful also sing. For me, being a choir member is first voluntary service, and for this reason it comes from the soul. We strive to make singing true devotion, which should first please God but should also permeate the hearts of the faithful and touch their souls.

In her testimony, Zsófia explicitly harkens back to the pedagogical ideology that informed and structured interwar Transylvanian Hungarian intellectuals' vocation to educational service in rural communities. She uses the specific words that denoted this model of intellectual calling and authority calling: service (*szolgálat*) and cultivation or education (*nevelés*), which contemporary historians combine to form the Hungarian technical term that I translate as "vocational service for the people": *népszolgálat*.

In this sense, parish choir members take a place alongside catechists in a growing cohort of lay assistants serving and helping priests in Catholic communities around the world. During the 1990s, anthropologist Andrew Orta studied with a group of rural Bolivian parish catechists who not only teach doctrine but, as organic intellectuals called to serve local communities, are caught up in contradictory judgments, "embodying [both] the failures of colonial evangelization and the promises of newer pastoral paradigms" (Orta 2004: 22). Bolivian catechists embody missionaries' hopes and fears for the project of rural evangelization, and when choir members reflect on the success of their pedagogical practice in service of renewing worship, they also express deep ambivalence. They go so far as to dramatize the vices that threaten not only their calling but also the entire project of renewing rural education.

For a few weeks during rehearsal, the basses told a joke that featured a whispered exchange during the Mass. In it, a priest stands before his altar with two servers, one of whom is the choir member. As the priest begins to dully intone, "In honor of Saint Stephen" the singer interrupts, "*Psst—* it's Saint László today!" The priest repeats, in the same dull tone of voice, "In honor of Saint László." The choir member then turns to the other altar server and adds, "I could have said 'Marty Smith' and we would have heard, 'In honor of Marty Smith.'"

When choir members made public statements about their work, declarations like the ones featured in the Tenth Anniversary Booklet, they tended to extol the value of persisting in their pedagogical mission; but through informal conversation and joke-telling they portray the fatalism and exhaustion that threatens the project of rural educational service. On the one hand, a priest could be an example of the Church's incomplete education of the countryside. While previous generations of Church leaders felt peasants to be sufficiently converted, sufficiently Catholic if there were clergy present to recite the liturgy, resulting in this priest who does not care to engage personally with the Mass, in the joke choir members implicitly claim that this approach to catechism is partial at best.

On the other hand, the priest's detached attitude in the anecdote is a troubling index of any vocational servant's greatest vices: exhaustion, frustration, despair. The church official is so bored by his work and the routine of rural service—in this case, saying the Mass, day in and day out, with little success to show for it among those villagers who remain unengaged—that he has given up. He cannot be bothered to remember which saint's holiday it is, much less identify with the saint's joy or agony. So it is left to a layperson, the choir member, to whisper at the priest, calling the cleric to task. The lay volunteer grows frustrated, though, and similarly admits defeat. In this way, the joke reveals a fate that the choir members themselves might face, since, like the priest, they are educators serving a rural community.

The Szekler Revival

While exhaustion had generally been a volunteer educator's frightening vice, Transylvania's ongoing Szekler revival has further destabilized the project of bolstering rural worship, specifically by encouraging choir members to embody what they saw as an uncivilized style of Szekler masculinity. In the 1970s, Harghita County's cultural office began funding Szekler-specific events and Szekler folk art revival groups that performed on a national festival circuit. The countrywide *Sing, Romania!* festival soon became the hallmark of the late-socialist movement to build a national and atheist revolutionary culture. Organizers at the highest levels of government demanded that the whole country be involved; every urban and rural work unit had to take part with musical content to perform. By the 1980s, according to historian Otilia Hedeşan, "the fever of fieldwork reached more and more people," leading urban intellectuals around the country to flock to the countryside where they took up the task of documenting folk traditions (Hedeşan 2008: 29; Mihăilescu et al. 2008: 65–66).[3]

Undertaken in many cases by village teachers who were already tasked with disciplining their research subjects—a pedagogical relationship toward a predetermined telos that informed the choir's own educational mission—singers and socialist-era teachers had a common methodological orientation even if they had different goals (see Luehrmann 2011). In the end, Sing, Romania!'s local officials and organizers were tasked with producing an atheist and national socialist culture, while the choir members were out to emotionally reengage believers in worship and revive the liturgical culture of the Catholic Church.

While secularism and culture-building were interconnected projects of the effort to build a revolutionary atheist culture, this system of cultural production also carried within it a gendered dimension (Luehrmann 2005: 37–8). Regional events associated with Sing, Romania! featured Szekler choirs and dance groups whose performances segregated roles between male and female choirs and they also had complementary repertoires. Male choirs specialized in "soldier ballads" (*katona dalok*), the thematic content of which focused on rebelliousness and conflicts with paternal authority figures; bar culture and alcohol consumption; joking and pranks; and longing for the maternal comforts of home.

As this genre was integrated into another folk revival taking place across the border in Hungary, according to folklorist Barbara Rose Lange it came to be seen as opposed to normative civilized and urban masculinity as a counter-hegemonic performance:

> When [Hungarian] revivalists traveled to Transylvania, they tended to see the way that the villagers behaved at the public parts of life-cycle rituals such as weddings, because the authorities in Transylvania would harass villagers for hosting the revivalists at home. The rituals entailed segmented gender roles, and they encompassed liminal behavior when men in particular might drink to excess, sing sentimentally, strike the musicians, or rowdily execute some traditional pranks. (Lange 2014: 43)

Szekler festivals created performative spaces for this liminal masculinity within the state's push to urbanize and civilize the populace.[4]

In the mid-2000s the leaders of the Csíksomlyó choir decided to form an NGO to gain access to funds that Harghita County was still dispensing to cultural institutions, no longer under the auspices of Sing, Romania! but rather as a way to support and preserve Szekler traditions. A county government grant, as well as funds from the Catholic Church, also went to the annual Ciuc Valley Catholic parish choir festival. I was late to my first festival, having hitchhiked to the village site hours after the choir had already arrived by its own rented bus. My driver let me out near the busses parked along the road just before the House of Culture, the government-owned building that in Ciuc Valley villages is used for official educational events.

Because of where I got dropped off, my late arrival turned out to be a learning opportunity. From the roadside, I walked past tables and a tent to poke my head into the main hall. The young man who greeted me seemed perplexed when I asked where the festival was. "Well, here," he replied before continuing, "but the concert [koncert] is in the church." He directed me up the hill to the parish church. As I followed its stone pathway, I wondered about the difference between festival and concert—how one took place here and the other, there. I didn't have a chance to ask, for just as I stepped into the church and slid onto the wooden pew beside my fellow choir members, another choir launched into their song from the altar.

Over the next three hours, groups from every village parish rose and processed across the stage. They were dressed in Szekler national costumes and presented a dignified style of Szeklerness while standing in lines on the risers to sing liturgical music. During these performances, I occasionally saw the members of Csíksomlyó's choir grimace or glance knowingly at each other, the nonverbal equivalent of the altar server's nudging about Saint László. At one point, for example, two basses exchanged a self-aware widening of the eyes when a group of singers noticeably pitch-slurred up to their opening note. This type of portamento, I would soon learn, was characteristic of masculine pub singing, but now the basses sent a surreptitious pedagogical message that technique of that variety was not appropriate for this performance.

This pattern of judgment extended also to rural singing in general, as for instance when choir members frowned at one group's harshly shrill sopranos. Lajos offered a similar judgment of distinction through positive encouragement when he whispered an approving comment at one choir leader as he led his group back into the pews behind us. Later, after our performance, we received praise from several priests on the walk back to our seats. "Very cultivated notes," one said, which seemed to confirm our ability to distinguish between good and bad singing and thus authorize our earlier judgments.

To end the concert performances, we heard speeches first from a representative of the Catholic Archdiocese of Transylvania (Alba Iulia) followed by an official from the Harghita County cultural office. The order struck me as significant, since the former's choice of words seemed to close the concert portion while the latter focused on what was to come next. He was releasing us to "the festival," but not before warning that, "If we don't preserve our culture, only the wicked will!"

The choirs then processed in a line out from the church, accompanied by the hum of conversation. On the path I had arrived on, still halfway from our destination back at the House of Culture, I also heard the sound of an upright bass pulling a syncopated rhythm. The music seemed to prompt Lajos, who was standing next to me: "This is how Szeklers party," he said with a sly smile. Attila from our group had gone ahead, and we guessed rightly that he found the wooden picnic table reserved for us. Once we were seated, a male server in Szekler costume handed over a colorless liquor in a glass bottle. The bottle went from person to person down the table, and we poured out and drank shots of a plum-flavored schnapps called *pálinka* that, so the server told us, was of local vintage.

I was not the only one hungry for the pork-stuffed cabbage leaves brought not long after. "That's it," Attila declared approvingly when the same server laid down a silver platter, heaped high. As we ate, the server visited us several more times, now carrying a jug of sweet white wine. The music stopped for a moment after the band had finished its first set and wandered off. Just then, somebody at the table's far end scooped up into a soldier ballad. He belted out a few notes, at which point other men joined in from tables scattered around the courtyard. They sang seated and looking ahead, matching in pitch and rhythm without acknowledging one another physically. Soon several Csíksomlyó men, one of them right next to me, were also singing, dipping and rising between notes in the masculine genre's typical style.

"Have you been to a Szekler wedding?" Lajos asked me later that evening as we walked in the dark to the bus. "Is it like this?" I inquired in return. "Well, yes, at traditional village weddings people will sing." I took Lajos's reference to singing to mean the ballads that the men, including many from the Csíksomlyó choir, had intoned throughout the evening. I then answered Lajos in the negative, because this was the first time I had heard this kind of performance.

Lajos next approached me about fifteen minutes later, going from seat to seat down the aisle with another stoppered bottle in his hand. When he pulled himself up beside me, Lajos held out a shot glass-sized white plastic cup: "This also belongs to our culture." Then he lowered his voice into the low whisper that, I was beginning to understand, meant a joke was coming: "Do you know what Szeklers think the letters stand for on the top of the cross? You know, I, N, R, I?" I said I didn't. "Drink it up, Uncle Nándi, because time is short!"[5]

By dividing the time and space of the church for properly civilized Szeklerness and the time and space of the government's House of Culture for its sloppy inverse, the choir festival authorized Csíksomlyó choir members' indulgence in the latter. A lexical distinction encouraged this pattern. As I learned from the young man in the main hall, "concert" referred to the church while "festival" meant the House of Culture. The choir members' more or less subtle pedagogical interventions only reinforced the division.

As volunteer teachers, we sent quiet messages disciplining other groups to be embarrassed about embodying the sloppy form of Szekler habituation in the context of the church concert. The basses' silent glances communicated a message about what did and did not constitute virtuous singing in their eyes, and our own excellence in embodying a cultured style of Szeklerness during our performance authorized this pedagogical work. Among the rest of the choir, they evoked the sense of obligation to each other and the group as a whole that some had spoken about in the Tenth Anniversary Booklet: the sense of responsibility to help the group, in Father Márk József's words, reach a "higher level" of artistry (nívósabb).

At the House of Culture, however, we embraced and performed a natural, boisterous, and coarse Szekler masculinity. The archdiocesan and governmental speeches began the transition between the Catholic and Szekler performative styles. Walking from one space to another, the group had enacted this transition in their bodies. The band's music also effected this transition. The musicians' rhythm reached the women behind me, setting their shoulders swaying in the style of traditional Szekler dance. Lajos's question on the point of Szekler weddings prepared me for this new type of gathering even as it conveyed his own anticipation of what awaited us at the House of Culture. Safe inside the bounds of Szekler performance, men passed around alcohol and exchanged ballads.

With his joke about the cross's inscription, Lajos had not simply identi-fied drinking with Szekler culture, he had also suggested that drunkenness was an outward sign of Szeklers' theological ignorance, if not irreverence. When the Szekler man in Lajos's joke misunderstood a Latin inscription on the cross, he took the Church's high liturgical language to be an exhor-tation to engage in a Szekler practice. INRI, the Latin inscription over Jesus' cross short for "Jesus of Nazareth, King of the Jews," became, for Lajos, a sign of Szeklers' incomplete embrace of Catholicism and the need for the Church to further prosecute a part-civilizational, part-evangelical mission.

This work to segregate civilized from sloppy, cultured from natural forms of Szekler masculinity, seemingly embraced and enforced by the choir in its pedagogical mission, was always incomplete and the line between natural and cultural modes of Szekler performance subsumed within the ambiguities of embodied experience. One evening, Lajos gave a two-word signal to transition from warm-ups into rehearsal. "Ave Maria," he said in his terse manner, and I began flipping through the sheet music for Franz Liszt's hymn to the Virgin Mary.

The piece features basses in solo for several bars, but Lajos whipped his arms down to stop us right after we began this passage. "Come on, what is this," he demanded. "We're not in some pub!" He then mocked our slurred timbre, how we had scooped up from a lower tone to the starting note. He used the word for a rural pub, *kocsma*, to underscore the unflat-tering comparison: We had unintentionally imitated the distinctively mas-culine and provincial style of soldier balladry, the uncivilized kind that some of us had harshly sanctioned during the annual parish choir festival.

During the festival, the choir members had confidently kept these forms of Szekler performance separate. In their pedagogical judgments of eye-rolling and smirking, the singers in my group had enforced the boundaries between the spheres of practice—church and House of Culture, civilized and sloppy—while also recognizing the pathway following the concert as the proper venue and occasion for making the transition between them. However, as Thomas Csordas has argued, the human body is irrevocably, ambiguously, and inseparably biological and cultivated, frustrating any attempt at distinguishing a natural realm or time from a cultural one (2002: 3–4). What the festival presented as a fait accompli—confidently separated spaces and times for natural and cultural forms of Szekler perfor-mance, a separation that furthermore seemed to manifest a conflict between the government institution of the House of Culture and the religious institution of the church—had become ambiguated in the flux of embodied experience, a state that called from choir members further pedagogical labor and discipline (see Rogers 2009).

Looking back to choir members' statements about losing consciousness while rising in sung prayer, these comments seem to call to mind—transposed into a liturgical framework—a mode of experience akin to uncivilized behavior: loss of self in a liturgical mode. Anthropologist Tanya Luhrmann argues that rural and racially "other" Charismatic and Pentecostal practices likewise helped a generation of baby boomer, middle-class white Americans experience God as vividly and sensorially real. But they first needed to recast these practices in a similar way, by understanding them as another form of the countercultural experimentation that had defined their generation's anti-bourgeois rebellion (Luhrmann 2012: 19–21).

The Ciuc Valley's latest village transplants are similarly ambivalent when they venture out onto the emotional margins of post-socialist urban middle-class culture, margins opened up to them by both questionably foreign Charismatic/Pentecostal Christianity as well as "their own" Szekler rural traditional culture; they deal with this ambivalence partly through exploring self-transcending experiences within the Catholic Mass's authoritative ritual framework, which they both identify with and stand apart from as activists seeking to renew Catholic worship. As rural educators reviving participation in the Mass, it was possible for them to combine the rebellious desire for vivid experience with an attitude of pedagogical responsibility that situated them as urban-based educational servants and leaders of a Transylvanian Hungarian tradition.

It would be problematically reductive, therefore, to claim that choir members are embodying either a Charismatic or Szekler subjectivity without attending to the way these efforts to change both self and other carry significant risks—making urban Transylvanian Hungarian singing groups appear foreign as well as backward—by virtue of their position within broader social fields. As I show in my analysis of the choir's joke about "Marty Smith," engaging in self-transcendence through liturgical pedagogy was never solely a solution to a problem but placed additional and uncomfortable burdens on its members.

However, not every singer could tolerate the multiple overlapping syntheses of identification involved in being a member of the Csíksomlyó choir. Gizella, my landlady in Miercurea Ciuc, stopped coming to our meetings sometime in the fall of 2010. I had moved into my own rooms, so I didn't immediately notice her absence. It was a surprise when Lajos sat down beside me after rehearsal to ask about her. The next week I phoned Gizella to stop by. When I arrived, she ushered me into the kitchen, where two red coffee cups were ready on the table. We exchanged pleasantries until I broached the reason for my visit. She laughed, happy to give her opinion about recent "conflicts" in the choir:

> When the choir became an organization and they started applying for sup-port, for money, that's when conflicts started. They started thinking about how to get supporters and patrons. And now I don't feel like going. I have had my own business. If I wanted another one, I would do that.

Gizella compared NGOs' relationships with the county government to a client's dependency on a patron's charity. Implicitly, she was harkening back to the socialist-era when state-owned firms competed against each other for investment funds. Explicitly, the choir's new involvement in competitions for government patronage reminded her of the culture of entrepreneurialism that she had once embraced in order to make the transition from socialist-era factory administrator to independent business owner. Such a relationship between government and conflict remains widespread in Eastern Europe. According to Susan Gál and Gail Kligman, under socialism a state is the paradigmatic domain where people compete against each other, whereas in Western capitalism the market has long been associated with agonism (Gál and Kligman 2000). Gizella complained that, once the choir began applying for state funding and competing for patrons, she began experiencing these characteristically conflictual social relations among the choir's members.

Gizella added an additional complaint that the choir was neglecting its pedagogical mission to rural believers by devoting too much time to celebrating Szekler culture. That afternoon we also spent time looking at a Hungarian tourist magazine, which featured an article about the choir. For Gizella, the magazine exemplified what was wrong with the group:

> For a long time, my opinion has been that there are a bunch of problems people just don't want to deal with. In these kinds of magazines, there's only light and nothing else. They don't write anything about or show any pictures of difficulties and everyday trials. At so many performances, they hold up the light and lighten the atmosphere, but they don't say anything about problems. Alcoholism, drinking, all the men who are drunk all the

time is what they don't talk about. Sure, you can see pretty things at dance
festivals and concerts, but I think they should also make things about what
life is really like here.

Gizella wondered how alcoholism could even begin to be criticized
when the Szekler revival had made masculine drinking part of "our culture." Gizella's embarrassment alludes to the degree to which this state-
sponsored style of representation holds sway over Szekler public life. The
authoritative status of Szekler authenticity leaves few options for those
who would question its celebratory tone. Nevertheless, Gizella worried
that the choir's greater integration into this system of idealized folk representation had impeded its civilizing mission; the dominance of Szekler
revival initiatives within the cultural field left some members, Gizella
among them, anxious about whether the choir was shifting its focus away
from rural ethical pedagogy and toward a revival-style valorization of
Szeklerness.

EUROPEAN-LEVEL CHRISTIAN HUNGARIAN ARTS

Lajos usually clapped his hands to begin rehearsal. A few weeks after the
festival, though, he caught the group's attention by waiving a printout
above his head. "I've got an invitation, news about the summer tour," he
began, then paused for dramatic effect. Choir members erupted in cheers
when he announced we were going to Székesfehérvár, a city in Hungary.
Beginning in the mid-2000s, the choir's officials had begun scheduling
these summer concert series. The choir's NGO funded the tours, submit-
ting applications for government support that Gizella had derided as a
deviation into competitive clientelism and a distortion of the choir's pedagogical mission to the peasantry.

A Hungarian tour was an additional innovation. This was only the sec-
ond time the Csíksomlyó group would cross the border for a concert series.
With the itinerary, Lajos had also received a letter of invitation from a
Fejér county government official, a politician from Hungary's right-wing
Christian Democratic People's Party (KDNP). "You are the true ambassadors of Hungarian culture," the official declared at the start, "since you
do the most to shape other nations' opinion about us as Hungarians."
And he closed with a compliment that inadvertently brought down the
house in laughter: "The Csíksomlyó choir, famous throughout Europe for
representing high artistic standards, has become a symbol of the solidarity
of Christian Hungariandom."[6]

The letter made it clear that for the choir the tour was much more than a simple change of geographical venues. The concerts marked a shift away from the choir's rural mission, the work to educate the peasantry to renew worship that we undertook throughout the year at Csíksomlyó and also during the valley parish choir festival. Performing in Hungary would bring these Transylvanian Hungarian rural educators face-to-face with audiences of Hungarians from Hungary, in much the same way that the orphanage director Brother Csaba addressed Hungarians in films, books, and speeches during his volunteer projects. While Brother Csaba had subjected himself to a seeker narrative style to convert post-socialist Hungarians into volunteers, the KDNP official's letter suggested that this choir of educator-servants to the countryside would face a different set of authoritative desires and goals that, while familiar, were also other.

These authoritative desires and goals were represented in the KDNP official's letter extolling the choir's European-level fame, which we had achieved as a chief artistic accomplishment of "Christian Hungariandom." The description fuses the Hungarian right-wing's Christian cultural politics with an older notion of "Europe-level Hungarian arts." The politician's reference to Christian Hungariandom fits with Hungarian conservatives' claim to be defenders of Europe's Christian culture, which in the right-wing view is under siege by secular Europeans and non-Christian refugee outsiders (Ádám and Bozóki 2016: 115; Kallius et al. 2016). This concept of a Christian Hungarian culture is then synthesized with an older goal of fashioning a musical tradition that is uniquely Hungarian but recognized as excellent on the European stage, a project that had been a controlling goal within Hungary's musical community as far back as the nineteenth century.

According to historian Kristina Lajosi, influential nineteenth-century musical journals contributed to the elevation of Hungarian music by fashioning it to European standards while at the same time emphasizing the importance of its national characteristics (Lajosi 2018: 149–51). Hungarian composers have long had a paradoxical need for European authorities to value what was supposed to be a self-evidently valuable Hungarian high-art tradition. Historian Carl Dahlhaus thus observes that, "The discovery (or the construction, as the case may be) of a national musical character, which was felt to distinguish a nation from the pan-European tradition, was itself a pan-European phenomenon" (Dahlhaus 1989: 90).

European-level recognition as an artistic aspiration itself harkened back to Hungary's marginal imperial position. Seeking greater independence in first the Habsburg Empire and then the Austro-Hungarian Empire, nineteenth-century Hungarian composers tended to judge the success of a national tradition against Austria's musical tradition, which had been powerful enough to define Europe's cosmopolitan and global perspective.[7] Hungarian classical music was supposed to be both grounded in ancient Hungarian tradition and sophisticated in the production and consumption of European-level excellence.

Choir members agreed that the KDNP official's claim that we had achieved European levels of excellence were exaggerated. They laughed at the idea that a group of lawyers, teachers, and bureaucrats, who sang part-time as volunteers, was going to impress the choirs that set standards of excellence within the world of European high-art vocal performance. Choir members seemed to recognize a discrepancy—on the level of our performative quality and refinement—between the goals of the Transylvanian Hungarian mission to educate the peasantry and the cultural, religious, and political agenda of the right-wing Hungarian state. Their laughter seemed to stand in for an implicit anxiety, that the project of making European-level Christian Hungarian arts had been imposed on the choir and its village educators from outside, with the potential to subject them to humiliating assessments.

Yet the singers generally agreed with the project of crafting a Christian Hungarian culture. Indeed, the engaged and personally intimate worship singers taught to peasants, to a certain degree, involved disciplining worship to a cultured and civilized style of singing. This embrace of civilized singing indexed a historical legacy that, like post-socialist desire for non-materialistic experiences, led Transylvanian Hungarians to be deferential to their cross-border ethnic cousins' tastes, powerfully disciplined by their encounters in Hungary where, as labor migrants in the tourism and service industries, they had observed (and had also served) Hungarians and foreigners enjoying Western-style touristic pleasure-seeking (Oláh 1996; Fox 2009).

The authoritative status of the Hungarian right-wing's agenda left choir members with little room to express open resentment about the KDNP's effort to subsume or reframe the Transylvanian Hungarian pedagogical mission within the project of crafting European-level Christian Hungarian arts. Instead of open resentment, the members' misgivings came out as anxiety about failing to live up to high artistic expectations, an internally oriented sense of inadequacy, and externally oriented awareness of others' unrealistic expectations. Choir members appreciated the Hungarian government's patronage; a free international vacation was hard to pass up. But it was a fraught reward.

There were many reminders throughout the trip, which we embarked on after boarding a rented bus one early July morning, of this complex mix of identification and pride, deference, gratitude, and anxiety. During the tour, choir members seemed to express anxiety about Hungarians from Hungary judging them (and finding them wanting) by simultaneously identifying with but also renouncing uncivilized Szeklerness. Suddenly, on the other side of the border and with the knowledge of the KDNP official's expectations, they were no longer the vocational intellectuals on a mission to teach peasants to revive worship; they were the rough Szekler peasants themselves.

These reminders were not formally organized performances or carefully planned teaching sessions. Choir members repeatedly, spontaneously reutilized tourism objects to recall and reenact uncivilized Szeklerness for each other. In Székesfehérvár, we stayed in a rather expensive hotel and we were served breakfast, lunch, and dinner at its well-appointed restaurant. The first day, as we were sitting down to breakfast, I overheard a male choir member ask, in an exaggerated rough tone "What are you doing with that *bicska*" while looking at the man across from him, who was getting ready to slice a sausage with his fork and knife. A *bicska* is the traditional Szekler pocketknife, famed for its role in drunken brawls and associations with outbursts of masculine pride and anger.[8] The men guffawed at the joke, an incongruous use of the term since it referred now to a piece of silverware that, far from being a brawler's weapon, was a blunt hotel restaurant butter knife.

The next day, the same choir member took the joke a step further with a different member of the bass section. This time, he took a fork and thrust it at the other man's chest, claiming that he was wielding a *bicska*. The choir member's victim responded by grabbing a butter knife from the table. "That's not a *bicska*," he shouted, "*This* is a *bicska!*"

After our arrival in Székesfehérvár, we passed the first full day of our stay being guided around—treated like the honored ambassadors that the Hungarian official had called us in his invitation letter. Elected and ecclesiastical officials led us through Fejér County's administrative building, the bishop's residence, and the historical downtown. After an evening reception with one of Székesfehérvár's parliamentary representatives, we made our way to the hotel through the downtown again. We walked along in clusters of four and five, chatting and laughing.

I was with Teréz and two other women when we passed by a knick-knack storefront. Next to the doorway was a gangly stuffed scarecrow, long limbs sliding off the seat of a wooden chair. One knee was on the cobblestones and his other leg clung precariously to the seat. Only his head, with the mouth smoking a corncob pipe, kept upright. "Oh, look, it's Old Man Szekler, loving his *pálinka*, drunk again," Teréz said as she palmed his cheek and tried, unsuccessfully, to shift him upright. Her voice then exaggerated pity, "Don't cry, Old Man Szekler, don't cry!" The other women laughed for a beat before continuing down the street, leaving Teréz to hurry and catch up.

Teréz's comment and the ensuing laughter said a great deal about the tour's effects on members' self-perception. In her own way, she was parodying the experience of being toured around Székesfehérvár's downtown by taking up and creatively distorting the tour guide's own practice of celebrating the city's cultural highpoints; instead of highlighting one of Székesfehérvár's architectural wonders, Teréz highlighted a disheveled and drunken Szekler man. While Teréz lampooned the guide, she did so in terms that evoked the anxiety-provoking specter of uncivilized Szeklerness: The Szekler scarecrow was so drunk he was slipping from his chair; and he was so overcome with emotion—perhaps also because he was so far from his Transylvanian home—that he was falling apart in maudlin sadness.

Trying to get him upright only to watch him collapse again, Teréz looked as though she were trying to pull the man together. Her failure echoed anxieties about the limitations of their civilizing mission that animated choir members' other spontaneous jokes, like the comment about celebrating the feast day of "Marty Smith." Her jibe at the Szekler man's drunkenness, despite being a spontaneous and fugitive sidewalk performance, continued what had by then become a pattern of using the trip to interrogate peasant and ethnic categories. Indeed, it took shape at the intersection of the choir's civilizing mission to reform rural education and the government's desire to appropriate the choir's work in order to celebrate the group as as a European-level achievement of Hungarian Christendom.

Neither of these spontaneous gestures—the *bicska* game, mocking the stuffed Szekler scarecrow—referred directly to the purpose of the trip: giving musical concerts. One additional episode involving our tour bus did seem to express the choir's anxieties about failing to be a European-level artistic achievement of Christian Hungarian culture. During one long stretch in the bus, when the windows were filled with the unremarkable scenery of expansive flat green fields, choir members turned their attention to each other, a typical effect of modern bus tourism that anthropologist John Urry calls "mobile privatization:" the sensation of being in a sealed and safe place as the vehicle moves through strange environments (Urry 2000: 62–63, 191).

Choir members sliced and shared home-brought sausages and vegetables on their pull-down trays, and men walked through the center aisle with bottles of *pálinka*; both evoked singers' identification with the Szekler culture of the county government's choir festival, but in the mode of domesticity and imagination that Michael Taussig associates with vehicular travel: "The automobile offers the fantasy of a safe space in a cruel and unpredictable world," Taussig writes, "a space of intimacy and daydreaming" (2011: 5).[9] Choir members were daydreaming their home in Szekler culture, at least as the cultural revival had been constructing this culture since the 1970s.

Yet as Urry and others have also noted, the sense of home that buses provide is unstable. As we raced along the highway, no local vendors could reach through the windows, a characteristic violation of the physical separation on which mobile privatization depends.[10] Instead, the one real nuisance came from the bus's air-conditioning system. Over the day, the bus' powerful air-conditioning threw out a stiff breeze of uncomfortably cold air on the singers up front.

Several times, I got up from my seat to chat with those behind the driver. With the two rows of sopranos behind them, Imola and her seatmate discussed how cold it was; Imola even said the chill was affecting their voices. I first noticed a change as we approached Budapest, hours before our arrival in Székesfehérvár, and asked Imola about it. Her bright chirr of a voice was now raspy. She explained that the air-conditioning caused the hoarseness, and it had happened before: "The last time I lost my voice like that was when I flew to Los Angeles. It was so cold on the plane, I practically got pneumonia."

On one level, the analogy between the conditions on the bus and a plane emphasized the fact that choir members associated the former vehicle with the tourism industry; but then Imola was alone among the choir members for having flown intercontinentally. Her analogy underscored that, for all their effort to feel at home, the air-conditioning caused some to feel not quite comfortable among the Hungarian government's trappings for honored guests. For Imola, this sense of unease existed at an embodied level; the chill air threatened her ability to sing, that is, to perform her role as a cultural ambassador.

Choir members were still able to reinstrumentalize this arrangement, recasting it within a Szekler context to entertain and amuse themselves. The group had turned boisterous that afternoon once we crossed the Hungarian border, but the high point was when the driver decided to play a Szekler folk band on the speakers. Up and down the bus choir members rose from their seats to watch, whistle, and whoop as others danced in the aisle, turning their ankles, pointing their heels, and slapping their thighs in the characteristically masculine style of Szekler traditional dance. I made short videos with my camera, and in the background of one clip, the green blur through the window showed that the driver had not slowed down. The laughter peaked when he took a turn and almost knocked the dancers off their feet; some did fall into the seats.

Attila was at the center of the revelry. He was the member of the bass section who had so eagerly led us to our table at the parish choir festival, and just as eagerly mock-threatened another man with a butter knife-cum-*bicska*. Now, he seemed to be in charge of instrumental pantomime. At first, he beat an imaginary *ütőgardon*, the distinctively Szekler cello-like instrument played with a stick instead of a bow; then he switched to playing the bus itself. In a feat of improvisation, Attila grabbed a pocketknife off his seat—truly the *bicska* symbol of Szekler masculinity—which he had just finished using for sausage. As he began running the knife's blade over a large air-conditioning vent, it produced a scraping sound not unlike the washboard used in American bluegrass bands' rhythm sections.

Attila's improvisation distilled for me the social significance of the choir's partying. It seemed to be a performance of Szekler identity shaped by and responsive to the way the Hungarian government had framed us as cultural ambassadors: the choir was enacting a style of masculine Szekler selfhood. The bus dance party was more raucous than the variety of masculine performance I had witnessed during the parish choir festival: the former was manic with dancers at liberty to throw themselves off their feet, while the latter was maudlin and singers were liable to slip from their chairs. Nonetheless, the two performances were qualitatively Szekler and of a piece.

The message from the choir members seemed to be that if the deal's terms amount to serving the Hungarian government's goal and meeting the unreasonable expectation to be "famous throughout Europe for representing high artistic standards," then choir members themselves will use the instruments of this ambassadorship to undermine this image. So they gave in to the intransigent air-conditioning system, insofar as the rented bus itself undermined their ability to live up to the government's expectations.

When Attila reinstrumentalized the air vent into a washboard, he took up, in the alternative context of Szekler cultural revival, an instrument that was negatively affecting the sopranos' ability to meet the Hungarian government's expectations. To that end, he refracted the choir's subjection to the bus as an extension of the government-run tourism system responsible for the choir's cultural ambassadorship. Attila's gesture invited others to enjoy themselves on their own terms, even if at home choir members did not entirely identify with the image of Szeklerness contained within these terms.

SZEKLER CATHARSIS

Although during the tour the choir performed many songs from our repertoire, members said that singing one piece in particular was the trip's high point. A shared catharsis during the Szekler national anthem sparked enthusiastic discussions among the singers. At the end of our second performance in Székesfehérvár's Church of Saint Sebastian, Lajos led us back onto the risers for an encore. Facing us so only we could hear, he whispered, "Szekler national anthem," and raised his arms.

I learned later that the choir members were actually surprised when the audience rose to their feet at the song's opening bar; they did not expect the crowd to know it. But when it became clear everyone was singing, I noticed Attila next to me, whose voice had begun to quaver; something seemed to catch in his throat, and then I noticed the bass on my other side faltering. By the time we neared the end, the crowd and choir were all weeping and singing together.

A few weeks later, during a meeting to debrief the tour, choir members were eager to talk about the anthem. Many remarked on the encore as we took turns speaking, sitting in a circle of portable school desks in the Csíksomlyó church's choir room. But a couple of comments garnered the lion's share of agreement. The first I have already described: Gizella's joke that contrasted a rural wedding with the concert performance of the Szekler anthem. To the group, she explained the latter was more civilized. To me, she mentioned that post-1989 weddings were drunken affairs where men sang sloppy and maudlin versions of the anthem. The concert offered choir members an opportunity to transcend the bounds of normal emotions, the experience that they wanted as Catholic liturgical assistants and leaders of a liturgical revival in the Catholic Church.

In Székesfehérvár, though, they had fallen apart as Szeklers, while singing the Szekler national anthem. This catharsis brought the choir dangerously up to the line of maudlin sloppiness. By crying through the encore, we had lost our composure before an audience of middle-class Hungarians from Hungary, and in our role as crowning achievements of Hungarian Christian culture: in robes, on choral risers, and at the altar of a cathedral of national historical import. In the process, the members had retained Szekler sloppiness in an experience that synthesized it with Catholic prayerful self-transcendence.

That encore was still on Lajos's mind in 2016 when I went back to Csíksomlyó for a visit. As we sat chatting with four other members in the rehearsal room, squeezed into the same portable school desks, we recreated the choir's post-tour discussion circle, albeit with a smaller circle of participants. At one point Lajos interpreted our experience as a form of social critique:

> We don't place a lot of importance on feelings, because the world pushes it deep inside us. [The world says,] 'Go! Get on, now! Faster! Faster! Progress! Success! Deep feelings aren't important. They're not essential.' It's not that this, this, catharsis, doesn't happen all the time. It's pretty common. It's just that we don't notice it and then don't slow down or talk about it when it does happen.

Lajos's complaint about urban life's fast pace echoes the rhetoric of the "slow food movement," which originated in Italy in the 1980s partly as a critique of modern capitalist urbanity (Thompson and Kumar 2018). The slow food movement has grown to include multiple critical perspectives—for instance, many Hungarian activists promote regional food cultures to resist globalization's cultural homogenization (Kovács and Zsarnóczay 2007).

According to Luc Boltanski and Eve Chiapello, who compare the slow food movement with other "artistic critiques" of capitalism, slow-food activists complain that the fast pace of urban lifestyles within bureaucratic workplaces produces not only homogenization but also, in the sphere of everyday human life, routinized and inauthentic social relations (2006: 197–201). The manifest content and purpose of Lajos's commentary positioned the choir as a critique of these aspects of city life. Lajos suggested that the experience on tour bolstered the choir's countercultural message. First, members showed Székesfehérvár's residents that deep feelings are essential. Later during the choir's group discussions back at home in Transylvania, members showed each other the value of authentic social relations by stopping to share these feelings.

Lajos shifted attention away from the conflict-inducing dynamic of the choir's ethical mission to rural Catholics, a mission to promote composure that the tour of Hungary had shown to be directed at the choir's own membership. When they worried how Hungarian audiences might identify them, the choir members expressed their ambivalence at the idea of being identified with the Szekler cultural revival through evoking rural Szekler vices—including disorderly public behavior—which many choir members felt they had an ethical responsibility to civilize. Although his comment was a tentative interpretive assay in an informal conversation, Lajos accomplished a rhetorical maneuver that opened up possibilities for the choir to expand its ethical mission beyond civilizing rural (Szekler) Catholics. At least in this moment, Lajos was moving beyond the rural pedagogical mission to ally the choir with an increasingly popular critique of urban middle-class culture, one that choir members could use to equip themselves during future encounters with Hungarians from Hungary.

Conclusion

In this chapter, I described how Csíksomlyó choir members understand liturgical performance as virtuous singing. Parish choir members take a place alongside catechists within the growing cohort of clerical assistants serving Catholic communities around the world. But based on my participant observation, the Csíksomlyó choir has a distinctive ethical bailiwick shaped by the group's multiple implications in the program of cultural construction that was Romanian urbanization. The choir's rehearsals and performances are a form of ethical cultivation toward composure and beauty, virtues that harken back to the post-socialist urban context. Members embrace virtuous singing as a means of honoring the project of civilization through urbanization that was part of their process of moving from natal villages to Miercurea Ciuc. Although they were taught that cultural projects help civilize rural peasants, today the choir receives funds from the same cultural offices that support an ongoing Szekler cultural revival. Complicating matters, the Csíksomlyó choir also sings at Szekler festivals, occasions that raise questions concerning the fate of cultural programs' civilizational mission.

In Chap. 5, I examine a Transylvanian Hungarian group's appropriation of a Hungary-based tradition: the cult of King Stephen, Hungary's first Christian monarch. My data comes from observing a contemporary group, the Knighthood Order of the Holy Crown, that is trying to extend devotion to this relic of King Stephen in Transylvanian Hungarian communities. King Stephen's cult has long played a significant role in political culture in Hungary. But after World War I, attitudes toward King Stephen diverged between Hungarians from Hungary and Transylvanian Hungarians.

Interwar Hungarian politicians used King Stephen's relics in monarchial religio-political spectacles, while Márton and his colleagues highlighted early Christian apostles as pedagogical ideals. The latter figures were ideal ethical intellectuals, and cultivated virtue in humbler educational media: They organized and taught in small groups, a model more apt than spectacle for the Transylvanian Hungarian community's new station as an ethnic minority. Spectacles featuring King Stephen's relics returned to a prominent place in Hungarian political life in the 1980s and 1990s. Extending the cult to Transylvania, I argue, requires overcoming these historical divergences to embed King Stephen's cult in the kind of small-group and virtue-centered educational program that Márton and others developed for the Transylvanian Hungarian intelligentsia. In Chap. 5, I develop my account of cultivating an ethical nation by examining how the Knighthood Order of the Holy Crown teaches Transylvanian Hungarians that King Stephen exemplified the virtue of courtliness.

NOTES

1. For analyses of the global "clash of civilizations" (see Brubaker 2017; Ádám and Bozóki 2016; Turda 2001: 203–5; Trencsényi 2010: 34–6; 2014).
2. Taussig finds a similar dialectic of barbarism and civilization. Barbarism, he argues, is channeled and elaborated by the local representatives of bureaucratic Enlightenment values: intellectuals, such as spirit healers, as well as by national elites (Taussig 1987).
3. See Magdó 2016: 86; Kligman 1988; Bíró et al. 1987. According to Demeter, "folk song and dance played the most significant role in the programs," to which cultural units at every level were required to contribute,

including dance troupes, choirs, poetry recitation groups, and brass and wind bands (Demeter 2011: 157).

4. While there were efforts to revive Szekler culture before the 1970s, only then did county-level Szekler cultural events become attached to participants' identification with urban civilization, primarily as a result of the Romanian state's efforts to foment regional divisions within Transylvania's Hungarian community. As Stefano Bottoni has shown, intellectuals created Szekler festivals to foster regional identity and combat labor migration as far back as the 1920s (Bottoni 2013: 499–501).

5. In Hungarian, "Idd meg, Nándi bácsi, mert Rővid az Idő."

6. The text comes from Lajos's printout that he provided the author.

7. In late socialist-era Hungary, this bidirectional orientation carried over into artistic traditions like architecture, which was equally influenced by the imperial dynamics of consumer production in socialist Eastern Europe. Through the 1970s Hungarian designers took over from the Soviet Union a "socialist modern aesthetic" of square angles, gray walls, and concrete materials, against which a group of marginalized dissident architects developed curvilinear, colorful, and organic designs that evoked Hungarian national themes (Fehérváry 2013: 155–8). After this latter style became the official aesthetic of the post-socialist Hungarian nation-state, the government sought European recognition for its new "Organicist" nationalistic aesthetic regime, selecting its chief proponents to represent Hungary in Europe-wide expositions (Fehérváry 2013: 156).

8. Museums have recently begun to mount *bicska* exhibitions, cementing its place in the movement to revive and preserve Szekler culture. See Márk 2016.

9. In her study of Hungarian consumer culture, Fehérváry calls the automobile a "heterotopic space" (2013: 50).

10. Kaell 2014: 166–8 describes this case.

References

Ádám, Zoltán and András Bozóki. 2016. State and Faith: Right-wing Populism and Nationalized Religion in Hungary. *Intersections: East European Journal of Society and Politics* 2 (1): 98–122.

Boltanski, Luc, and Eve Chiapello. 2006. *The New Spirit of Capitalism.* New York: Verso.

Bottoni, Stefano. 2013. National Projects, Regional Identities, Everyday Compromises Szeklerland in Greater Romania (1919–1940). *Hungarian Historical Review* 2 (3): 477–511.

Brubaker, Rogers. 2017. Between Nationalism and Civilizationism: The European Populist Moment in Comparative Perspective. *Ethnic and Racial Studies* 40 (8): 1191–1226.

Csordas, Thomas J. 1994. *The Sacred Self: A Cultural Phenomenology of Charismatic Healing.* Berkeley: University of California Press.

Dahlhaus, Carl. 1989. *Between Romanticism and Modernism: Four Studies in the Music of the Later Nineteenth Century.* Berkeley: University of California Press.

Demeter, Csanád. 2010. "Városrendezés" Csíkszeredában ["Ordering the City" in Csíkszereda]. *Korunk* 2: 101–108.

Dunn, Elizabeth. 2004. *Privatizing Poland: Baby Food, Big Business, and the Remaking of Labor.* Ithaca, N.Y.: Cornell University Press. Thomas J. Csordas. Body/meaning/healing. New York: Palgrave Macmillan, 2002.

———. 2011. Falusi urbanizáció és városi ruralizáció a Székelyföldön [Village Urbanization and Urban Ruralization in the Szekler Land]. *Korunk* 4: 101–107.

Fehérváry, Krisztina. 2013. *Politics in Color and Concrete: Socialist Materialities and the Middle Class in Hungary.* Bloomington: University of Indiana Press.

Fox, Jon. 2009. From National Inclusion to Economic Exclusion: Transylvanian Hungarian Ethnic Return Migration to Hungary. In *Diasporic Homecomings: Ethnic Return Migration in Comparative Perspective,* ed. Tsuda Takeyuki, 186–207. Stanford: Stanford University Press.

Gal, Susan, and Gail Kligman. 2000. *The Politics of Gender After Socialism: A Comparative-Historical Essay.* Princeton: Princeton University Press.

Gog, Sorin. 2020. Neo-Liberal Subjectivities and the Emergence of Spiritual Entrepreneurship: An Analysis of Spiritual Development Programs in Contemporary Romania. *Social Compass* 67 (1): 103–119.

Jowitt, Ken. 1983. *Soviet Neotraditionalism: The political corruption of a Leninist regime.* Soviet Studies. 35 (3): 275–297.

Kaell, Hillary. 2014. Age of Innocence: The Symbolic Child and Political Conflict on American Holy Land Pilgrimage. *Religion and Society: Advances in Research* 5: 157–172.

Kallius, Annastiina, Daniel Monterescu, and Prem Kumar Rajaram. 2016. Immobilizing mobility: Border ethnography, illiberal democracy, and the politics of the "refugee crisis" in Hungary. 43 (1): 25–37.

Kligman, Gail. 1988. *The Wedding of the Dead: Ritual, Poetics, and Popular Culture in Transylvania.* Berkeley: University of California Press.

Kligman, Gail, and Katherine Verdery. 2011. *Peasants Under Siege: The Collectivization of Romanian Agriculture, 1949–1962.* Princeton: Princeton University Press.

Kovács, Ágnes, and Gabriella Zsarnóczay. 2007. Protected Meat Products in Hungary – Local Foods and Hungaricums. *Anthropology of Food* 2 (2): 1–7.

Lajosi, Kristina. 2018. *Staging the Nation: Opera and Nationalism in 19th-Century Hungary.* Leiden: Brill.

Lange, Barbara Rose. 2014. "Good Old Days:" Critiques of Masculinity in the Hungarian Folk Revival. *The World of Music* 3 (2): 39–58.

Luehrmann, Sonja. 2005. Recycling Cultural Construction: Desecularisation in Postsoviet Mari El. *Religion, State, and Society* 33 (1): 35–56.

———. 2011. *Secularism Soviet Style: Teaching Atheism and Religion in a Volga Republic.* Bloomington: Indiana University Press.

Luhrmann, Tanya. 2012. *When God Talks Back: Understanding the American Evangelical Relationship with God.* New York: Alfred A. Knopf.

Magdó, Zsuzsanna. 2016. "Romanian Spirituality in Ceaușescu's 'Golden Epoch': Social Scientists Reconsider Atheism, Religion, and Ritual Culture." In *Science, Religion, and Communism in Cold War Europe*, eds. Paul Betts and Stephen A. Smith. London: Palgrave, 77–101.

Márk, Boglárka. 2016. "Tusványos: megalakult a Székelyföldi Értéktár Bizottság" ["The Tusványos Festival: The Committee to Preserve Szeklerland Cultural Treasures Has Been Formed." *Maszol.hu.* https://maszol.ro/kultura/67408-tusvanyos-megalakult-a-szekelyfoldi-ertektar-bizottsag. Accessed 22 Dec 2021.

Mihăilescu, Vintilă, Ilia Iliev, and Slobodan Naumović. 2008. *Studying Peoples in the People's Democracies II: Socialist Era Anthropology in South-East Europe.* Berlin: LIT-Verlag.

Oláh, Sándor. 1996. A székelyföldi migráció előtörténetének áttekintése [A Sketch of the Pre-History of Migration from the Szekler Land]. In *Elvándorlók? Vendégmunka és életforma a Székelyföldön* [Emigrants? Labor Migration and Lifestyle in the Szekler Land], ed. Juliánna Bodó, 15–36. Miercurea Ciuc: Pro-Print Könyvkiadó.

Orta, Andrew. 2004. *Catechizing Culture: Missionaries, Aymara, and the "New Evangelization".* New York: Columbia University Press.

Rama, Angel. 1994. *The Lettered City.* Durham: Duke University Press.

Rivkin-Fish, Michele. 2005. *Women's Health in Post-Soviet Russia: The Politics of Intervention.* Bloomington: Indiana University Press.

Rogers, Douglas. 2009. *The Old Faith and the Russian Land: A Historical Ethnography of Ethics in the Urals.* Ithaca: Cornell University Press.

Schweizer, Peter. 1988. *Shepherds, Workers, Intellectuals: Culture and Centre-Periphery Relationships in a Sardinian Village.* Stockholm: University of Stockholm Press.

Taussig, Michael. 2011. *I Swear I Saw This. Drawings in Fieldwork Notebooks, Namely My Own.* Chicago: University of Chicago Press.

Thompson, Craig J., and Ankita Kumar. 2018. Beyond Consumer Responsibilization: Slow Food's Actually Existing Neoliberalism. *Journal of Consumer Culture* 0 (0): 1–20.

Trencsényi, Balázs. 2010. Imposed Authenticity: Approaching Eastern European National Characterologies in the Inter-War Period. *Central Europe* 8 (1): 20–47.

———. 2011. Civilization and Originality: Perceptions of History and National Specificity in Nineteenth-Century Hungarian Political Discourse. In *Encountering Otherness. Diversities and Transcultural Experiences in Early Modern European Culture*, ed. Guido Abbattista, 305–338. Trieste: Trieste University Press.

Taussig, Michael. 1987. Shamanism, Colonialism, and the Wild Man. Chicago: Univesity of Chicago Press.

Turda, Marius. 2001. Deciding the National Capital: Budapest, Vienna, Bucharest and Transylvanian Romanian Culture. In *Tradition and Modernity in Romanian Culture and Civilization*, ed. Kurt W. Treptow, 95–114.

Urry, John. 2000. *Sociology Beyond Societies*. London: Routledge.

Zigon, Jarrett. 2010. HIV is God's BlessingRehabilitating Morality in Neoliberal Russia. Berkeley: University of California Press.

CHAPTER 5

Courtliness

PERSISTENCE IN A VOCATION

Midway through my fieldwork, I moved from Miercurea Ciuc, an urban county seat, to a nearby village where I rented a room from a former director of the local House of Culture. Emil had worked as director for several years but had lost his position after he failed in his signature initiative to create a local museum, compounded by a shakeup in the village government and complaints that he did not have a college degree. Indeed, before teaching, Emil had been a skilled laborer in a state-owned copper mine, once touted as a crown jewel of socialist progress (Pozniak 2013a, 2013b; Ghodsee 2009; Barabási 1996)

However, in the 1990s, post-socialist governments insisted that either privatizing or shuttering heavy industry was the best way to transition from socialism to capitalism. Miners' unions organized strikes that turned violent and tarnished their public reputation (Kideckel 2008). Amid the chaotic political situation, for many Transylvanian Hungarians working-class identity also became attached to Romanian national identity, intellectuals in the Ciuc Valley came to see miners as Romanian outsiders, agents of the Romanian state's national assimilation policy, within their homeland.

In the late 1970s when he went to work in the mine, Emil had expected a secure financial future and a good public reputation as a member of a

© The Author(s), under exclusive license to Springer Nature Switzerland AG 2022
M. R. Loustau, *Hungarian Catholic Intellectuals in Contemporary Romania*, Contemporary Anthropology of Religion, https://doi.org/10.1007/978-3-030-99221-7_5

group of industrial laborers whom the government celebrated as paragon socialist workers. In the 2000s, he took a government contract buyout as Romania's leadership began a campaign to slander miners for undermining the country's transition to capitalism. Emil used the money to take night school classes and begin a new career in cultural administration, but he was dogged by his industrial working-class past, which local political opponents eventually used to depose him.

In this chapter, a biographical case study of Emil, a village intellectual, I turn to the method of biographical analysis keeping in mind that the chief architects of the Transylvanian Hungarian intellectual tradition placed great emphasis on the virtue of persistence, which they understood to be manifest in a life of dedicated and tireless service to the people. Thus, Áron Márton, when he founded *Transylvanian School*, wrote that he was seeking a new type of village teacher, one who would "embrace a driving fever for work," anticipate opposition, and persist despite failure. Teachers are supposed to see responses to difficulties not only as tests of personal virtue but also signs of the nation's ethical self-awareness and generative revelations of God's collaborative presence. In this chapter, I explore the social experience of a pedagogical vocation by analyzing the meanings Emil imparted to his history of conducting village educational work. I argue that with his story, Emil initially tried to present the worldview of the industrial working class and resuscitate a socialist-era practice of using working-class identity to enter the ranks of middle-class intellectuals.

During my fieldwork, professors at a Hungarian-speaking university's ethnology department in Budapest invited me to speak about my research. With Emil's consent and help to craft the Hungarian text of lecture, I presented his narrative to this academic audience. Some audience members responded by questioning Emil's national identity. Although Emil was not present to witness this response, he received a similar message via other conversations about his story, which, in the wake of losing his teaching position in the House of Culture, led him to reflect more deeply on his calling to village teaching. I use my observation of the conflicts that emerged during this process to explore how Emil understood that opposition in relation to his class background, then how he drew on institutional and discursive resources to demonstrate to others his virtuous steadfastness to his vocation.

Over the past twenty years, numerous anthropologists have remarked on an irony of contemporary Eastern Europe intellectual life. Intellectuals who once led anti-religious propaganda classes under socialism now claim that, after converting and being hired to teach in growing churches, they are helped by the very classroom methods they once used to eradicate belief. In this chapter, I build on this body of research about the religious "recycling" of socialism's cultural practices (Luehrmann 2005, 2011). I examine the legacies of the socialist government's valorization of industrial labor and laborers' practice of using government benefits for industrial workers to improve their social position. This particular case, however, allows me to reframe a problematic, rational choice-style assumption of research on religion after socialism: that subjects choose to engage in religious practice according to whether doing so results in social benefits.

I do so by focusing on the relation between religious intellectual practice and working-class identity, which the national politics of privatization tarnished and left highly problematic. While I question the implicit assumption in this literature that religious practice should help subjects strengthen their class status, I do not draw the opposite conclusion that religious practice hurts teachers' class standing. I explore Emil's reaction to the experience of having his narrative turned into a lecture: privatizing his narrative, claiming it was irrelevant to his teaching initiatives, and comparing his vocation to Jesus's pedagogical approach. I argue that these are creative responses through which he deepened his identification with the Transylvanian Hungarian intellectual tradition's view that pedagogical setbacks are a test of one's virtue.

His village museum failure did not end Emil's teaching career, though. Eventually, Emil began an apprenticeship with a Hungarian Catholic knighthood order and chivalric association, the Order of the Holy Crown, a group of volunteer intellectuals just then creating a new rural educational initiative. In this chapter's first section, I summarize the history of the Hungarian cult of King Stephen and the Knighthood Order. As with the orphanages and choirs that I describe in previous chapters, the Knighthood Order is led by Transylvanian Hungarian intellectuals who collaborate with and draw financing from Fidesz, Hungary's ruling right-wing Christian party.

While interwar writers like Márton and Venczel seemed to draw a distinction between apostolic educators and intellectuals who organized monarchical spectacles about the Holy Crown, the Knighthood Order overcomes the divide between the Transylvanian Hungarian pedagogical tradition and this devotional cult by innovating small-scale educational events, during which they cultivate King Stephen's courtliness and other noble virtues. During my stay in Emil's home, he spent a year's volunteer service organizing lectures about King Stephen's Holy Crown relic for residents of area villages.[1]

My understanding of the cult's recent history therefore represents a departure from post-1989 Hungarian research on this topic, which has been limited by a preoccupation with (dis)proving the historical authenticity of devotional traditions.[2] My portrait is also more plausible than anthropologist Chris Hann's overly-broad speculation that we are dealing with a crisis cult. If, as Hann has argued, Hungarians were drawn to participate in this movement because they desire effective symbols of political authority following a crisis of confidence in the post-socialist state, we would expect the Knighthood Order to have a far larger membership and its events to have mass appeal. Neither appears to be the case.[3] Beyond these unsatisfying options, it is possible to develop a more convincing, if more modest, portrait of the contemporary cult of King Stephen: a small, committed minority using state resources to correct what it sees as the cult's previous mistakes by highlighting different themes from Hungarian history, namely King Stephen's ethical and devotional relationship with the Virgin Mary.[4]

In the second section, I present my analysis of this oral biography followed in the final section by my participant observation of Emil's village organizing. At one of his first Knighthood Order events, held in Emil's home, his elderly father-in-law became uncomfortable and disrupted a lecture by trying to leave. This incident put Emil in the position of choosing between conflicting ethical values—hospitable care on the one hand and courtly service on the other—a surprise experience of being pulled in two directions at once. The conflict disrupted his participation within the prayer evening and, as I show in a subsequent ethnographic vignette, made him reluctant to combine hospitality and service at future Knighthood Order events.

KING STEPHEN, ETHICAL SERVANT

While Transylvanian Hungarian interwar writers distanced themselves from the project of using monarchical spectacles to conduct cultural education, by lavishing praise on their own humbler, apostolic intellectual tradition, contemporary Transylvanian Hungarian intellectuals overcome this apparent divide. Like Csaba Böjte as he cultivated volunteers for his orphanages through manipulating the seeker subjectivity of Hungarians from Hungary, they are motivated to alter the cult's trajectory in a humbler direction, giving the cult's pedagogy a distinctively Transylvanian Hungarian orientation. Specifically, while the Hungarian right-wing has long been preoccupied with recreating King Stephen's former empire, a revisionist or irredentist goal, today's conservative Transylvanian Hungarian Catholic activists are trying to add to this cult an emphasis on ethical statecraft and the monarch's political virtues, which village intellectuals might embody and cultivate.

Hungary's interwar politicians delivered speeches insisting that by remembering King Stephen—the first Hungarian monarch to convert to Christianity—Hungarians could convert their current culture, thus defending it against non-Christian enemies from within and without (Hanebrink 2006). In irredentist pamphlets and propaganda, King Stephen's kingdom was also the image of the political state that these political activists aspired to recreate by rewriting the borders to reunite Transylvania with a Hungarian nation-state (Christian and Krasznai 2009). When the Hungarian constitution recognized the First and Second Vienna Accords, which restored parts of Slovakia and Romania lost after World War I, as territories "returned to the body of the Hungarian Holy Crown" (quoted in Péter 2003: 460), King Stephen seemed to justify irredentists' successes in the language of the law.

More recently, during the late socialist period, political and religious leaders in Hungary installed the Holy Crown in a display in the Hungarian National Museum in Budapest and later organized a national tour of the relic (Hann 1990: 6; Kürti 2015: 249).[5] According to Hann, tour organizers acknowledged that the Holy Crown was serving a new educational purpose:

> The article went on to quote the bishop's clear awareness that, in consigning to the exhibition room many of the cathedral's most treasured objects, he was launching them into new contexts which would include cultural education within Hungary, the edification of tourists, and the circulation of the objects through the national network of museums. (1990: 18)

Politicized cultural education now lay at the heart of a revived cult of King Stephen.

During the post-socialist period, according to Hungarian historian László Péter, the revived cult's pedagogical methods came to be seen as inadequate. While King Stephen did many admirable things in his life, simply viewing his Holy Crown behind glass would not facilitate deep personal identification with this virtuous figure. Stephen's only son died just as the king was growing old. Because he had no other heirs, members of the royal court began scheming to divide the kingdom among themselves. A stale museum exhibition did not clarify how his actions demonstrated his virtue as he prayed to the Virgin Mary to preserve his kingdom, nor did it promote a deep sense of identification with King Stephen's character. In historian Péter's words, throughout the 1990s, "Holy Crown societies" made a mark by arguing that the relic was not "something to be tucked away in a museum" but rather "a *living* tradition and a part of national identity in this sense" (2003: 502, emphasis in original).[6]

Besides that, the socialist-era touring exhibition only visited sites in Hungary. Border restrictions prevented Transylvanian Hungarians from learning to venerate King Stephen's character. Although anthropologist László Kürti has written about the current right-wing Hungarian government's mimetic reproduction of the 1980s tour, the groups that Péter refers to as "Holy Crown societies" take up this practice while also correcting its past mistakes (Kürti 2015: 247–9).[7] Both in terms of type of impact and reach into Transylvania's rural enclaves, the Knighthood Order came to look like a better method for educating Hungarians' devotion to King Stephen and the Holy Crown.

The Knighthood Order's effort to inject ritual veneration of King Stephen's virtues into the cult took shape against the backdrop of the growing popularity of chivalric groups in Hungary (Visnovitz 2008).[8] The Knighthood Order's effort to encourage veneration of King Stephen's character draws upon the programs of other groups that occupy this field, especially the Hungarian *Ars Ensis* movement. *Ars Ensis* teaches the medieval courtly martial art of sword fighting, and through these exercises, members cultivate medieval knights' exemplary ethical attributes, what the group calls "courtly" or "knightly" virtues (*lovagi erények*).

In a publication entitled "What makes a knight a knight," an *Ars Ensis* author lists the chief courtly virtues and their contemporary manifestations: courage (*bátorság*), wisdom (*bölcsesség*), loyalty (*hűség*), and courtliness (*udvariasság*). For *Ars Ensis*, these are intellectual virtues that govern an individual's habits of thought and speech: "Courage is not just in actions but in words too, like when one is not afraid to give an opinion," the *Ars Ensis* author explains. "Wisdom is when one has a true and authentic picture of the world. Courtliness is the desire to preserve others' (and one's own) respect and honor."[9]

Although Knighthood Order members receive the touch of a sword during their initiation rite, there's nothing in the group's practice like *Ars*

Ensis's elaborate physical-education program of medieval swordplay. Instead, the Order teaches courtly virtues to its members through one-on-one mentoring relationships. Amid the group's emerging pedagogical mission to the countryside, these mentoring bonds, which pair urban-based group leaders with newer village trainees, makes the Order something like the urban dormitories that interwar intellectuals imagined using to turn peasants into rural intellectuals. After a Knighthood Order candidate petitions for admission, they are paired with a mentor. During their initiation year, prospective members must submit themselves to intensive spiritual direction and personal examination, with special attention to "the transformation of their lives and seriousness of their intentions in light of the strictures, virtues, and commitments of the chivalric life."[10]

Once the governing body judges that an initiate has successfully cultivated those courtly virtues identified in the Order's constitution, an initiation rite follows in order to publicly recognize the transition to full knighthood.[11] In Emil's case, the group's leaders recognized that he had completed the initiate year in an urban Catholic milieu where they had a base of support. For the event, he traveled from his village to a Miercurea Ciuc parish, recreating the folk educator's journey, as the Transylvanian Hungarian intellectual tradition had imagined it, from village to city and back.

Not only his mentor's home church, but the parish priest was also an Order member. Over the course of a typical initiation ceremony, according to public documents, new members dedicate themselves in service to the Virgin Mary and commit to cultivating the virtues of King Stephen. The Knighthood Order's constitution further states that, "Knights strive to follow traditional courtly virtues and comportment [...] This means not simply putting on the knight's robe but rather transforming one's way of living."

The Knighthood Order's emphasis on King Stephen as client-servant to his patron, the Virgin Mary, marks another departure from earlier cult practice in Hungary. In Chris Hann's account of the Holy Crown's 1987/8 tour, he writes that exhibit organizers construed Mary and Stephen through the lens of gender complementarity, as partner queen to his king (Hann 1990: 20).[12] In contrast, Order members cultivate what they see as King Stephen's servant attitude, as in this sentence from Knighthood Order's mission statement: "We commit to giving every bodily and spiritual capacity and endowment in the service of the Holy

Crown of our Queen, the Great Lady of Hungary, the Mother of the Savior."

Order lecturers, for instance, focus on King Stephen's petition for the Virgin Mary's help, describing it as a virtuous response to place himself in her service while outwitting his plotting courtiers. In a lecture I heard in early 2012, Ernő Bíró contradicted what he called a "common mistake" about King Stephen's decision, after his son and heir had died, to pray to the Virgin Mary to protect his kingdom against enemies in the royal court who were scheming to divide up the realm:

> Some say that he made this decision out of fear, that he couldn't see what was coming. He feared that he won't have a successor and that his kingdom will be short-lived. It looks to many like he petitioned Mary out of fear. But this isn't true.

Bíró countered a view that King Stephen wasn't wise after all, but rather a fearful, impulsive, and short-sighted ruler. He went on to provide evidence for this interpretation, including King Stephen's decision to make his petition in full view. In fact, King Stephen gathered important members of the nobility and clergy around him to witness his act: "If it had happened this way," Bíró argued, "then he wouldn't have offered up the crown in a ritual in front of the most important people of the country."

Some of King Stephen's courtiers had indeed hatched a plot to assassinate him, while others planned to divide up the kingdom upon the king's death. In the hands of the Knighthood Order's storytellers, the Catholic devotional narrative about King Stephen's petitionary prayer to the Virgin Mary is an allegory of the virtuous Christian and political leader. In its developed form, according to Walter Benjamin's study of Baroque-era theater, the genre's characteristic style of allegorical storytelling "carries with it a court" (Benjamin 2019: 201). Benjamin here points to Baroque-era allegorists' obsession with the social relations between monarchical patrons and the nobility that served in their courts.

The Knighthood Order's allegories thus focus on actions that reveal personal character within a particular type of political context forming these servant-patron bonds, what Benjamin calls "the testing and confirmation of princely virtues, the exposure of princely vices, the insight into diplomatic affairs, and the operation of political machinations" (Benjamin 2019: 46). The Knighthood Order's lecturers discourage audiences from repeating the vices of King Stephen's disloyal servants while highlighting for emulation his virtuous courage and composure.

EMIL'S TESTIMONY AND A TEACHER'S PERSISTENCE

I spent most of 2010 in the city of Miercurea Ciuc, renting a room from a retiree named Gizella and, as I described in Chap. 4, singing with her in the official choir of the nearby Our Lady of Csíksomlyó Catholic shrine. By the beginning of 2011, I wanted to recenter my fieldwork in a rural setting; I began asking around about finding another host. A priest acquaintance put me in touch with Emil, a devout Catholic who lived in a Ciuc Valley village.

After a short phone conversation, two days later I found myself kicking concrete shards against the wall of Miercurea Ciuc's transit station while waiting for the regional bus that stopped close to Emil's home. Hopping off the final step onto a grass-lined ditch, I noticed Emil waiting outside the gate that framed his tidy courtyard of fruit trees and grass. That night over dinner with him and his wife, Zsuzsa, I explained that part of my research was on Catholic testimonial practices, how people talk publicly about petitionary prayers to Our Lady of Csíksomlyó. Emil replied that he himself had petitioned Mary for help, when he suffered a work accident deep in the shafts of a nearby state-run copper mine.

Until receiving an early retirement package, he explained, he had worked as a welder in the copper mine in the Ciuc Valley city of Bălan. He confessed that he had never shared this testimony outside of his family; but he pulled up his sleeve and slid his thumb across his arm. Slowly, he measured the scar that ran fully around the width of his bicep. While doing a repair underground he noticed a rock-ore conveyor was about to jam up. Grabbing a hose to wash down the runners beneath the bulky rubber belt, his shirt's cuff hung too close and caught; the force nearly severed his arm. Emil said he had called out, "Help me, Virgin Mother," after which his sleeve came free. He did see the Virgin Mary or hear her speak, as if she had appeared to him in an apparition, he told me that first night we met. Nevertheless, he survived and as he demonstrated from a position at the head of his kitchen table, he could still use his arm.

In January, one month later, I rented a room in Emil's house and soon his village became my fieldwork base for the next year. While Emil introduced me to those he considered friends and allies, a previous acquaintance who also hailed from the area connected me to others in the village, some of whom turned out to be Emil's intellectual and political rivals. One of these individuals, a former member of the village parish governing council named Tamás, seemed intent on reinterpreting Emil's testimony about his petitionary prayer: "There were some women, about five years ago, who said they saw someone, a woman, I don't know what, out around the village's edge." He speculated, "That could have been what Emil was talking about."

Parish councils are elected bodies of lay Catholics who, in addition to performing administrative duties like fundraising, take on pedagogical roles in the community. In his recollection of serving on the parish councils, Tamás positioned himself above Emil: He was the educator while Emil was the "simple" peasant, the one to be educated.

When I asked Tamás to fill in some details, he mentioned the women's stories about people who had escaped dangerous accidents after praying to the Virgin Mary and explained that he had intervened to educate a group of elderly women when they came to the council to testify about seeing this apparition.[13] He restated arguments parish council leaders had used to instruct them about official Catholic doctrine concerning apparitions.[14] Implicitly, Tamás compared Emil with the women to whom, in his capacity as parish council member, he had given catechist-style instruction.

Emil invoked the virtues of the Transylvanian Hungarian vocational intellectual in his own defense when, a few days later, I related my discussion with his competitor. First, Emil expressed surprise that I had even visited Tamás. Emil claimed Tamás had shown himself to be less than virtuous after losing his position on the parish council: "He had been a member of the council for a long time," Emil explained, "but then he ran and didn't win. He hasn't done anything since then. He hasn't organized anything. His part of the village is dead; no life, no programs."

Emil's focus was on Tamás's pedagogical service, the complaint being that Tamás lacked an enduring desire to serve. For interwar intellectuals like Áron Márton, the collapse of Hungary's state bureaucracy in Transylvania, which included the Hungarian state's educational system, revealed the need for a new generation of Transylvanian Hungarian intellectuals whose authority, like the early Christian apostles, would be rooted in vocation and virtue. Emil drew an implicit comparison between Tamás's declining interest in organizing pedagogical, religious, and cultural programs and the lost election. Tamás had not even taken on new educational projects to benefit his smaller section of this village, which, if he had, would have been the external sign of his internalized vocation.

That summer I received an invitation to give a lecture, delivered in Hungarian, at a Budapest university. Emil and I were in the midst of preparing his testimony for this lecture when one morning, as I was sitting at the kitchen table, I caught sight through the window of a black sedan gliding into place before the house. Two middle-aged couples, dressed in suits and ties, skirts and blouses, stepped through the front gate, and Emil said they were from Cursillo.

This educational movement by and for lay Catholics originated in Spain in 1944 out of a program of short courses—or *cursillos*—which featured theological lectures preparing pilgrims for journeys to shrines (Nabhan-Warren 2013: 4). Cursillo spread from Western Europe to Hungary and finally to Transylvanian Hungarian communities by the 2000s, at which time Emil attended a weekend conference that inspired him to become something of an informal catechist to Catholics in his village: a lay substitute teacher in place of overcommitted and exhausted priests. Like the Knighthood Order, Cursillo structured and authorized Emil's village educational activities, his pedagogical service to rural Transylvanian Hungarians.

The appearance and behavior of these Cursillo colleagues seemed to invite class-and status-based comparisons with Emil's mentor in the Knighthood Order. I recognized their car and attire, in particular, as evidence of their urbane and middle-class status.[15] Emil himself looked this way when he prepared for Cursillo educational events. However, caught off guard by their unannounced visit, he was now in a white undershirt and dusty blue overalls; in Ciuc Valley villages, this is akin to a peasant and working-class uniform. After yanking open the door, Emil pulled out the table for our guests, who sat facing the kitchen from the pew-like bench nailed to the exterior wall. By the time they were sipping from four small coffee cups, I understood they were on their way to a weekend Cursillo workshop. They had pulled off the main road to visit Emil and invite him to speak during a seminar on marriage and family scheduled for next month.

Amid the business and pleasantries, Emil explained my presence at one end of the kitchen table, pointedly including himself in my research: "He is going to deliver a paper in which we are reworking my story about my accident; you know, so to say, my little miracle, in relation to Marian devotionalism." The conversation throughout had been stilted, and even more so now with this comment. Emil looked especially abashed at this mention of a miracle, delivering the word with a shrug and inclining his eyes. The acquaintances, appearing at the house as Cursillo activists recruiting Emil to lead an educational session, did not give thanks for this testimony. As silence ensued, Emil quickly changed the subject back to their invitation. During their visit, he made no other attempt to integrate his testimony into their discussion about Cursillo.

What had been tentative hopefulness that his fellow teachers might recognize his miracle, a few weeks later turned into a fearfully defensive demeanor expressed in once-and-for-all renunciations. Back home after speaking at the Cursillo marriage seminar, during a conversation about my lecture, Emil denied that his miracle was at all relevant to his pedagogical service in the village. After dinner one evening, he declared that, "No one has to believe that this miracle happened to me." He continued:

> Take Jesus. Jesus didn't care at all about whether people accepted that he was the savior. He just went about his business and did what he had to do. He did God's work, preached and taught. For me it's the same, I don't care if anyone else believes that this happened to me. There don't have to be any conversions. If they accept my miracle, who cares, it doesn't affect me. I believe in it. And that's that. The rest doesn't matter.

Emil first renounced the typical end—conversion—to which Catholics use Marian miracle testimonies; then his reference to Jesus's service recentered him in his preferred role as teacher.[16] Thus, this refusal doubled as a reconfirmation of his catechist-style, Cursillo-inspired educational service.

I first thought it was deference that made Emil say yes when I asked if I should still include his story in my lecture. But while recording a fuller version of the miracle narrative, I came to see that the story indexed a conflict, situated within the context of Romania's post-socialist politics of industrial privatization, between class ambition on the one side and workers' collective pride and solidarity on the other. In the latter case, Emil recalled miners' sense of togetherness. "Underground no one was Hungarian or Romanian," he explains on the recording. "There was no nationality in the shafts. It was dangerous, you just had to help each other and rely on each other if there was a problem."

Other former miners tied this danger to a sense of solidarity over and against the mine's educated managerial class. One mutual acquaintance, for instance, described his job as a mineshaft elevator operator as "shirt-and-tie" work (*nyakkendős*). Even though he worked in the shaft, he had felt himself more like an administrator. In his phrase, distinctive clothing came to stand for their entire style of work. When I asked him if Emil had done "shirt-and-tie work," the former coworker thought for a moment and said, "No, he went underground a lot, so, no, you can't say that he did shirt-and-tie work."

Meanwhile, Emil also said that alcohol consumption created a sense of labor solidarity against the managerial class (Kideckel 2008: 198). He bristled at the interview's end when I asked him if he had fit the stereotype of a heavy-drinking miner. "It's not true," he retorted, "the bosses and engineers drank as much as we did. There were three of us on my crew called Emil, and so there was always a lot to drink on my name day. But the bosses got as much as we did, and then some." When it came to drunkenness, one of the most frequently cited violations of socialist-era workplace morality, Emil could mobilize a clear sense of solidarity against the mine's authorities.

Emil reported that the most shameful experience associated with his accident was when he became subject to a medical professional's arrogant condescension. The incident occurred at Miercurea Ciuc's main hospital. After being sent for an x-ray, Emil ended up waiting in a hospital hallway.

> The poor nurse, she would have liked to get me through quicker but the x-ray doctor, he, well, he was annoyed. I don't know what his problem was. No idea. But he looked at me, when he came out. Well, you know, they say that a miner's clothes are never clean. Muddy. Smelling like sweat. Stinky. And so he looked at me like I was a piece of shit. And it was really humiliating.

When he blamed his bosses for drinking just as much as the miners did, Emil recalled passing bottles of liquor with his fellow workers during a name-day ritual act. In this case, the ritualized creation of solidarity with other men allowed him to recast the humiliating judgments of mining company professionals in an us-versus-them vein. But this humiliation, under the gaze of authoritative and educated professionals, reflects the absence of the emboldening presence at the Miercurea Ciuc hospital of other fellow workers.

While in the run-up to my lecture I questioned whether Emil's rural educational calling would be strengthened were an audience of Budapest intellectuals to hear this story—so full of contradictions like identification and alienation, pride and shame—he did not object to my plans. Yet this consent was also destabilized by the deference that I observed in other interactions between Transylvanian Hungarian teachers and audiences of Hungarians from Hungary. I recognized the mix of enthusiasm, submission, and resentment that I had seen among Csíksomlyó choir members when a Hungarian politician claimed that they were ambassadors of Hungarian Christendom to Europe. When invited to perform a series of concerts for an audience of Hungarians from Hungary, they felt the imposition of a high-art standard of aesthetic judgment on their pedagogical work, but were not about to refuse the opportunity; after all, they also admired and even embraced the Hungarian state-endorsed goal of building a Christian Hungarian culture that audiences in Hungary were going to judge them by.

Emil's testimony was not going to be judged according to high-art aesthetic standards; it was not a musical performance, after all. However, even before I presented it to a Budapest audience, other Transylvanian Hungarian intellectuals subjected Emil's voice—as we had recorded it on the paper I would read from—to the kind of disciplining correction that Lajos had requested from choir members during rehearsals. On my way to Budapest, I visited Cluj-Napoca, home to Transylvania's largest university, and showed the lecture text to several Hungarian ethnologists.

One scholar, Salamon, worried that my audience would not understand Emil's description of mine work. Emil had gone into detail explaining the conditions underground: the machines' dimensions and the force that the conveyor belt was carrying when it caught his sleeve. I interpreted Emil's explanation as an attempt to cross class boundaries, to translate a working-class life-world to middle-class urban intellectuals in Budapest. But as I sat with Salamon in his office, surrounded by the bookshelves and filing cabinets of a church's historical archives, he took a blue pen to a different section of the printout.

For example, Salamon crossed out words like *tambur* (drum) and *flux* (flow). "These are Romanian words," he explained, "You need to change these because they won't understand them." Then he replaced them with Hungarian translations. Salamon's edits amounted to a form of "language policing," which Brubaker et al. note is a commonplace practice among bilingual ethnic minority groups that receive schooling in both majority and minority languages (Brubaker et al. 2007: 247–50). When particular ethnic minority groups recast their collective history as an effort, often championed by intellectuals and educators, to reproduce the minority community against the threat of assimilation, ethnic membership becomes an accomplishment that must be constantly renewed. Transylvanian Hungarians routinely interrupt conversations to correct others' Hungarian vocabulary and grammar, leading to widespread belief that membership is "achieved" (Brubaker et al. 2007: 229).

Language policing, however, was an uncommon practice among miners. In Emil's case, he learned to use the Romanian words for many technical terms during his professional training in the 1980s, when the Romanian socialist government was embracing an aggressively nationalizing educational policy (Brubaker et al. 2007: 75–80). Bălan, home to the copper mine where Emil had worked, had had Hungarian schools. It retained a large Hungarian minority through the 1980s. Still, many technical subjects were primarily taught in Romanian (Barabási 1996: 57; Kideckel 2008).[17] Years later in the mine, Emil continued to use these terms even when speaking with his Hungarian colleagues. When Emil used the Romanian word for "drum" with me, as we were preparing the lecture, he slipped back into the class-coded, commonsense, unremarked-on speech habit of his everyday life, with which he interacted with the many former industrial workers living in his village and the surrounding environs (Brubaker et al. 2007: 259–60).

The post-socialist politics of ethnic assimilation further destabilized Emil's identification with the labor movement. Throughout the 1960s and 1970s, Bălan's mine employed laborers like Emil from Hungarian-speaking villages in a region that, until 1968, was officially designated as a "Hungarian Ethnic Autonomous Region" (Barabási 1996; Bottoni 2008). The state continued to grow Bălan, even in the 1980s, by directing workers into the ranks of the mining company from Romanian-speaking villages across the Carpathian Mountains; by the 1980s, what had been Hungarian effectively "became a Romanian city" (Brubaker et al. 2007: 109). Romania's late-socialist industrial labor policy during the period was over-determined, such that demographics and nationality policy dovetailed. Because the largest surplus population available for industrial work was to be found in Romanian-dominated villages, "urbanization was bound to entail nationalization" (Brubaker et al. 2007: 112–3).

The reemergence of public ethnopolitical contention in Romania during the 1990s—including violent street clashes between Romanians and Hungarians in Târgu Mureş—led many intellectuals involved in the Szekler cultural revival like Emil to simplify this history. With pathways into the scholarly class increasingly open to ethnoculturally identified intellectuals, those based in Ciuc Valley's Hungarian-dominated villages and county seat, Miercurea Ciuc, tended to view Bălan's miners through the lens of Nicolae Ceauşescu's widely publicized efforts at ethnic assimilation; efforts to combat it then became the basis for assistance and solidarity provided by Hungarians from Hungary. In the process, a personal and biographical working-class history became an obstacle rather than a pathway to becoming an intellectual.

After reviewing Emil's narrative, Salamon accompanied me onto Cluj-Napoca's city streets with a colleague, a university historian. We were walking with this acquaintance to a bus stop when the man, a Hungarian, referred to his identification card as a *buletin*, a Romanian word. The colleague shared Salamon's middle-class position, and Salamon let the Romanian word slip by without comment. Reading Emil's speech, Salamon had rigorously substituted Hungarian for Romanian, a practice known to linguists as "collaborative repair" (Schegloff, Jefferson, and Sacks 1977). Salamon's comments combined such substitutions with an implied questioning of Emil's class and ethnic identity, a skepticism to which he did not subject his university professor colleague when this man used a Romanian word. While marking up the printout, he had explained Emil's use of Romanian terms in a short but highly critical assessment of the Ciuc Valley's "very poor" Hungarian educational system that, Salamon alleged, did not do enough to prevent "corruption" by the dominant Romanian language.

With this commentary, Salamon showed how ethnic minority language policing often works on multiple social levels simultaneously, especially when it involves purist efforts to protect against influence from a dominant national language. "Class, status, and ethnicity," Brubaker et al. observe, "are often intertwined in such efforts [to enforce language purism]" (2007: 261). To illustrate this point, Brubaker et al. use the hypothetical example of a Transylvanian Hungarian teacher chiding a student by saying, "We are not the kind of people who speak like that" (Brubaker et al. 2007: 261). Such comments encourage students not only to distinguish themselves from class and ethnic others but also associate this distinction with an ethical judgment: "References to speaking 'pure' or 'impure' Hungarian invoked class differences and, at the same time, made salient distinctions between 'good' and 'Romanianized' Hungarians" (Brubaker et al. 2007: 262). For Transylvanian Hungarian village intellectuals, these intertwining factors of class, status, and ethnicity became salient in the hearing of audiences of Hungarians from Hungary.

When I returned from Budapest, I did not discuss Salamon's changes with Emil. However, other comments about how he converted the ambition that made him a miner into the ambition to teach suggested that he would have both accepted the rationale for the edits even as he would have also resented that a fellow Transylvanian Hungarian intellectual had called him a class and ethnic outsider. In fact, he was proud of his shift, following employment with the mine company, from industrial laborer to Director of his village's House of Culture:

> I used the money, you know, that ordinance, to do some continuing education. I went to Sapientia [the Hungarian-language university in Miercurea Ciuc] and took a class to be a cultural manager. And then I got the job as the Director of the House of Culture. So I used the money to develop myself and to better my family's life. But the others, here in the village but also in Bălan, they just took the money and bought televisions and fancy things, or they did what they always did when the mine was running. They partied and got drunk, and then sat around.

Emil seemed to say that he had reached this position because he embraced hard work and self-denying asceticism. He identified with these values because they indexed the post-socialist culture of entrepreneurialism but also, insofar as this enterprising hard work launched his cultural education career, with the Transylvanian Hungarian pedagogical tradition.

Emil's commentary on leaving behind one medium for social ambition, industrial labor, for another, cultural administration, is in line with David Kideckel's argument about the individualizing effect of post-socialist labor policy. As Kideckel puts it, "Where socialism sought to plan the distribution of resources and awards, thus giving workers collective access to education and upward mobility, postsocialist states show renewed faith in private ownership and markets and leave individuals to make their own way in society" (2008: 10).[18] Kideckel calls the buyouts—the Romanian government terminated miners' labor contracts in return for severance pay—the quintessential post-socialist policy because it was so divisive, producing resentment and recrimination between the "bought-out" and those who stayed on the job (2008: 81–4).

In Emil's retelling of post-socialist industrial privatization, the Hungarian-government-supported Sapientia University seems to have exacerbated the buyout's individualizing effects while speeding a shift among some former workers toward identification with the Transylvanian Hungarian community. Under socialism, Emil had trained for his mine job in Bălan, getting to know his fellow workers and building up the sense of solidarity that he had manifested in comments about the togetherness that transcended ethnicity in the shafts. He had received this training in line with the government's collective provision of education; the socialist government had distributed worker education as a collective resource by locating them in its model socialist towns, the settlements designed to fulfill the socialist state's goal of creating a new socialist working class and where life revolved around a single large factory that employed a large portion of the population (Fehérváry 2013; Pozniak 2013a; Loustau 2020). Now, however, the university course in cultural administration demonstrated his personal, virtuous reinvestment of the state's resources.

Emil's project to "develop myself" sounds like an updated form of Weberian middle-class worldly asceticism. In embracing this attitude, he identified himself with economic rationality and discipline, a strategy that the European middle class has historically used to distinguish themselves from the profligacy of both the aristocracy and the working class (Gal and Kligman 2000: 43–5). But Emil's claim also lends a personalist interpretation to capitalism's middle-class ethos of the rational reinvestment of resources. Emil's decision to invest in himself rather than a firm aligns him with Elizabeth Dunn's view of post-socialism as a "privatization of the person," the distinguishing mark of the post-socialist middle-class being one's embrace of the project of remaking ethical subjectivity and selfhood (2006: 94–129; see also Gog 2020).

Transylvanian Hungarian-Romanian ethnic animosity could have also played a role in Emil's explanation. He may have worried that, in the Transylvanian Hungarian view, the funds were tainted. It was "Romanian" money. He had received it from the government in return for aiding a project—the mine—that the state had used to move Romanians into the area and speed the assimilation of the Transylvanian Hungarian ethnic minority. By claiming that he used the buyout to aid the Szekler cultural revival, Emil might have legitimized his decision to take this money.

But as with many sociological and political explanations that reduce ethics to legitimacy, this account is flat and simplistic.[19] The concept of legitimacy carries implicitly therapeutic and conservative meanings; whatever legitimizes helps subjects react and accommodate themselves to a preexisting social action.[20] Emil's case highlights how these assumptions can actually foreclose questions about core pedagogical virtues—dedication, persistence—that lie at the heart of the Transylvanian Hungarian intellectual tradition. The concept of legitimacy invites social analysis to presume that subjects are trying to resolve social conflict and strengthen their weakened social status, thus drawing analytical attention away from an action's unintended consequences.

Although Emil had successfully used his mine buyout to complete a course in cultural administration and get an educational job in his village government, he actually spent a short time at the House of Culture. Emil tried unsuccessfully to found a small museum to display traditional agricultural tools, in local parlance a "house-museum" (*tájház*). One evening while he was doing farm chores in his backyard, he explained what happened:

> I wanted to create the house-museum here. Like they did in Csíkszentmarton [Sânmartin Ciuc]. They made a nice one there. And I tried to get the council to set aside some land for it. First by the main road. And then by the police station. But neither of the ideas worked. I wanted to move the police station into another building just next door. But when I proposed it to the council it was, 'No, we can't move the police station. No, that's not possible.' And there was Marti and his friends on the council, they kept saying no, no, no.

While the Romanian government's money had led to another, legitimate career in support of Transylvanian Hungarian cultural education, this did not mean that Emil was now free from social conflict. In fact, using the money this way led him deeper into a tug-of-war between village council factions over his proposed project. Emil lost this contest and eventually his job.

Emil's commentary reveals his insecure social position in his village, perhaps a consequence of the years he spent working in Bălan. Over thirty years of work in the state mining company, Emil had numerous opportunities to develop deep reciprocities with employees. Some employees were from his village, and these relationships proved an asset when he became director. But he was not as knowledgeable about village alliances as he might have been had he not spent so much time working outside the village. The government buyout helped him get an educational degree, but it did not help him to revive his atrophied village relationships, to renew reciprocities and alliances in his local community. Emil and I continued to chat more about the political conflicts that derailed this project. We were stacking firewood—most villagers heated houses with wood because declining state subsidies had made gas too expensive—when I asked what he thought had gone wrong. "The director of the culture house is like the mayor," he explained, "there's always some people who aren't going to be happy. No matter what the culture organizer does, no matter what he says, people are always going to get annoyed. That's the essence of politics."

Emil's abortive career as a village cultural official sheds light on how local political processes mediate post-socialist economic policies to produce unintended consequences. In one way, his decision to use the miners' contract buyout to become a cultural professional was an ideal outcome, based on the government's aspirations for this program: Emil used the buyout for its designated purpose, making the transition from miner to cultural official just as the government was beginning to privatize or dismantle Romania's industrial economy in favor of its tourism sector. While the government's job retraining program led Emil into a highly politicized professional field, it did not provide him with necessary skills for building the house-museum: working behind the scenes to build political support and negotiating compromises with opposing factions.

BETWEEN COURTLY SERVANT AND CARING HOST

Emil first encountered the Knighthood Order of the Holy Crown at one of the group's exhibitions. In the main hall of his village's House of Culture, two knights had stood guard beside the replica Holy Crown

Knighthood Order members with the replica of King Stephen's crown. (Credit: Marc Roscoe Loustau)

while a lecturer spoke about its history. The next evening over dinner Emil declared, "For me, the Holy Crown is like the Ten Commandments." Cursillo had inspired him to read the Bible for its moral laws, and I took this statement to indicate that he wanted to find similarities between the Order's pedagogy in regard to the Holy Crown and Emil's established approach to teaching. Knighthood Order leaders viewed Emil as a potential asset in their plan to expand the group's rural educational programming. During Emil's initiate period, the group was eager to develop a type of small-group prayer and lecture session called "prayer evenings" (*Imaeste*), which the leaders hoped would provide face-to-face educational opportunities for peasants, whom they called "simple folk" (*egyszerű emberek*).

I was staying with Emil's family in 2012 when Bíró visited the day before an exhibition in a nearby village. Twenty to thirty individuals attend each session, Bíró told Emil that afternoon, which usually lasts for two hours in the evening. It was essential that during the session Knighthood Order members adequately exemplify the knight's properly courteous demeanor so that uneducated participants might also learn this attitude. Knighthood Order members dressed in their official robes for the procession, forming a line behind the most senior member, who carried the replica Crown; and they faced the relic while the senior member lowered it onto a table. Audience members are expected to remain standing with the entrance of the knights and dames. They take seats on either side of the Holy Crown, chairs turned toward the audience in a semi-circle, before leading the whole group in the Rosary followed by the lecture.

That evening, Bíró began the question-and-answer session following his lecture by saying that this program was actually a core part of the group's overall project to educate peasants:

> We have started holding these prayer evenings, mostly in believers' homes, to complement the lectures that we hold for simple people in churches and houses of culture. We have made a decision to bring out a book including the information in this presentation, a book that has long needed to be published to aid the understanding of simple people. The problem is that previous books have had information intended for intellectuals; these books are not meant to sit on the simple person's kitchen table. We see this as a problem. One way to reach those people who come to hear our basic presentations in churches and houses of culture is to publish a small-format,

100-page book, which will include for instance the lecture I just gave as well as others.

Bíró suggested prayer evenings worked in concert with the group's lectures and exhibitions, which the Knighthood Order often scheduled to coincide with local holidays. However, Emil's prayer evening was a spontaneous affair, as Bíró was returning to Cluj-Napoca with the Holy Crown the next day. Emil and Zsuzsa rushed to extend invitations, eventually gathering the group that included Zsuzsa's father, whose attempt to leave the lecture early I described in this chapter's Introduction.

In the days following, I had a chance to ask Emil's guests about that disruption. Zsuzsa's mother, for instance, batted away my suggestion that her husband's exhaustion had proven the lecturer went on too long. We were in her kitchen, down the road from Emil's house, when I gave my opinion: "I thought it was really long, an hour and a half. That wasn't long for you?" She demurred,

> For me, it didn't seem long, but perhaps for Daddy it was long. Because he felt, 'My God, can I endure this?' But I was able to endure it. It was very interesting. I learned a lot. But for him, he was so tired that he could barely wait to get home for us to help him lie down.

Her response was artful for not taking my bait; she avoided criticizing this volunteer teacher and deferred to his authority to instruct. Instead of joining me in complaining, she turned my comment around to suggest that it showed I had poor stamina. I was as weak as her infirm husband was. In contrast, she herself had not been affected by the duration. On a deeper level, though, it revealed the village community's view of my own embodied social status in the context of hospitality. As a guest, I offered hosts a challenging burden of responsibility, akin to the challenge of caring for a stroke-hobbled relative.

Emil was to serve at another prayer evening about the Crown in July, this one hosted by the village government of Voşlăbeni, about an hour's drive north. I expressed interest in attending while we were eating lunch, joined this time by Emil's brother-in-law, Dénes. My request launched the men into competitive boasting. "I don't think so," Emil said first. "I mean, it's fine with me, but there are rules. The problem is that we ourselves, we're guests. It's the rule to register at the local parish how many people are going, four people, right, and other things like that."

Emil was searching for justifications, and I suspected underlying his reluctance was the memory of his recent difficulty hosting the prayer evening. His circumspection indicated that he was insecure as to whether he could take responsibility for me at the event. After all, his mother-in-law intimated that I was about as weak as his father-in-law. If Emil suspected as much, then he might also have worried about facing another difficult choice between tending to an exhausted guest and serving the Holy Crown. The prayer evening had proven that he had difficulty carrying out both duties.

At this point Dénes broke into our exchange with a boast. "I used to have so many friends in Vasláb [Voşlăbeni]," he claimed. "I could have found a place for us to stay." As Emil's guest, Dénes was at a disadvantage. In rural Romania's agonistic cycle of exchange, which persisted and adapted through the socialist-era's collectivization of agricultural property, guests put themselves in a position of dependency by eating at a host's table (Kligman 1988; Kligman and Verdery 2011: 185–190). Dénes's claim to be the superior host thus redressed this dependency.

Emil's braggadocio was all the more effective for calling attention to the burden that my request for hospitality posed. He boasted that, at least in the past, he could have done both: cared for a guest and served the Crown. Making light of seemingly unmovable obstacles is, according to anthropologist Michael Herzfeld, a key part of rural Greek masculine performances, which challenge modern assumptions about sociality by combining the seemingly incommensurable relational modes of opposition and amiability. Men express their commonality—in Herzfeld's words, "their ability to stand up to life's travails as well as to each other"—by blustering in the face of their burdens and showing they can overcome these challenges where other cannot (Herzfeld 1985: 127).

Providing good hospitality to one's guests is one such task, a burden one must make to look impossible for others in order to overcome it oneself, and with flair (Herzfeld 1985: 128). Dénes's comment thus challenged Emil and demanded a riposte. While Emil insisted that hosting me at the Voşlăbeni event was impossible, he looked ahead and offered to host me at a future event. "How about this: We're going in three weeks to Bucsin [Bucin]; I'll ask about that. Do you want to go to Bucsin [Bucin]?" I said yes but added that I had never heard of the village. "Me neither," added Dénes. Emil threw his shoulders back as he told us that the village was "next to Gyergyó [Gheorgheni]." He projected pride and pleasure at besting Dénes, turning aside his brother-in-law's boastful challenge.

Whereas Dénes claimed he once had "so many friends" in Voşlăbeni, Emil was now offering to host me in a place Dénes was unfamiliar with; in other words, he had proven that his relational network was more extensive than Dénes's. But the real victory lay in the improvisational creativity that Emil had demonstrated. Initially, he had professed incapacity in the face of the Knighthood Order's rules and regulations. But now he had used the means offered by membership in the Knighthood Order to prove a superior hospitality. Masculine performative excellence is defined by "the ability to improvise, to make the most of what chance offers," according to Herzfeld (1985: 135). Turning a weakness into a strength—in this case, transforming another man's aspersion that he was a weak host into a tentative claim that he could provide hospitality where his challenger could not—is the defining characteristic of agonistic rural masculine hospitality.

Emil had not found a final solution to the problems posed by hosting prayer evenings in his village. He was likely to encounter the tension between hospitable care and courtly service again were he to organize additional local Knighthood Order events. But in this moment, an interactional victory over Dénes allowed him to claim excellence in a realm of local contestation and demonstrate his continued dedication to village values like hospitality. At the same time, he also expressed the durability of his vocation to rural education, his virtuous commitment to keep on teaching even though he had run into problems and difficulties. And Emil had even managed to impress Dénes with his inner knowledge of the Knighthood Order's future plans.

Conclusion

I have portrayed the Knighthood Order of the Holy Crown as a small group of voluntary intellectuals who use the cult of King Stephen, Hungary's first Christian monarch, to transform themselves into an ideal of courtly virtue. While incorporating other chivalric orders' focus on virtue into the cult of King Stephen they also extend the cult's reach into Transylvania's rural Hungarian communities. I have argued that this represents a shift of emphasis in the cult's history: Satisfying the populace's desire to restore the Empire's borders, not cultivating virtue, was the interwar cult's main goal. Although the Holy Crown became the cultural educational tool it is today during socialism, as a touring museum exhibit the cult had limited effect on viewers' subjective experience, and only reached urban areas in Hungary. Now a small but committed group of intellectuals labor to correct these limitations and lead the Transylvanian Hungarian minority to embody King Stephen's virtues.

I have also described one individual's journey to become a knight and assume a leading role in the Knighthood Order's rural educational programs. This biographical case study of a man I refer to as Emil first revealed how he came to view the Knighthood Order's pedagogical mission through the initial stages of becoming a knight. Emil found parallels between his performances at the Knighthood Order's programs and the lectures he had spent years giving for the Cursillo movement. He treated the former as an opportunity to enact the legalistic style of ethical pedagogy he learned while teaching classes on Catholic marital and family doctrine. From the Knighthood Order's perspective, Emil was an appealing prospective member because he could potentially advance their mission into Transylvania's Hungarian villages. As a former director of his village's House of Culture and current Cursillo activist, Emil had experience organizing educational activities in area villages. What I ultimately show is that Emil did not look to either Cursillo or the Knighthood Order to compensate for political and economic dispossession. Both pursuits took shape at the unstable meeting point of rural Marian devotional culture's contestational social dynamics; normative expectations with regard to hospitality; details of Emil's personal history; and the more encompassing structures of the post-socialist political economic moment.

The next chapter shifts sites once again to focus on a different intellectual group active at Csíksomlyó. I describe a close circle of ordained priests, a kind of underground network of Catholic clergy friends who worked on the edges of a Csíksomlyó-based orphanage network known as the Black Sheep Foundation. Like the many other intellectuals I profile in this book, they too consider themselves teachers with a vocational mission: to promote the virtue of penitence. The next chapter therefore represents one more variation on this book's core theme of intellectual authority as the enactment of a vocation to ethical cultivation through voluntary service.

NOTES

1. The full name is the Order of the Holy Crown of the Great Lady of Hungary and Victorious Queen of the World. Emil was one of the Order's first Ciuc Valley members from outside the main city of Miercurea Ciuc. Those from farther afield lived in even larger cities like Cluj-Napoca. Emil's initiate master and the Order's main lecturer, Ernő Bíró, lived in a Cluj suburb.

2. Voigt (2004) and Magyar (2001) debate whether devotion to King Stephen is a recent elite invention or it had survived unbroken within some mystical vernacular substrate.

3. In Hann's words, "as soon as the economy began to go seriously wrong, compensating efforts in the symbolic dimension were called for" (1990: 24). Hann also states that, "Such symbols are the ones most likely to gain in prominence at times when powerholders have no ready answers to pressing political and economic problems" (1990: 7). See also Péter 2003: 501. Hann's argument shows the limits of political economic anthropology when confronted by religious agency. Rather than grasp the creative processes by which Catholic intellectuals' use Hungarian public culture to reveal new sources of divine presence, as Brother Csaba does when he reveals God's collaborative laboring to spiritual seekers, Hann and others presume that once religious actors have restored their economic status or come up with the needed solutions to pressing political problems, they will disappear again from the public stage.

4. My argument is inspired by Hackett's observation about elaborating the Virgin Mary's virtues through comparison with Elizabeth I in post-Reformation England: "[T]here was not a complete transformation of belief, but rather 'the ground shifted a little and the argument moved forward'. Change was promoted by a small but committed minority, who contended with extreme reluctance from most of the populace" (Hackett 1994: 9).

5. The government first repatriated the relic from the American government, which had held it since World War II.

6. For a comparable case, see Russian Orthodox complaints that teaching Orthodoxy from a cultural perspective threatens to make it "boring" (Köllner 2016: 377).

7. These include the ceremonial installation of the Holy Crown in the Hungarian Parliament and the relic's one-day visit to the Hungarian Cardinal's residence in Esztergom.

8. There are over 150 chivalric orders active in Hungary.

9. This document, titled "A lovagi erények mai értelmezése és integrációja a vívásoktatásban," is in the author's private collection and is available online: https://www.arsensis.hu/pdf/S3_17_SZ.pdf

10. Szent Korona Lovag Rend, "Constitution of the Order," http://www.szentkoronalovagrend.hu/rendi-alkotmany/

11. These ceremonies typically take place on October 8th, which is the anniversary of the feast given to celebrate the day King Stephen offered the Hungarian Crown to the Great Lady of Hungary.

12. Hann states that Mary and King Stephen fit like puzzle pieces within Hungarian Catholicism's "sexual division of religious labor," with a virile father-figure complementing a compassionate mother-figure (1990: 20).

13. In the modern period, ecclesiastical officials frequently publicized the miracles that follow such visions, promoting in the process both the regional Transylvanian shrine to Mary, Queen of Light, in Seuca as well as globally famous sites like Our Lady of Lourdes in France and Our Lady of Fatima in Portugal. See Apolito 1998; Valtchinova 2009; Zimdars-Swartz 1991; Nabhan-Warren 2005.

14. There is an extensive literature on shrine culture and the politics of contestation. See Eade and Sallnow 1991; Halemba 2015.

15. Later, when we accompanied them to the car they had parked outside, the couples' middle-class status seemed to be confirmed by that well-kept car, which was furnished with dark leather seating.

16. See, for example, Zimdars-Swartz 1991: 57; Kaufman 2007: 86.

17. The same holds for Cluj-Napoca. See Brubaker et al. 2007: 259.

18. See also Barabási's comment that in Bălan during the 1990s "The mine's social network suffered a certain degree of breakdown" (1996: 175).

19. See, for instance, Hann 2011.

20. See, for example, Köllner's argument that legitimacy obscures the creative role that the recent revival of Orthodoxy plays in Russian public life.

REFERENCES

Apolito, Paolo. 1998. *Apparitions of the Madonna at Oliveto Citra: Local Visions and Cosmic Drama*. Trans. Jr. William A. Christian. University Park: The Pennsylvania State University Press.

Barabási, László. 1996. *Balánbánya története* [History of Balánbánya]. Miercurea Ciuc: Barabási.

Benjamin, Walter. 2019. *Origin of the German Trauerspiel*. Trans. Howard Eiland. Cambridge: Harvard University Press.

Bottoni, Stefano. 2008. *Sztálin a Székelyeknél. A Magyar Autonóm Tartomány Története (1952–1960)* [Stalin and the Székelys: History of the Hungarian Autonomous Region]. Miercurea Ciuc: Pro-Print Könyvkiadó.

Brubaker, Rogers, Margit Feischmidt, Jon Fox, and Liana Grancea. 2007. *Nationalist Politics and Everyday Ethnicity in a Transylvanian Town*. Princeton: Princeton University Press.

Christian, William A. Jr. and Zoltán Krasznai. 2009. The Christ of Limpias and the Passion of Hungary. *History and Anthropology* 20: 219–242.

Eade, John, and Michael Sallnow. 1991. *Contesting the Sacred: The Anthropology of Christian Pilgrimage*. Eugene: Wipf and Stock.

Fehérváry, Krisztina. 2013. *Politics in Color and Concrete: Socialist Materialities and the Middle Class in Hungary*. Bloomington: University of Indiana Press.

Gal, Susan, and Gail Kligman. 2000. *The Politics of Gender After Socialism: A Comparative-Historical Essay*. Princeton: Princeton University Press.

Ghodsee, Kristen. 2009. *Muslim Lives in Eastern Europe: Gender, Ethnicity, and the Transformation of Islam in Postsocialist Bulgaria.* Princeton: Princeton University Press.

Gog, Sorin. 2020. Neo-Liberal Subjectivities and the Emergence of Spiritual Entrepreneurship: An Analysis of Spiritual Development Programs in Contemporary Romania. *Social Compass* 67 (1): 103–119.

Hackett, Helen. 1994. *Virgin Mother, Maiden Queen: Elizabeth I and the Cult of the Virgin Mary.* New York: St. Martin's Press.

Halemba, Agnieszka. 2015. *Negotiating Marian Apparitions: The Politics of Religion in Transcarpathian Ukraine.* Budapest: Central European University Press.

Hanebrink, Paul. 2006. *In Defense of Christian Hungary: Religion, Nationalism, and Antisemitism, 1890–1944.* Ithaca: Cornell University Press.

Hann, Chris. 1990. Socialism and King Stephen's Right Hand. *Religion in Communist Lands* 18: 4–24.

———. 2011. Moral Dispossession. *InterDisciplines* 2 (2): 11–37.

Herzfeld, Michael. 1985. *The Poetics of Manhood: Contest and Identity in a Cretan Mountain Village.* Princeton: Princeton University Press.

Kaufman, Suzanne. 2007. *Consuming Visions: Mass Culture and the Lourdes Shrine.* Ithaca: Cornell University Press.

Kideckel, David. 2008. *Getting by in Postsocialist Romania: Labor, the Body, and Working-Class Culture.* Bloomington: Indiana University Press.

Kligman, Gail. 1988. *The Wedding of the Dead: Ritual, Poetics, and Popular Culture in Transylvania.* Berkeley: University of California Press.

Kligman, Gail, and Katherine Verdery. 2011. *Peasants Under Siege: The Collectivization of Romanian Agriculture, 1949–1962.* Princeton: Princeton University Press.

Köllner, Tobias. 2016. Patriotism, orthodox religion and education: Empirical findings from contemporary Russia. *Religion, State and Society* 44 (4): 366–386.

Kürti, László. 2015. Neoshamanism, National Identity, and the Holy Crown of Hungary. *Journal of Religion in Europe* 8 (2): 235–260.

Loustau, Marc R. 2020. Transgressing the Right to the City: Urban Mining and Ecotourism in Post-Industrial Romania. *Anthropological Quarterly* 93 (1): 1555–1578.

Luehrmann, Sonja. 2005. Recycling Cultural Construction: Desecularisation in Postsoviet Mari El. *Religion, State, and Society* 33 (1): 35–56.

———. 2011. *Secularism Soviet Style: Teaching Atheism and Religion in a Volga Republic.* Bloomington: Indiana University Press.

Magyar, Zoltán. 2001. *Halhatatlan és visszatérő hősök. Egy nemzetközi mondatípus Kárpát-medencei redakciói.* Budapest: Akadémiai Kiadó.

Nabhan-Warren, Kristy. 2005. *The Virgin of El Barrio. Marian Apparitions, Catholic Evangelizing, and Mexican American Activism.* New York: NYU Press.

———. 2013. *The Cursillo Movement in America: Catholics, Protestants, and Fourth-day Spirituality.* Chapel Hill: University of North Carolina Press.

Péter, László. 2003. The Holy Crown of Hungary, Visible and Invisible. *Slavonic and East European Review* 81 (3): 421–510.

Pozniak, Kinga. 2013a. Generations of Memory in the "Model Socialist Town" of Nowa Huta, Poland. *Focaal—Journal of Global and Historical Anthropology* 66: 58–68.

———. 2013b. Reinventing a Model Socialist Steel Town in the Neoliberal Economy: The Case of Nowa Huta, Poland. *City & Society* 25 (1): 113–134.

Schegloff, Emanuel A., Gail Jefferson, and Harvey Sacks. 1977. The Preference for Self-Correction in the Organization of Repair in Conversation. *Language* 53 (2): 361–382.

Valtchinova, Galia. 2009. Introduction: Ethno-Graphing "Divine Intervention". *History and Anthropology* 20 (3): 203–218.

Visnovitz, Péter. 2008. "Saját szigetről álmodnak és zsíroskenyeret kennek a magyar lovagok." *Origo.com*, October 9. https://www.origo.hu/itthon/20081008-lovagrendek-magyarorszagon-lovagi-cimek-karitativ-tevekenyseg-maltai-lovagrend-es-tarsai.html. Accessed 7 Jan 2022.

Voigt, Vilmos. 2004. *A vallási élmény története. Bevezetés a vallástudományba* [The History of Religious Experience: An Introduction to the Study of Religion]. Budapest: Timp Kiadó.

Zimdars-Swartz, Sandra L. 1991. *Encountering Mary: From LA Salette to Medjugorje.* Princeteon: Princeton University Press.

CHAPTER 6

Penitence

"Let us bring our penitential acts to this place because the crowned queen of heaven will complete [them]."
—Inscription at a shrine installed at the Csíksomlyó *pilgrimage* site,
June 2010.

FROM JUST JUDGE TO LOVING SERVANT

Halfway up the Csíksomlyó pilgrimage site's most prominent natural feature, a steep hill that rises alone from the valley floor to provide dramatic mountain views, is a large wooden cupola. This gray-colored architectural feature rests on eight thick wooden columns set into a square concrete platform and topped with a bent cross, making it recognizable as the Holy Crown of King Stephen (975–1038), Hungary's first Christian king. Beneath the larger-than-life cupola, but only visible from up close, is another Hungarian national and Catholic symbol. A statue of the Virgin Mary sits atop the stone base in the shape of a map of "Greater Hungary"— when Hungary included Transylvania within its borders. The structure's only written inscription is carved into a gray wooden sign leaning against the hillside: "Let us bring our penitential acts to this place," it says, "because the crowned queen of heaven will complete [them]."

© The Author(s), under exclusive license to Springer Nature Switzerland AG 2022
M. R. Loustau, *Hungarian Catholic Intellectuals in Contemporary Romania*, Contemporary Anthropology of Religion, https://doi.org/10.1007/978-3-030-99221-7_6

163

While attending Csíksomlyó's 2010 annual pilgrimage event, I noticed people milling about the structure and several lines snaking up toward it from various directions. Curious, I climbed the hill. Once there I heard the shrine's architect give a short speech saying that, while volunteers from Hungary had built it, the shrine was the brainchild of a former Transylvanian Hungarian Catholic priest, Father Pál, who ran an orphanage and educational NGO.

After the speech, I spent an hour observing people at this site. Some commented on King Stephen's Holy Crown and the map of Greater Hungary. Others took in the view, posing for photographs with the valley in the background. Still others, though not everyone, studied the inscription—in relative terms, a small and obscure feature within the whole. The shrine's explicit meaning, according to the sign, was penitential. Yet it seemed by design to make penitence one reason among others for visiting the site, even going so far as to exhort people to offer their strenuous labor in return for forgiveness only after they had arrived.

Father Pál's shrine to the Virgin Mary at the Csíksomlyó pilgrimage site. (Credit: Marc Roscoe Loustau)

This chapter develops an earlier claim that the social conditions that destabilize Transylvanian Hungarian intellectuals' service also set the stage for creatively renewing and reviving this intellectual tradition. As I argued in Chap. 3 in my analysis of Brother Csaba's outreach to spiritual seekers, Transylvanian Hungarian intellectuals confront the differing socialist legacies of Hungary and Romania in and through their habit of deferring to Hungarians' authoritative consumer taste. In this chapter, I examine a similar process at work in Father Pál's volunteer construction project to build the new hillside shrine to the Virgin Mary. In fact, as I learned in conversations with Father Pál, his Hungarian volunteers surprised him by delivering the unexpectedly huge, crown-shaped cupola. His decision to go ahead with the project demonstrated Transylvanian Hungarians' habit of deferring to Hungarians—in this case, deferring to the affinity for using King Stephen's cult to construct large-scale, monarchical pedagogical spectacles.

However, the shrine project also renewed Father Pál's identification with the Transylvanian Hungarian intellectual tradition—it demonstrated the intellectual virtues of dedication, commitment, and persistence in one's vocation—at a time when observers in the media were questioning the effectiveness of his service. The year before he mounted this project, after Father Pál had publicly disobeyed an order from his Archbishop, he had been suspended from the priesthood (Rédai 2011). In the wake of his suspension, one journalist asked Father Pál, "Do you still feel like you're able to be successful in the charitable arena?"[1] Amid these doubts, the shrine became a valuable public demonstration that Father Pál could mobilize Hungarians from Hungary to volunteer resources and labor.

This chapter also renews my ethnographic reflection on the social conditions of vocation and the practice of pedagogical virtue that I explored in Chap. 5. Indeed, Father Pál faced a situation with parallels to Emil's case. Both men had lost their teaching positions and wondered how they would continue to serve amid opposition to their educational initiatives. This was the fate that interwar educators had warned about when they counseled intellectuals not to rely on institutions like state governments to guarantee either their authority or the success of their work. While Emil persisted in and through the Knighthood Order's programs, Father Pál renewed his service using the shrine's ambiguously materialized ethical meaning.

As he had during his years as a priest, Father Pál exhorted his audiences to perform penitential acts. In the subdued form of the sign's text, he continued to tailor this message to the desires of his right-wing audience in Hungary, among them Catholics who were reluctant to view a pilgrimage journey as a penitential act for the forgiveness of sin and just as uncomfortable with taking time during such a trip to confess personally to a priest. By placing the exhortation to view the journey as a penitential act on a humble and nearly hidden sign and expressing this demand in absentia, he distanced himself from the role of confessor. Just as important as how Father Pál carried forward a key element of his former service, I also note that this effort did not entirely solve Father Pál's problems following his suspension.

My narrative in this chapter extends across three chronologically organized sections. Material for the description of Father Pál's early career in Csíksomlyó and his 2007 transfer comes from print and online news sources. In the second section, I examine the texts of three prophetic dreams featuring Father Pál; these originated in emails from one of his former parishioners and they were eventually circulated among Father Pál and a small group of his clergy friends. By interpreting these dreams, Father Pál deepened his preferred vocation of loving, charitable service even while acknowledging a need to perform penitential labor. In the final section, I describe Father Pál's post-hoc regrets over the shrine's construction, a process that reinforced an unequal relational dynamic existing between Transylvanian Hungarian intellectuals and Hungarian volunteers.

LOVE OR OBEDIENCE

During Father Pál's early ministry in the 1980s, strict pro-natalist laws and policies, which among other things severely restricted access to abortion, were the key element of the socialist government's drive to control the extraction and redistribution of human labor resources. Nicolae Ceaușescu, rising to the position of Party Secretary in the mid-1960s, determined that legally restricting access to abortion would not only remedy a growing demographic crisis—after World War II, population growth throughout Romania began to decline inhibiting the growth of Romania's capital-poor, labor-dependent economy—but also solidify his control over the Romanian Communist Party.[2,3] Anthropologist Gail Kligman has demonstrated vividly how Romania's abortion restrictions had far-reaching effects, remaking the extractive relationship between state and citizens according to the idealized model of a paternalistic peasant family: "The typically gendered dependency relations that are created through this type of family organization were elevated to the level of the socialist state's 'legitimate' rule over its citizens" (Kligman 1998: 30).[4]

In rural communities the *pater familias* controlled all household members' labor, which included the ability to extract and redistribute women's reproductive labor; this control rested partly on the *pater familias*'s personal sense of justice, with his ability to discern how much each member either owed or was due based on the household unit's common good (Kligman 1988). Nicolae Ceaușescu was presented as the personalization of the redistributive state, the Romanian nation's just father figure (1998: 137). Government propaganda represented citizens of the socialist state as if they were children who owed obedience to their patron Ceaușescu in return for his paternal care (1998: 30). In Kligman's words, "the paternalist state would look after family welfare in return for filial gratitude manifest through obedience" (Kligman 1998: 124).

Patron-client relationships also drove urban population growth—the centrally planned redistribution of human resources from villages to cities—after the Romanian socialist state created a county system of governance in 1968. In Chap. 4, I described the way that the county government in Miercurea Ciuc, capital of Harghita County, established patron-client relationships with new urban subjects. Bureaucrats in county governments kept industrial and educational funding close to where they lived in the county seats, ensuring they would be the primary beneficiaries of this investment, and the city's population began to grow rapidly with an influx of workers needed to fill positions in these new schools and factories. These new urbanites were often young villagers from the Hungarian-speaking Ciuc Valley who from the beginning created or inserted themselves into patron-client chains with the government bureaucracy, using their connections, talents, and proletarian backgrounds to gain access to the positions in Miercurea Ciuc's government-owned schools and factories that allowed them to leave the village in the first place.

While Brother Csaba's volunteer recruitment film, *Travels with a Monk*, called Hungarians from Hungary to serve government-abandoned populations of peasants-cum-workers, Father Pál's publicity literature portrayed him discovering his calling to serve in encounters with former residents of state orphanages living on city streets. The state abandoned these children not only by retreating from its program of industrialization and urbanization, but also by failing to enact pro-natalist policies. While every citizen was in effect one of Ceaușescu's dependents, the patron-client, *pater familias*-dependent bond appeared most clearly in propaganda about state-run orphanages. The government claimed orphans as wards of the state and used propaganda to celebrate plans for modern institutional orphanages to provide care in accord "with the state's exercise of its paternalistic obligations" (Kligman 1998: 85).

By law, orphans were fed, housed, and educated in these institutions, which were often situated close to urban county seats. For example, Harghita County's government orphanage in Csíksomlyó was in a former Catholic elementary school, established after Csíksomlyó was administratively incorporated into the capital Miercurea Ciuc in 1968 (Demeter 2009, 2011). Transferring rural orphans to urban centers helped government bureaucracies maintain efficient control of these institutions while also cementing the state's patron-client relationship with its citizens and aiding the process of industrialization and urbanization. Former orphanage residents could be easily transferred to Miercurea Ciuc's nearby tractor and knitwear factories at the age of eighteen, when they received their guaranteed state employment and apartment housing through these institutions.

In practice, the socialist government struggled to live up to the image of the just extractive and redistributive *pater familias*, failing to provide for its citizen-clients amid Ceauşescu's effort to pay off the country's foreign debt. Through the 1980s, as the government extracted increasingly large portions of the country's material and human resources for conversion into salable exports, the populace suffered with widespread shortages of even the most basic necessities. The government's shortage economy resulted in appalling living conditions in state-run orphanages, which North American and Western European reporters subsequently revealed in the early 1990s. These institutions had originally been touted as the shared property of a workers' state and privileged sites of Ceauşescu's paternalistic justice, but they ended up devoid of ownership; the state's wards were likewise forsaken, "virtually ignored" and "victims of systematic, institutional neglect" (Kligman 1998: 227).

Father Pál's NGO, called the Black Sheep Foundation, aims its publicity mostly at audiences in Hungary, much like the way Brother Csaba's films and interviews are intended to recruit new volunteers from Hungary. The Black Sheep Foundation's official history begins against the backdrop of Romania's late-socialist shortage economy, when the government was depriving citizens of basic necessities to increase the country's exports. In this period, Father Pál moved to a parish close to Csíksomlyó's state-run

orphanage. But Father Pál did not meet with the orphans in his church—
he encountered them on Miercurea Ciuc's streets.[5] "I ran into these children by chance on the side of the road," he recalls in one article, "because
they weren't allowed to come to my parish and meet with me"
(Forró 2010).[6]

According to Father Pál's story, after the state abandoned children
within these orphanages, it did so again by turning them out at the age of
eighteen to fend for themselves. Father Pál's reference is significant
because roadsides, like orphanages, were abandoned publicly owned
spaces. Roadsides were the equivalent of empty town squares and the hallways of high-rise apartment buildings. In anthropologist Krisztina
Fehérváry's words, they were "supposed to be collective spaces but in
practice were spaces no one claimed" (2013: 16–7).

The detail about the rule forbidding children from visiting Father Pál's
parish, however, adds an active disciplinary twist to the narrative of compensating for state neglect that structures both Father Pál and Brother
Csaba's narratives about being called to serve. In the name of educating
wards into the state's atheistic socialist culture and forming them in the
model of the "new socialist man," the state forbade orphans from entering
the premises of the local Catholic parish. Father Pál's statement, in con-
junction with numerous similar references in material detailing his ministry, suggests that Romania's socialist-era cultural and educational politics
are equally crucial in informing contemporary religious leaders' charity.
Thus, Romania's socialist state lives on in the imaginary of contemporary
Transylvanian Hungarian servant intellectuals, motivating and shaping
their service. They teach not only to compensate for the state's material
abandonment but also to rectify state-driven ethnoreligious assimilation.

The Foundation's website called these early conversations a form of
service in sharing. "These young people who were getting kicked out of
the state orphanages presented a great challenge," the organization states,
"They had no place to turn, so Father Pál made the daring decision to
share his life with them" (Csibész Alapítvány 2017). Like Brother Csaba,
Father Pál then took the step of institutionalizing his ministry to erstwhile
peasant children in the form of an NGO orphanage network that operated
in cooperation with Brother Csaba's Saint Francis Foundation.

Father Pál's NGO occupied a social structural position analogous to
Brother Csaba's Saint Francis Foundation. Both religious organizations
took over a compassionate and caretaking role from the shrinking post-
socialist welfare state, serving the needs of an abandoned rural population.

In the process, they also performed a key function in the Transylvanian Hungarian educational system, circulating young rural students to the city and cultivating the virtues of these future village teachers. The similarities extend even to their socio-spatial positioning, as the Black Sheep Foundation's flagship educational institution is located inside a house across the street from Brother Csaba's Csíksomlyó orphanage. Thus, the Black Sheep Foundation can be seen as another contemporary institution laying claim to the role interwar Transylvanian Hungarian Catholic intellectuals imagined for the Collegium Transylvanicum—not only a locus of apostolic pedagogy and educational service to the rural populace, but itself in its institutional form an index of the ethnic minority community's national self-consciousness.

Against the backdrop of Father Pál's description of educating the former child residents of shuttered Romanian state institutions, the Black Sheep Foundation seems to be intentionally replacing the state as a non-sectarian, public provider of aid. Sonja Luehrmann and others have argued that the growing number of religious NGOs in post-socialist countries have supported themselves through finding common cause with Western European political conservatives, who claim that Eastern European state-socialism's flaws prove that Western Europe's governmental welfare systems are doomed to failure and must be dismantled (Luehrmann 2011: 16; see also Muehlebach 2012); but the Black Sheep Foundation also addresses its narratives closer to home—to Hungary's consumeristic middle class. While Transylvanian Hungarians do seek solidarity with politically conservative Hungarians from Hungary, significant differences between the two communities' understanding of the ethical basis of Catholic clerical authority have the potential to destabilize the project of attracting volunteer support to an NGO headed by a priest.

Father Pál's sense of his pedagogical vocation in the Black Sheep Foundation also takes shape in response to Hungarian Catholics' changing feelings about priests' role in the sacraments. Father Pál began his ministry at a time when Catholics in Hungary, according to anthropologist Bertalan Pusztai, preferred to encounter priests serving in the Mass rather than hearing confession (Pusztai 2004: 77). A priest in the Mass fed believers by serving them communion; in confession, he extracted their labor by commanding them to perform penitential acts. According to official Catholic doctrine, priests draw on complementary virtues to perform the two sacraments: the former exemplified the priest's abundant love and the latter, his justice in determining what the sinner owes to God.

Catholics' growing preference for the former took place over time alongside shifts in pilgrimage practice. Historically Catholics viewed the often expensive and arduous journey to a shrine within the framework of the sacrament of confession (see Frey 1998: 98). In the medieval period, many pilgrims were criminals and the journey itself was penitential labor in return for sin (Pusztai 2004: 77). However, Hungarians grew increasingly disinterested in confession and penitence during the 1980s amid a number of transformations wrought by the New Economic Mechanism, including consumeristic tourism's growing role as the sign of socialism's victory over capitalism (Fehérvéry 2013). Although the state did not organize religious pilgrimages, small groups informally visited shrines while taking advantage of the faster, more efficient transportation options that had emerged with the late-socialist Hungarian tourism industry. Socialist-era Hungarian ethnologist Gábor Barna, for example, describes Hungarians who rented buses to visit spas and then stopped at shrines on the way (Barna 1991: 347).

During his fieldwork with Hungarian Catholic shrine visitors in the 2000s, Pusztai observed that priests at shrines rarely offered confession and visitors often neglected to ask for it. Generally, the packed driving schedule did not allow for such lengthy individual conversations at the shrine (Pusztai 2004: 54). Building on this observation, Pusztai comments, "the journey to and from, the *via purgativa*, lost much of its significance, and the mass celebrated at the shrine gained import…" (Pusztai 2004: 88; Barna 1987: 233, 1991, 2001). Improved travel infrastructure coincided with the growing appeal of the Mass, compounding Hungarian Catholic pilgrims' declining interest in confession and the performance of penitential labor.

When Brother Csaba described Jesus stopping into the priest's passenger seat for a spontaneous conversation, Brother Csaba does not actually say he was undergoing confession. He refers to this as a "conversation" and "dialogue" with Jesus, even though it has all the hallmarks of the sacrament, including the fact that, according to the dogmatic imagination, priests in confession are *in persona Christi*. By demonstrating the ethical benefits of confession under a different name and in a middle-class context of one's personal vehicle, Brother Csaba appears to be teaching his readers, who might view confession as superfluous to their practice or even be skeptical of its personal and social benefits, to regain their enthusiasm for or comfort with the ritual. Insofar as Father Pál deemphasizes his role in extracting penitential labor through the sacrament of confession and

instead emphasizes how confession helped him develop his calling to educate children, this narrative is a construct that looks two ways at once.
Through his emphasis on vocation, Father Pál identifies with the
Transylvanian Hungarian intellectual tradition, but as a Catholic priest
lovingly sharing God's abundance, he defers to middle-class Hungarians'
preferred, love-based ethical model for picturing Catholic priests.

Today, Church officials continue to rely on the model of priest-as-just-
judge—extractor and redistributor of labor—that Hungarians from
Hungary increasingly see as old-fashioned or backward, a remnant of the
time when the Catholic Church embraced a starkly anti-modernist cultural stance. Midway through his twentieth year at Csíksomlyó, newspaper
reports announced that the Transylvanian Archdiocese was transferring
Father Pál to a tiny parish more than 300 kilometers away (Gondola.hu
2007). According to American Catholic theologian Avery Dulles, in the
act of transferring parish priests, bishops exemplify the virtues of justice
and obedience proper to "the institutional model of the Church" (Dulles
1974: 36). During the mid-twentieth century, Dulles advocated for democratic reforms in the Church and, to this end, criticized those he saw as
placing too much emphasis on this institutional model. Some Catholics,
Dulles alleged, have become "overly concerned with fulfilling ecclesiastical
obligations and insufficiently attentive, at times, to fulfilling the law of
charity" (Dulles 1974: 43).

Father Pál himself understood the transfer order in this light—as a conflict between loving service and obedience. In his farewell homily at
Csíksomlyó, he declared that his ecclesiastical mission had been defined by
service: "I have strived to serve the people according to my fullest ability.
I had and still have this feeling and capacity within me" (Nagy 2014).
Despite his continuing calling to serve, Father Pál also expressed a commitment to obey. "No matter what," he wrote in an August 2007 press
release, "I will submit myself to the archbishop's decision and I will go
wherever he orders" (Gazda 2007). Father Pál found himself bound by
the virtue of obedience to a bishop who exercised justice through extraction and redistribution of priests' labor.

Father Pál translated this conflict of ethical values into an existential
impossibility, a demand to be in two places at once. Obedience to the
Archbishop required that he be in his new parish, while his patronage-style
pedagogical service to the Black Sheep Foundation's wards demanded he
remain in Csíksomlyó. A 2007 newspaper article, "Father Pál accepts his
fate," summarized the ethical conflict that defined this moment in Father

Pál's life. After commenting that Father Pál's clerical service (*diakóniai szolgálat*), including the Black Sheep Foundation, ties him to Miercurea Ciuc, the reporter quotes Father Pál admitting that he faces a new challenge. "[T]he distance of 300 kilometers will no doubt cause problems," Father Pál says, "Still, there isn't a lot of work to do during the week. Therefore, I can come home quite frequently" (Gazda 2007). Father Pál confidently looked forward to a practical solution that would mediate the tension. If he arranged his schedule properly and secured frequent transportation, he could still perform his charitable service at Csíksomlyó.

PENITENCE WITHOUT SCHISM

The first winter after leaving Csíksomlyó, Father Pál began to abandon this hope. The first signs of Father Pál's shift came when a young Miercurea Ciuc lawyer named Tünde reached out to him concerning a prophetic vision, a message from a divine source she had received in a dream. Tünde contacted Father Pál through a mutual acquaintance, a priest named Father Albert, who forwarded me the email that contained the text of Tünde's dream-vision:

I saw the following dream 4/20/2008. Location: The Church (I always see the same church; built on a hill, old big church). Many priests were inside the church, praying (I recognized several among them but I know that they were all presently living, serving, and real personages). There were some who during the prayer stood up and left the church and there were some who were constantly glancing toward the exit. I saw on their faces and I sensed their uncertainty. One priest could not take it anymore. He jumped up from the pew, but I chastised him, saying that he had not finished the prayer. He looked at me angrily and then knelt before the altar, said a quick "Our Father," stood up, and rushed out of the church. On the other hand, I just stood there (the shocking disappointment and pain that I felt is indescribable) and I watched as the church quickly emptied out. And only then did I notice that one side of the church was totally black, as if a thick soot had covered it. I asked the Father (he is always there, approx. 70 years old and like this church's caretaker), if this church was always like this and if I am not remembering it correctly, or if something has happened? To which, hanging his head in sadness, he shook his head, no, and said quietly: It has not been like this, my child. At that moment, it was as if an internal voice said: Someone (someone or some people) wants to tear down and destroy the WORK that the priest(s) began at Csíksomlyó. They are working on this right now! I went out into the open air and I saw a young couple: they could have been approx. 18 years old. The girl hung her head. She had brown hair, unremarkable (I felt this). I was looking at the boy when I heard the following: If she lives in darkness, not seeing the light, she is nevertheless blessed, because she sees what others cannot! The Lord, God, loved the world and decided to gift it with Tanja Popovice seeing the light. At the sound of this name, the boy looked towards the girl and squeezed her shoulder, saying: that is you! The girl answered: I know and raised her head. She was blind. On her face, however, was some kind of indescribable glory! Since then I have seen this face in front of me. Albert, I know that I have gone on for a while, but when I woke up, I had the feeling that I have to tell this to you. I waited on it for 5 days but since this feeling did not pass, I have written it down. I hope that you can understand more of it than me. This has or must have some kind of meaning.[7]

Father Albert, who lived in a city near Father Pál's new parish, visited Father Pál to discuss it. Afterwards Father Albert forwarded the text to two other Catholic priests, declaring that it was a divine message calling on them to gather for a "penitential rite and Mass" (*engesztelő szertartás és mise*) at the Csíksomlyó shrine.[8]

The men perhaps chose this location for this rite because, as anthropologists argue, Catholic shrines are historically and doctrinally associated with penitential labor. Shrines have long had a distinctive power to transmute the experience of sin in one domain into another, blurring the boundaries between individual and collective national identities and making a person or group's suffering objectifiable as well as manipulatable at other scales of social experience.[9] While Father Pál's ethical tribulation was translated into a personal wish to be in two places at once, both Tünde's message and the proposed penitential rite seemed to expand the scope of the misfortune he was experiencing.

In 2012, I interviewed several of these priests—Father Pál's clergy friends whom Father Albert had emailed about the dream-visions—to learn more about Father Pál's vocation to serve Transylvanian Hungarian orphans as it related to his relationship with this group of clerics. Father Albert, for example, insisted that Tünde's message related to all of the men to whom he sent emails, especially since the men shared Father Pál's perspective on Marian spirituality; some had also been transferred during the summer of 2007. The coincidence pointed to a broader conflict in the Catholic Church.

In Father Albert's words,

We also need to make a broader connection. Tünde saw that when Father Pál left, the new priest who came in was rational, without spirituality. So it's not just about that parish. I think that the message is symbolic. Spirituality is getting attacked by modernity and rationalism.

The forces of spirituality, including Father Pál, had suffered a setback against modernity and rationalism. The penitential rite would redress a sin, unnamed in Father Albert's commentary, that had sapped their strength for this battle. At Csíksomlyó, they could win back divine favor and regain their momentum.

Father Albert noticed a pattern in the archbishop's actions that tied the events in the Csíksomlyó parish to a broader battle for the Church's soul. According to this interpretation, the transfer aided the forces of rationalism. Father Pál identified with Marian spirituality too, and he believed his initiatives for fostering devotion to Mary were under attack. "Because we had begun many new initiatives at Csíksomlyó. We had begun spiritual programs for young people and teenagers. And summer camps and prayer groups," he told me, "They were trying to ruin all that." Both men suggested that the archbishop's transfers hid an ulterior motive or at least gave their antagonists an opportunity to take the upper hand.

Moreover, when Father Pál spoke about the archbishop's transfer, which had opened up an avenue for the unnamed enemies of Tünde's dream-vision to ruin his spiritual initiatives, he implied that the archbishop had lost sight of the community's common good—an essential condition of personal justice. As Father Pál returned to Csíksomlyó to perform a penitential rite, he articulated an alternative account of the archbishop's transfer. Besides being a sign of the latter's justice, to which Father Pál owed his obedience, the transfer had aligned him with an intimate group of clergy friends in an intra-Church battle between Marian spirituality and rationality.

Although this group of Marian priests wondered about alternative explanations for Father Pál's transfer, casting doubt on the archbishop's virtue, they never contemplated mobilizing a coalition to leave the Church; the priests even found ways to distance themselves from a passage in Tünde's message that might have been construed as commending such an act. Their interpretive engagement with Tünde's first vision petered out after the caretaker's sorrowful comment about the old stone church's sooty walls and the elderly priest's admission that the building had not always been so dark, narrow, and claustrophobic. The ensuing second scene then begins with the words, "I went out into the open air." The rest of the action then takes place outside the old stone church and features a new character, a seer named Tanja Popovice.

I conducted several interviews with Father Albert, Father Pál, and a third priest, Father Henrik, and each time it was necessary to remind them about the details of the subsequent scene outdoors, waiting while the men read the printout I had brought. Even Father Albert, from whom I originally received the text, admitted to having neglected this part. He rambled distractedly about possible etymological and cultural sources for the young seer's name, Tanja Popovice. "This name occurs more frequently in Romania than Hungary," he speculated, "because the Romanian Orthodox Church was under Serbian control. I forgot about this. The connection to Slavic culture and to Orthodoxy as well." I was struck by how different their responses were, compared with their strongly declarative and confident statements regarding the dream's first section. Instead, the men said they had been confused by the events depicting a group of people *outside* the old stone church.

In the Catholic imagination, schism and disobedience are linked with one's physical positioning within church buildings. When the pope speaks authoritatively—making statements that require believers' faithful obedience—he is said to do so ex cathedra, from his seat of authority in the space of a cathedral (Coleman and Bowman 2018). The priests' responses to the gathering outside the old stone church, as related in Tünde's story, suggested they wanted to distance themselves from a potential interpretation that they too represented a movement to leave the Church. They did so first by ignoring this passage. But when I urged them to consider it, they highlighted how this gathering of people *outside* a Catholic church was profoundly foreign. In the dream, the visionary at the group's center, Tanja Popovice, was outside what Tünde had described fondly as a familiar old stone Catholic church building. Popovice was outside, according to Father Albert, in two additional senses: she was ethnically Slavic and religiously Orthodox.

Father Pál and the others placed her on the far side of multiple social boundaries, impeding their ability to identify themselves with her role and her words; by deferring the discovery of this scene's personal and practical meaning, they avoided the question as to whether the dream called them to behave disobediently, much less to lead a schismatic movement that would have rendered them doubly foreign to the Church. The content of Tünde's dream played a crucial role in forming Father Pál's precarious middle position. To the extent that he cast aspersions on the archbishop's virtue, he did so while avoiding direct suggestion of leading a schismatic group outside the Church. Instead, the men tried to insist that Father Pál's departure from his new parish, return to Csíksomlyó, and renewed commitment to serving the orphans of the Black Sheep Foundation were not the beginnings of a schismatic movement.

PENITENCE AND PATRONAGE

A few months after her first vision, Tünde emailed Father Albert again. She had dreamt another divine message, which Father Albert took to elaborate the meaning of the "penitential rite and Mass" called for in the first text. "Two weeks ago," Tünde wrote,

> I was sent a message in a dream and it said, 'Tell him (that is, you) that the triad means that the three of you, by strengthening each other, will constitute a truly strong unity. Whoever is above must always know and support the other two people from two sides, and vice versa.' While I was hearing this, a triangle appeared. I can't make sense of any of this. The two sides of the triangle were like a support reaching down from the highest point and holding the lower two together.

Father Albert again visited Father Pál, this time with Father Henrik, to discuss the second message. In his email summarizing the discussion, Father Albert highlighted the Trinitarian character of the image: "We must strengthen the Christly unity between each other," he urged,

> in the mode of the 'priestly holy trinity' modeled on an equilateral triangle, so that, at any given time, the stronger members, those who are 'at the peak of the triangle, that is, just there at the top,' will strengthen and lift up the other two weaker members of the triadic unity.

The second vision thus identified friendship as the object on which the priests' penitential rite could depend.

By comparing their bond to the Christian Trinity, Father Albert implied that the bonds within this intimate group were like patron-client relationships. The Trinity, in Catholic thought, is a unity of three mutually dependent unequal persons: the Father, Son, and Holy Spirit. Father Albert's hint that this inequality may shift "at any given time" indicates the biographical and temporal perspective implicit within their Trinitarian social imaginary.

Participants in unequal patronage relationships, anthropologist China
Scherz has shown, often value this inequality because they situate charitable donations in a biographical temporality. Scherz points out that, "a
person might be a giver or a receiver at different moments in life," an
observation that resonates with the social impact Father Albert claimed for
the upcoming ritual gathering (Scherz 2014: 75). Although things might
change, Father Albert and Father Henrik would participate in this act of
penitence as the triangle's stronger persons supporting the weaker
Father Pál.

Looking back on their penitential ritual during an interview I conducted in 2011, a period when Father Pál had regained his position in the
Black Sheep Foundation, Father Pál claimed that with his clergy intimates
he had renewed his vocation to serve, his calling to redistribute from
God's abundance. The men met at night on a hillside at the Csíksomlyó
pilgrimage site, he explained. All night long they prayed. Although when
I spoke with Father Pál he reported they had not celebrated the Mass, he
still likened the penitential rite to this sacrament:

> What do I compare this to? It's like when priests celebrate the Mass
> together, and when the host is consecrated, the priests will get some kind
> of extra something. A feeling of being spiritually filled. Afterwards these
> priests belong to each other, feel closer to each other. If I have a problem,
> an intimate problem or any kind of problem, then they will give me help.
> And I to them. It's much more than simply belonging to a prayer group.
> Because…because they understand me. No, better than that – they help
> me. That's better. They will help me. It's a trust, a more profound trust.

Father Pál likened the priests' public prayer for forgiveness to priests jointly
celebrating the Mass, a practice known as "concelebration."[10] Before it
was introduced into Catholicism in the 1960s, some clergy complained
that rule that a priest is not allowed to celebrate the Mass outside his parish was a bureaucratic and jurisdictional obstacle to cooperation.

Father Pál allied this friend group of clergy intimates not only with the
practice of concelebration but also with a practice of sharing God's abundance. Indeed, he claims that the penitential rite's essence amounted to an
"extra something": a spiritual feeling that exceeded one's typical experience of celebrating the Mass. In this case, Father Pál was extending his
past service into the present. His earlier ministerial service led him to share
himself by talking with and helping abandoned former orphans. In the

process, this love went on to exceed the boundaries of his parish, such that his service had become tied to the entire region around Csíksomlyó. This same sense of serving by offering excess now shaped ritual life with his emerging group of clergy intimates, who during the penitential rite shared in that "extra" of God's abundance.

Father Pál also told me about a third prophetic message from Tünde. She shared this one only with him, whereas before she had sent texts to him through Father Albert. None of the other priests reported any familiarity with this vision. This prophecy differed by featuring a command that required Father Pál to disobey the archbishop:

> She told me this vision's, dream's – whatever we should call it – first part was that I have to come back. The same place where she had her feeling, dreams, visions. I have to come back to the same place where she got this message. She always saw the same place. The Blessed Lady needs to be present there. We need to bring our penitential acts to her. And she needs to be crowned. She said, '*You* need to build a chapel.' I asked, 'How?' She said, 'You have to come back – no delay!' No conversation, no discussion. And not just anywhere around here, but right here. She didn't know any of the details about how I was going to do this. But she knows for sure that I needed to come back.

Father Pál underscored the individual nature of the Virgin Mary's command by stating that Tünde had "called me personally," while the request that Tünde go back to confirm the order only underscores the commanding nature of this prophecy. There is no room for interpreting this message by ignoring part of it or deciding that a triangle merely referred to the familiar interpersonal relations of the Trinity. The Virgin Mary was now communicating by fiat.

At first glance, this case is an example of a commonplace phenomenon in Catholic visionary culture, wherein Catholics call down higher divine powers to abrogate the will of ecclesiastical authority figures when it suits them. For some anthropologists the idiosyncratic character of the third vision might raise further suspicions about the nature and purpose of this text. Perhaps Father Pál made up the vision on his own, as opposed to those other texts produced in the relational space formed by the bonds between himself, Tünde, Father Albert, and the dream's divine disembodied voice. If he did invent this third dream, should we understand the message as a more transparently direct effort to justify fulfilling his desire to return to Csíksomlyó, disobeying the archbishop?

Another interpretation is possible that captures more of the nuance evident in Father Pál's understanding of friendship and patronage, one that avoids this interpretation's crass instrumentalism. The final message is not just a tool, a means for Father Pál to justify his decision to move back to Csíksomlyó. In the process, we can move toward an understanding of ethical conflict that draws on and extends Simon Coleman's observation on theory in pilgrimage studies, that paradigms of cultural contestation tend to "flatten out" pilgrimage sites' complex socialities (Coleman 2014: 285).

Father Pál's account of the message illustrates the internally contradictory practice of friendship. Michael Taussig notes a seemingly universal characteristic, evident in numerous anthropological accounts, of people who are thought to be "good at friendship," that they are often just as likely to withhold information, act dishonestly, and dissemble. The practice of friendship is a matter of oscillating between disinterestedness and instrumentality, Taussig concludes, because intimacy does not aim at eliminating the contradiction between ends and means so much as it endeavors "to blend the energies of these opposed principles" (Taussig 1999: 61). Even if Father Pál had chosen to disobey the archbishop, he remained bound to his circle of intimate clergy friends who, as priests, held fast to the virtue of obedience. A personal prophecy gave Father Pál an avenue to help his friends: they would avoid the ethical conflict he himself had to face, preserving and extending the bonds established in their shared experience of sacred power.

A POETICS OF THE MASS

Despite this attempt to avoid personally breaching a vow of obedience, the Archdiocese punished Father Pál after he returned to Csíksomlyó in 2011, saying that it had suspended him from the priesthood. The Archdiocese's public announcement did not fail to note the most important consequence of this decision, which was that Father Pál was now forbidden from celebrating the Mass. Even so, in the weeks after Father Pál explained to reporters that he still served the community as a ritual leader.

A blogger for a Hungary-based teachers' association published an interview titled, "It's impossible to destroy a calling…lives and destinies: Father Pál," in which Father Pál claimed that his service had recently intensified:

Over the events of the last few months, my calling has only deepened and, from this perspective, it has yielded a different kind of light, you might even say more light and commitment. The rituals and prayers that I perform in my own way are more mature and as a result are more fruitful. In particular, the people [*nép*] are constantly seeking me out and asking me to put this difficult task on my shoulders. I have not been divested of my calling but rather invested with it. (Székely János Pedagógus Társas Kör 2014)

The interview's title implies that the Archdiocesan suspension had called into question the effectiveness of Father Pál's volunteer work, but also praises Father Pál's determination. The dialectic between persistence, external challenges, and one's calling is a core concern of the Transylvanian Hungarian intellectual tradition, formed as it was during a period of crisis following World War I. Commitment [*elkötelezettség*], maturity [*érettség*], and enthusiasm for hard work were virtues that Áron Márton once claimed for village intellectuals and ethnic minority educators; Father Pál claims them, too, although he claimed them after facing a kind of adversity—disobedience to his archbishop, suspension from the priesthood—that Áron Márton certainly did not imagine when this future bishop of Transylvania counseled his readers about persisting through their difficulties (Bárdi 2015: 23–5).

During an interview I conducted with Father Pál, he specified that the "rituals and prayers" he refers to the blogger's article were in fact the Mass:

I still celebrate the Mass today, just in my own way. I open the heavens. The light shines down and flows out. I ask it for myself, drawing it to the place where I am, and I try to expand it so that it should reach as big an area as possible, to embrace the area. I link the earth to the heavens and vice versa. And I try in that light, in that vision to remain sober and sentient, avoiding bad feelings. Because, you know, every day I have bad feelings, resentments and other stuff like it. If I do this, then it burns the bad feelings out of people. One can come to this holy place, which still attracts others, and they can be purified there. For instance, take the nuns across the street. In truth, I am angry at them, too, because what they did, it hurt me too. But now I'm a little ashamed of myself because I wanted to hurt them, too, and I feel like it wasn't necessary.

In this commentary, Father Pál offers a simultaneously familiar and unfamiliar definition of the Mass. Beginning this statement with the simple declaration "I still celebrate the Mass today" (*Még most is misézek*), he goes on to describe opening the heavens to call down a light whose primary effect is not the ontological transformation of material substance into God's presence but rather an emotional and ethical miracle of purification. Through all this, Father Pál omits the very act that—in the eyes of officials in the Transylvanian Archdiocese if not most Catholics—would have made this ritual a Mass: the transformation of bread into the real body of Jesus Christ. Playfully reinterpreting a ritual's normative meaning by distorting, reframing, and obscuring its various elements, according to anthropologist Michael Herzfeld, is a hallmark of the expressive mode he calls "social poetics," although in this case the term "sacramental theological poetics" may be more apt, since Father Pál's was reinterpreting a sacramental ritual's theological meaning.

While Herzfeld highlights cursing and slandering divine beings in his list of social poetic forms, Father Pál is subtler than to blaspheme against the normative theology of the Catholic Mass, just as he was reluctant to disobey blatantly his archbishop (Herzfeld 1984). He subjects himself to reporters' queries suggesting the archbishop's action cast doubt on a calling. Father Pál also uses these very questions to draw new attention to a theme in the Transylvanian Hungarian intellectual tradition's understanding of pedagogical authority: that a calling is the basis of pedagogical authority and its most authentic expression for ethnic minority teachers lies in voluntary rural education.

In Father Pál's account of his poetic interpretation of the Mass, he strikes a familiar note about serving out of God's abundance: the light that purifies his bad feelings overflows out into the world. Father Pál also expends his own energy in attempting to broaden the extent of God's abundance and, in his words, "reach as big an area as possible." He admits the light is also overwhelming, considering how he struggles to stay sober and sentient while he serves others. In and through God's abundance, individuals can be drawn to the place where Father Pál has opened up the heavens and receive purification.

This amounts to an argument that God's abundance purifies mundane resentments, which would have afflicted not only his relations with the archbishop but also his bond with the erstwhile orphanage collaborator Brother Csaba. After years of working together, Father Pál's suspension had soured the relationship between these fellow patrons and vocational teachers.[11] A friar in Brother Csaba's Franciscan order once gossiped to me that Brother Csaba had denounced Father Pál's Csíksomlyó hillside shrine, which Father Pál had built with the volunteer labor of Hungarians from Hungary. Brother Csaba's project for Hungarians from Hungary to build a shrine to Mary, which I described in Chap. 3, was partly a reaction to Father Pál's shrine. In this sense, Brother Csaba's project was a type of pilgrimage politics and contestation as well as an effort to appropriate Mary as a "competitive spirit" in the religious market for volunteer labor (Eade and Sallnow 1991; Chesnut 2003).

Yet Coleman's admonition to avoid reducing pilgrimage-mediated social action to strategic agonistic competition is apt in this case, as well, since the conflict between the erstwhile colleagues actually opened up opportunities for their former wards to make new appeals for patronage, subjecting Father Pál *qua* patron to a kind of manipulation by his orphan clients (Coleman 2014). After Father Pál's return, as the orphanage leaders' rift became widely known, their wards seemed to actually encourage tensions between the men.

During my 2013 interview with Father Pál, a young woman named Monika stepped into his office for help finding a job. I sensed these two were already on familiar terms, which Father Pál confirmed when he explained to a prospective employer over the phone that Monika had "grown up here at our place," meaning in one of the Black Sheep Foundation's homes. She was unmarried with a young son, had her own apartment in Miercurea Ciuc, and sounded responsible as well as talented; that is, I learned of these characteristics from overhearing Father Pál speaking on her behalf to the man whose company was probably going to hire her.

But he left out certain other details: before Father Pál picked up the phone to find her a job, Monika had spent a few minutes detailing how she lost a job cooking at a college cafeteria in Miercurea Ciuc, leading to fruitless inquiries with companies that advertised positions they had already filled. Advertising for applicants, she complained to Father Pál, was only for show, a way to satisfy legal requirements.

"This is why I'm wailing like this to you," Monika confessed, "because I can't bear it anymore. Truly, I try and try." Amid this breathless lament, Father Pál managed to slip in a few questions, including whether she reached out to Böjte Csaba. Monika replied with a veiled criticism. "He's not even bothering to pick up his phone," she said, "I tried several times."

Orphans in Uganda, anthropologist China Scherz observes, often foment competition among different charitable organizations, exploiting the organizations' embeddedness within a patronage ethical system based on hierarchical relations of mutual dependence (Scherz 2014: 90–5). The young woman asking Father Pál for help cast ethical aspersions on Brother Csaba to heighten this competition, implying that Father Pál had been the more responsive patron; that is, like Father Pál had proclaimed in the interview, he was more willing to take on the task of serving "the people" when they seek him out for help.

Monika's comment appeared to spur him to action. Immediately after her reply, Father Pál started dialing. Perhaps sensing that slandering Brother Csaba had been an effective strategy, Monika returned to this topic even after Father Pál had found her a job, saying just as he was putting down the receiver, "I tried several times to get in touch with Csaba Böjte. But I don't know why he's not picking up?"

Monika's appeal to Father Pál sheds light on a hidden competitive calculus behind Brother Csaba's own relationships with his former wards. This calculus was evident in the way he related to Ambrus, the older teenager who had participated in the volunteer building project for Hungarians from Hungary. Ambrus belonged to the same social cohort as Monika; they were both young former residents of local orphanages and lived in Miercurea Ciuc's urban apartments. I described how Brother Csaba spoke of Ambrus in his lectures to the Hungarian volunteers, ultimately concluding that it was to indulge their desire for spontaneity. Except recall that he also promised to find Ambrus a job near Csíksomlyó so that they could "build God's kingdom together." A story centered on Ambrus thus also took shape within an emerging competition between Brother Csaba and Father Pál, also actively trying to find jobs for his former wards.

Brother Csaba had formerly collaborated with Father Pál, insofar as they seemed to occupy distinct niches within the field of Transylvanian Hungarian educational NGOs; Brother Csaba worked primarily with school-aged orphans, whereas Father Pál built his reputation working with orphans in their late teens and early twenties who had been abandoned, first by the socialist state and later Romania's post-socialist governments. Meanwhile, Brother Csaba's offer to Ambrus signaled that he now wanted to help those orphans whom Father Pál had made his reputation serving; and former orphans like Monika, in search of patronage, used complaints to exploit this competitive bond. The archbishop's decision to remove Father Pál's ordination came to shift the tenor of his bond with Brother Csaba as the men no longer related to each other as collaborative partners but rival patrons.

Ambient Penitence

As his interaction with Mónika demonstrated, part of his authority as leader of the Black Sheep Foundation depended on his ability to serve former wards as patron, to recirculate valuable resources like jobs by calling on business owners and friends. In the wake of the Church's censure, which led some journalists to wonder if he was still capable of doing effectively charitable work, community members would have been justified in wondering whether he could still extract charitable resources from Hungarians from Hungary. Since the new shrine at Csíksomlyó was built with materials and labor donated by Hungarians, it constituted a public, highly visible statement that, in the wake of his punishment, he could still mobilize these resources; to do so, Father Pál cleverly tapped into right-wing Hungarians' fascination with King Stephen.

As I describe in Chap. 5, the iconography of Hungary's first Christian monarch, including the Holy Crown he offered to the Virgin Mary's protection, has played a prominent role in twentieth century Hungarian religio-political spectacles (Hann 1990; Hanebrink 2006). Despite the Knighthood Order of the Holy Crown's program of small-group lectures and prayer sessions—an effort to integrate devotion to the Holy Crown into the Transylvanian Hungarian intellectual tradition's model of humble, rural apostolic pedagogy—other Transylvanian Hungarian teachers adopted the Hungarian tendency to embrace pomp, grandeur, and spectacle in celebrations of the Holy Crown (Fülöp-Székely 2021). Father Pál confronted this tendency when he asked friends in Hungary to build a cupola in the shape of the Holy Crown to cover a modest meter-high statue of the Virgin Mary, which had been installed on the hillside the year before.

The cupola featured brightly stained strips of plywood that led to a pinnacle topped with the Holy Crown's distinctive bent cross; the plywood rested on a wooden frame, painted light gray to create a figure-ground form, and the metal bent cross on top was also a tin-like shade. Because the cross angled off a small pillar resting on a flat metal base, the large curves of wood appeared to dip away from the edges, leaving them exposed. White light bulb-like ornaments ringed another plywood strip, forming the cupola's base where it rested on eight wooden pillars. Getting a closer look, one could make out other design elements of the shrine not directly related to King Stephen's cult, including tulips carved into the pillars by a local artisan and that evoked the late nineteenth-century

Secessionist designers' use of the tulip as a symbol of the Hungarian people (Fehérváry 2013: 149). But viewing the shrine from far off, all of these
details disappeared. What remained to attract visitors was the oversized
Holy Crown-shaped cupola.

The new shrine succeeded in convincing people in the area that Father
Pál, despite ecclesiastical censure, could indeed make use of donated
resources from Hungary. This was the meaning Ápor, an architect and
artisanal carver from Miercurea Ciuc, took from the shrine. Ápor had
designed the structure, and when I called to arrange an interview, he suggested we discuss the shrine at an outdoor café across from his office.

Our glasses of beer on the plastic table were half gone when Ápor began
listing the materials that went into building the shrine:

All the materials were donated through Father Pál. The cupola itself came
from Hungary. Someone Father Pál knows in Hungary brought it here. The
whole thing, in pieces, which they assembled on the hillside. The wood for
the columns also came from Hungary. Also some other pieces of wood that
you can't see now, but they are under the cupola. You know, it isn't a small
thing to have all these materials donated because they are so expensive. And
it costs money to bring them here.

In Ápor's words, "it isn't a small thing" to coordinate and organize a hillside shrine. It had impressed Ápor that Father Pál was able to mobilize
resources for such cultural initiatives. Even though the Transylvanian
Catholic Church no longer recognized him as a priest in good standing,
Father Pál had no trouble calling on Hungarians to donate costly materials
as well as labor.

While the project excited a handful of business owners like Ápor, all
potential patrons of Black Sheep Foundation wards, the shrine upset
Catholic ecclesiastical leaders. Shortly after Hungarian volunteers had
erected the cupola, during Csíksomlyó's 2010 pilgrimage, I leaned against
one of its columns as an associate of Father Pál's gave a speech before a
gathered crowd; toward the end, he included a short and oblique reference to "some [who] have said that it should be torn down." When I
brought this up to Father Pál later during an interview the following year,
he acknowledged but downplayed the conflict: "Many people are angry
about it," he said. "Some of the Franciscans were actually happy about it,
but there was one who said that it should be torn down with a tractor."

As we talked further, Father Pál disputed the specific criticisms I had heard in regard to the cupola's design; but our conversation also revealed the ways in which he was subject to his Hungarian volunteers' tendency to express their devotion to King Stephen in the pomp and grandeur of monarchical spectacle. Father Pál disagreed that the cupola's narrow and bulbous shape made the Holy Crown look rather onion-like, similar to the ornamental tops on some Eastern Orthodox church buildings. Instead, he claimed that the cupola, like the Holy Crown, evoked medieval Hungarian designs from the period of King Stephen's reign. Father Pál ardently defended the choices Hungarian volunteers had made in designing and constructing the cupola while at the same time admitting that, given the voluntary nature of the project, he had lost some control over the design. The cupola turned out different from what he expected: "I had pictured it smaller. But when the Hungarian man brought it, I saw that it was really quite big. So that was a surprise."

Father Pál gives voice with these comments to Transylvanian Hungarians' broad sense that their Hungarian ethnic kin's consumer tastes are authoritative. As I describe in Chap. 2, since Transylvanian Hungarians first began visiting Hungary to buy Western consumer goods in the 1970s, they have understood themselves to be subject to their ethnic kin's consumerist desires. The subsequent growth of Hungary's village tourism industry only deepened this tendency, while I argue in Chap. 3 that Brother Csaba attempted to synthesize aspects of the Transylvanian Hungarian intellectual tradition with his Hungarian volunteers' seeker mentality. Through affirming his readers' spiritual search, even as he recast enlightenment as the recognition of God's collaborative presence, Brother Csaba continued to treat Hungarians' desires and interests as authoritative.

Like him, Father Pál avoided openly and explicitly criticizing the taste of his Hungarian volunteers. Left to satisfy their own desire to materialize devotion to the Holy Crown, Father Pál's collaborators produced an unexpectedly large cupola—so large that it drew the Church leaders' ire. Although Father Pál succeeded in his effort to dispel doubts over his access to Hungarian resources and labor, the effort became mediated through the unequal field of post-socialist consumer culture that shapes even the Hungarian right-wing's preference for monarchical spectacle. The cupola revealed his Hungarian volunteers' divergent taste in religio-political symbolism and made plain to him, furthermore, that he was subject to this divergence.

Woman enjoying the view at Father Pál's shrine. The sign with the inscription is on the far left. (Credit: Marc Roscoe Loustau)

Father Pál called the site a "place of penitence" (*engesztelő hely*), in addition to its role as a shrine celebrating the Holy Crown, Greater Hungary, and Hungarian national solidarity. As a former Catholic priest, Father Pál would have known that penitence is enacted in offering labor for the forgiveness of sin. Likewise, in what Pusztai calls the normative and traditional model of pilgrimage, this ritual is the via *purgativa* and one can combine pilgrimage with penitence by completing an arduous physical task at the shrine like walking up a steep hillside. However, the shrine's explicit references to penitence were muted and thus ambiguated. The shrine's penitential purpose was indicated only by a meter-long carved wooden sign, which read, "Let us bring our penitential acts to this place because the crowned queen of heaven will complete [them]."

The sign, planted into the earth on a thin stick, lies behind a statue of the Virgin Mary; and from a distance the Holy Crown cupola can seem to stand for the shrine per se, since it is the only feature visible from the base of the hill. Were Hungarians from Hungary being invited up the hillside for the promise of enjoying the beautiful and magical Transylvanian view? Were they being invited by the Holy Crown-shaped cupola to honor Transylvanian Hungarians' work to preserve Hungarian national culture and its heroes? Or as the visitors discovered when they finally arrived—huffing and panting—had they just completed a laborious act of collective penitence that the Virgin Mary would accept and complete?

This material arrangement of a penitential exhortation beneath the Holy Crown seems to be a right-wing nationalist variation on an evangelizing strategy that Mathew Engelke has called "ambient faith." According to Engelke, in Western Europe Christians feel they must express belief by exhorting others to convert but also must accommodate secular norms that admonish them to treat conversion as a personal choice (Engelke 2012, 2013). In Hungary, public displays of right-wing religio-political iconography are by no means interdicted; Hungary's right-wing government legitimizes its rule by routinely funding displays of Christian national iconography.

However, not all right-wing Hungarians who visit such sites embrace official Church practice. There are also plenty of right-wing Hungarian nationalists who aren't Catholic or are nominally so, and thus not familiar with the sacrament of confession. They may be turned off or simply bored were a priest to demand that they undertake personal physical labor on behalf of the Hungarian nation in return for God's forgiveness. Furthermore, as Pusztai and Barna both note, socialist-era consumer culture and tourism has shaped the tastes of even those Hungarians who are interested in traditional Catholic practices at traditional religious sites, leading them to view penitential labor for sin as an option to undertake, but only if one has time during a pilgrimage trip (Pusztai 2004; Barna 1991). Father Pál faced the challenge of calling for penitential labor from some visitors who might feel they simply didn't have time to walk up the hill.

The sign instructing visitors to offer their penitential acts to the Virgin Mary. (Credit: Marc Roscoe Loustau)

Thus, even when addressing a right-wing audience which, among other things, has crossed the Romanian border to celebrate Hungarian national solidarity, Transylvanian Hungarian Catholic intellectuals like Father Pál still defer to this audience's authoritative preferences. Father Pál exhorted visitors to penitence within conditions set by various intertwined processes, which together have led Hungarians on both sides of the border to distrust priests who rooted their public-facing persona in the ritual of confession and extraction of penitential labor.

The ambiguous design continued Father Pál's effort to shift ethical models of sacramental ministry. Over the course of his career, Father Pál had repeatedly defined his clerical mission as sharing both *his* resources as well as God's abundance. This change took shape as an effort to move beyond an idea of the priest as a confessor-judge and corresponded with a shift of emphasis within Catholic sacramental practice away from confession. The Csíksomlyó shrine bolstered Father Pál's effort to ally himself

with the trend within Catholicism to deemphasize the priest's role in organizing and authorizing penitential labor; but he did so while still exhorting people to perform it. He effectively hid a call to Hungarians to
strenuously make up for their sins beneath a conspicuous celebration of
King Stephen and the Holy Crown.

In addition to hiding and ambiguating the shrine's penitential message,
Father Pál also sought to remove the priest *in persona Christi*—in the person of Christ—entirely from the process of confession. The sign's text
urged visitors to make their offerings to her, for she will complete them.
Father Pál declared that the Virgin Mary accepts all such labor. He suggested that confession need not depend on the participation of a virtuously just priest who determines how much the believer owes. Whatever
the believer is willing to give to the Virgin Mary, she will accept it and
complete it.

Father Pál recast the Virgin Mary in this role and reframed justice as
generosity and acceptance. He urged visitors to be confident that the
Virgin Mary will receive however much retributive labor they offer. The
shrine contributed to Father Pál's lifelong suspicion of what, in Hungarian
culture as a whole, was coming to be seen as an older view of penitential
labor: from the confession-based notion that priests use penitence to
extract believers' labor, making up for one's sins is now an opportunity for
Hungarians to remember their nation's special bond with the Virgin Mary.

CONCLUSION

In this chapter, I examined the role that penitence plays in a Transylvanian
Hungarian intellectual's exhortations to rural Transylvanian Hungarians
as well as a broader audience of Hungarians from Hungary. Father Pál
cultivated an ethical nation by urging both groups to perform penitential
labor for their sins, even though a fraught relationship with the
Transylvanian Catholic Church nearly destabilized this effort. I described
the crisis Father Pál faced in 2007 following two decades of developing his
clerical persona as a loving servant, mediating God's gifts through sharing
his life with displaced former residents of Romania's state-run orphanages.
Out of virtuous obedience, in 2007 Father Pál submitted to the archbishop's order to move to a distant parish.

Over the following year, Father Pál received prophetic messages that
called for a new penitential mission at Csíksomlyó's pilgrimage site, where
he then performed a penitential rite with a group of clergy friends. In this

rite, the priest's friends cultivated a penitential attitude, an orientation that contributed to Father Pál's ability to stand apart from an alternative model of clerical virtue—justice performed in redistributing resources—embodied in the archbishop's transfer order. This process of negotiating between models of the clerical vocation took shape in relation to changing views governing the sacraments of confession and Mass. Father Pál's references to the Mass offer a chief example of this ritual's fluctuating status, such that even after the Transylvanian Archdiocese declared he was ineligible to celebrate the Mass, Father Pál could still claim to do so. His account of celebrating the Mass refashioned his view of ministry as the ethical practice of sharing God's abundance.

NOTES

1. In the words of one journalist, "Do you have a sense for how successful your charitable programs are now that you are a layperson?"
2. Historians of Romania's socialist period have argued that post-World War II economic factors drove Romania's policies concerning abortion, noting further that religious arguments were absent from nationally and ethnically focused justifications legitimating the state's need for increased fertility.
3. In 1965, he issued Decree 770, which determined that abortion in most cases became punishable by severe fines and jail sentences (Gal and Kligman 2000; Kligman 1998). A typical Romanian woman was eligible for an abortion only if she was above the age of 45 or had four living children. In 1985 a new decree raised that number to five living children and stipulated further that they all had to be "under her care" (Kligman 1998, 68).
4. Kligman refers to the "wizened guidance of the pater familias" (1998: 30).
5. Kligman states that under Romanian socialism, youth homelessness did not exist, but historical accuracy does not limit this narrative about Father Pál's calling and ministry (Kligman 1998: 237).
6. Father Pál opened himself to talking with these children, who spent their time begging or engaging in petty crime. "Several young orphans reached out to the parish priest in secret," reported the *Transylvania Diary* (Erdély Napló) online news site in 2016, "and these conversations gave birth to his commitment to serving their cause" (Makkay 2016).
7. All typographical irregularites are part of the original text.
8. He called it a "vision" (*látomás*). Tünde's social and educational class position reflects the blending of Catholic "visionary culture" and the Charismatic movement within Catholicism, which Thomas Csordas has written about extensively (Csordas 1994, 1996).

9. See, for example, Orsi 1996 as well as the voluminous literature on the Lourdes Catholic shrine (Harris 1999; Kaufman 2007; Christian and Krasznai 2009).
10. Before it was introduced into Catholicism in the 1960s, clergy complained that the rule stipulating priests can only celebrate in their own parishes was a bureaucratic obstacle to collaboration. Father Pál's interpretation of this ritual dovetails with those theologians who argued it would unite the clergy in bonds of unity that exceed "artificial" jurisdictional lines (Seasoltz 1980: 13). See McManus 1987. During the pre-Vatican II era, concelebration had been limited to special occasions, such as a priest's ordination.
11. While filming a documentary about his charitable work, Brother Csaba stopped an interview to take a call from Father Pál. Not only did he make sure to announce that it was Father Pál on the line, he also used Father Pál's very informal nickname when he picked up. See "Travels with a monk," https://www.youtube.com/watch?v=PU6e_cAUpcw, 19:40-19:50.

REFERENCES

Bárdi, Nándor. 2015. A népszolgálat genezise és tartalomváltozása. In *Népszolgálat: A közösségi elkötelezettség alakváltozatai a magyar kisebbségek történetében* [Service to the People: The Elementary Forms of Community Commitment in the History of the Hungarian Minority], eds. Nándor Bárdi, Tamás Gusztáv Filep, and József D. Lőrincz, 11–48. Pozsony: Kalligram Kiadó.
Barna, Gábor. 1987. Egy szokáskör: a búcsújárás strukturális változásai kisalföldi példák alapján [A Circle of Practice: The Structural Varieties of Pilgrimage on the Basis of an Example from Kisalöüld]. *Folklór és tradíció* 4: 228–237.
———. 1991. A magyarországi búcsújárás változásai [The Varieties of Hungarian Pilgrimage]. *Vigilia* 56 (5): 345–347.
———. 2001. *Búcsújárók: kölcsonhatások a magyar és más európai vallási kultúrákban* [Pilgrims: Exchanges of Influence Between Hungarian and Other European Religious Cultures]. Budapest: Lucidas.
Chesnut, Andrew R. 2003. *Competitive Spirits: Latin America's New Religious Economy.* Oxford: Oxford University Press.
Coleman, Simon. 2014. Pilgrimage as Trope for an Anthropology of Christianity. *Current Anthropology* 55 (S10): S281–S291.
Coleman, Simon, and Marion Bowman. 2018. Religion in Cathedrals: Pilgrimage, Heritage, Adjacency, and the Politics of Replication in Northern Europe. *Religion* 50 (1): 1–23.
Csibész Alapítvány. 2017. Rólunk [About Us]. http://www.csibesz.ro/wordpress/en/about-us/. Accessed 2 Jan 2020.

194   M. R. LOUSTAU

Csordas, Thomas J. 1994. *The Sacred Self: A Cultural Phenomenology of Charismatic Healing*. Berkeley: University of California Press.

———. 1996. Imaginal Performance and Memory in Ritual Healing. In *The Performance of Healing*, ed. Carol Laderman and Marina Roseman, 91–114. London: Routledge.

Demeter, Csanád. 2009. *Területfejlesztési- és modernizációs politika Székelyföld elmaradott régióiban* [The Politics of Regional Development and Modernization in Backwards Regions of the Szekler Land: Harghita and Covasna Counties in "the Multilaterally Developed Socialist Society"]. Ph.D. dissertation. Department of History, Babeş-Bolyai University, Romania.

———. 2011. Falusi urbanizáció és városi ruralizáció a Székelyföldön [Village Urbanization and Urban Ruralization in the Szekler Land]. *Korunk* 4: 101–107.

Dulles, Avery. 1974. *Models of the Church*. New York: Doubleday.

Eade, John, and Michael Sallnow. 1991. *Contesting the Sacred: The Anthropology of Christian Pilgrimage*. Eugene: Wipf and Stock.

Engelke, Matthew. 2012. Angels in Swindon: Public *Religion* and *Ambient Faith* in England. *American Ethnologist* 39 (1): 155–170.

———. 2013. *God's Agents: Biblical Publicity in Contemporary England*. Berkeley: University of California Press.

Fehérváry, Krisztina. 2013. *Politics in Color and Concrete: Socialist Materialities and the Middle Class in Hungary*. Bloomington: University of Indiana Press.

Forró, Gyöngyvér. 2010. Csíkszereda: húszéves a Csibész Alapítvány [Csíkszereda: The Black Sheep Foundation is 20 Years Old]. *Krónika Online*. January 13. https://kronikaonline.ro/erdelyi-hirek/csikszereda_huszeves_a_csibesz_ala-pitvany. Accessed 2 Jan 2020.

Frey, Nancy. 1998. *Pilgrim Stories: On and Off the Road to Santiago, Journeys Along an Ancient Way in Modern Spain*. Berkeley: University of California Press.

Fülöp-Székely, Botond. 2021. A Szent Korona felnagyított mását állították ki Székelyudvarhelyen [Exhibiting the Oversized Copy of the Holy Crown in Odorheiu Secuiesc]. *Szekelyhon.ro*, August 2. https://szekelyhon.ro/aktualis/a-szent-korona-felnagyitott-masat-allitottak-ki-szekelyudvarhelyen. Accessed 27 Dec 2021.

Gal, Susan, and Gail Kligman. 2000. *The Politics of Gender After Socialism: A Comparative-Historical Essay*. Princeton: Princeton University Press.

Gazda, Árpád. 2007. Tiszti vállalja a sorsát [Father Pál Shoulders His Fate]. *Kronika Online*, July 4. https://kronikaonline.ro/erdelyi-hirek/tiszti_vallalja_a_sorsat_/print. Accessed 2 Jan 2019.

Gondola.hu. 2007. Csíksomlyó ragaszkodik plébánosához [Csíksomlyó Sticks to Its Priest]. *Gondola.hu*, July 4. https://gondola.hu/cikkek/55093-Csiksomlyo_ragaszkodik_plebanosahoz.html. Accessed 2 Jan 2020.

Hanebrink, Paul. 2006. *In Defense of Christian Hungary: Religion, Nationalism, and Antisemitism, 1890–1944*. Ithaca: Cornell University Press.

Hann, Chris M. 1990. Socialism and King Stephen's Right Hand. *Religion in Communist Lands* 18 (1): 4–24.

Harris, Ruth. 1999. *Lourdes: Body and Spirit in the Secular Age.* New York: Viking.

Herzfeld, Michael. 1984. The Significance of the Insignificant: Blasphemy as Ideology. *JRAI* 19 (4): 653–664.

Kaufman, Suzanne. 2007. *Consuming Visions: Mass Culture and the Lourdes Shrine.* Ithaca: Cornell University Press.

Kligman, Gail. 1988. *The Wedding of the Dead: Ritual, Poetics, and Popular Culture in Transylvania.* Berkeley: University of California Press.

———. 1998. *The Politics of Duplicity: Controlling Reproduction in Ceausescu's Romania.* Berkeley: University of California Press.

Luehrmann, Sonja. 2011. *Secularism Soviet Style: Teaching Atheism and Religion in a Volga Republic.* Bloomington: Indiana University Press.

Makkay, József. 2016. Csíksomlyói árva csibészek [The Orphan Black Sheep of Csíksomlyó]. *Erdélyi Napló*, March 25. https://erdelyinaplo.ro/aktualis/riportok/csiksomlyoi-arva-csibeszek. Accessed 10 Jan 2019.

McManus, Frederick R. 1987. *Thirty Years of Liturgical Renewal: Statements of the Bishops' Committee on the Liturgy.* Washington, DC: United States Catholic Conference.

Muehlebach, Andrea. 2012. *The Moral Neoliberal: Welfare and Citizenship in Italy.* Chicago: The University of Chicago Press.

Nagy, István. 2014. Az elhivatottságot megtörni nem lehet...Életsorsok: Gergély István "Tiszti". [It's not possible to destroy a calling: Life and destinies: István Gergély "Tiszti."]. http://szjptk.iif.hu/toronyor/V_evf_4/tiszti.htm. Accessed 1 Dec 2021.

Orsi, Robert A. 1996. *Thank You, Saint Jude: Women's Devotion to the Patron Saint of Hopeless Causes.* New Haven: Yale University Press.

Pusztai, Bertalan. 2004. *Religious Tourists: Constructing Authentic Experiences in Late Modern Hungarian Catholicism.* Jyväskylä: University of Jyväskylä.

Rédai, Botond. 2011. Nem gyakorolhatja papi hivatását Gergely István [Father Pál Cannot Practice His Priestly Calling]. *Szekelyhon.ro*, April 19. https://szekely-hon.ro/aktualis/csikszek/nem-gyakorolhatja-papi-hivatasat-gergely-istvan. Accessed 2 Jan 2020.

Scherz, China. 2014. *Having People, Having Heart: Charity, Sustainable Development, and Problems of Dependence in Central Uganda.* Chicago: University of Chicago Press.

Seasoltz, Kevin. 1980. *New Liturgy, New Laws.* Collegeville: The Liturgical Press.

Székely János Pedagógus Társas Kör. 2014. Az elhivatottságot megtörni nem lehet...Életsorsok: Gergely István "Tiszti" [It's Impossible to Destroy a Calling...Lives and Destinies: Father Pál]. http://szjptk.iif.hu/toronyor/V_evf_4/tiszti.htm. Accessed 5 Jan 2020.

Taussig, Michael. 1999. *Defacement: Public Secrecy and the Labor of the Negative.* Stanford: Stanford University Press.

CHAPTER 7

Conclusion: A Challenge to Anthropologists of Christianity to Write for Christian Publications

In 2019, Pope Francis, head of the global Catholic Church, celebrated a Mass for half a million pilgrims at the Csíksomlyó pilgrimage site. People I met during my fieldwork, including Emil the village intellectual I described in Chap. 5, contacted me when the news broke early that year. In an email I received on January 29, 2019, he wrote that, "You can imagine. The entire Szekler Land is preparing to welcome the pope. Everyone is excited." The announcement thrilled Hungarians everywhere, but especially my acquaintances in the Transylvanian Hungarian community.

A month before I received this message about the pope's visit, Central European University (CEU) in Budapest announced that Hungary's right-wing government had forced it to relocate. Founded in 1991, CEU has offered affordable English-language higher education to students from more than 100 countries, including many Hungarians and Transylvanian Hungarians. I had been in residence in 2013 as a guest researcher in the Sociology and Social Anthropology Department. In a sped-up "emergency" legislative process, the government revoked the institution's ability to issue US-accredited degrees in Hungary. While CEU bent over backward to comply with the new law, Fidesz politicians approached these negotiations in bad faith. Finally, CEU's administration announced the university was moving most of its programs to Vienna, Austria.

© The Author(s), under exclusive license to Springer Nature   197
Switzerland AG 2022
M. R. Loustau, *Hungarian Catholic Intellectuals in Contemporary Romania*, Contemporary Anthropology of Religion,
https://Doi.org/10.1007/978-3-030-99221-7_7

I mourned this loss from Hungarian intellectual culture. I mourned even as I pursued my research about the slippages of meaning and miscommunications that destabilized Transylvanian Hungarians' collaborations with the Hungarian government, collaborations that ultimately tightened the latter's ideological control over the educational field. In the words of CEU philosophy professor Maria Kronfeldner, writing on the blog of the American Philosophical Association, "it is Hungarians who will pay the highest price." I felt whiplash reading statements like this right after receiving excited emails from Ciuc Valley acquaintances about the pope honoring all Hungarians with this upcoming visit.

In February, I reached out to *America: The Jesuit Review*, known as the primary voice of the US Catholic progressive intelligentsia. I had never pitched an editorial before, but the editors wrote back and invited me to write an article about the pope's visit to Csíksomlyó. I called it, "A message to Pope Francis: Be wary of right-wing populists when you visit Romania" (Loustau 2019). Sending a message to Pope Francis was a journalistic conceit. I had no pretensions he would read this article. Journalists write all the time as if they had the ear of a church leader about to make an important appearance, but really, they are informing their audiences—in my case, progressive American Catholics—about what's at stake in a speech. I wanted progressive American Catholics to read whatever news might come from the pope's visit with a discerning eye.

I guessed that *America*'s readers would have a vague sense that Hungary's government was right-wing and maybe that it had recently succeeding in ejecting CEU from the country; but most would not know that there is a Hungarian ethnic minority in Romania, much less that Hungary's right-wing has justified its rule as a way to defend the collective interests of the Transylvanian Hungarian ethnic minority. I wanted readers to know what the pope was risking and what he might accomplish with this visit, and how those with a stake in Hungarian politics might interpret his presence at Csíksomlyó. As has since become my habit when writing for popular Catholic publications, I highlighted internal dissent within the Hungarian Catholic Church.[1] In the article about the pope's visit, I raised awareness and urged support for Hungarian Catholics who have heeded the pope's call to provide radical hospitality for migrants and refugees as well as activism in defense of human rights for the marginalized.

In the years leading up to this piece in *America*, I had published several flagrantly heretical articles in academic journals—including pieces in Hungarian translation—and fielded no responses whatsoever from

Catholic Church officials. In one of these articles, for example, Catholic women and men talk about committing mortal sins like terminating pregnancies. They say flagrantly blasphemous things, like for example that the Virgin Mary helped them obtain these abortions. For a while, I worried that my academic research might upset Catholic officials. My fears were unfounded. I have yet to hear a peep about research articles that have appeared in academic journals from anyone in a position of authority in the Catholic Church.

In contrast, within two weeks of appearing on *America*'s website, "A Message to Pope Francis," was covered by journalists for secular and Catholic publications in Lithuania (Žiugždaitė 2019), Hungary (Lázár 2019), Romania (Dungaciu 2019), Italy (Giantin 2019; Grieco 2021), Brazil (Rabolini 2021), and France (Senèze 2019). The leader of Hungary's Jesuit Order, who was born in Miercurea Ciuc, criticized me in an open letter (Jezsuita.hu 2019). Hungary's Ambassador to the Holy See, Eduard Habsburg-Lothringen, pressured the Jesuit Order's headquarters in Rome to publish a reply, which appeared as a Letter to the Editor in *America*'s next issue (Habsburg-Lothringen 2019).

These were the more reasoned critiques of my article. On Facebook, Twitter, and Instagram, I heard from many right-wing commentators who speculated on the state of my soul, my political ideology, my national identity, and even my sexuality. Apparently, based on the images on my professional website, I also have demonic facial features. Other faculty at College of the Holy Cross regularly receive this type of public harassment—sometimes much worse—which is perhaps why my colleagues were understanding when they received emails slandering my research and academic publications. If I sound like I am exercising my privilege by making light of the online harassment I received, I assure readers that I did not have lighthearted conversations with my family when I received hate mail suggesting the writers had knowledge of my home address.

The members of the Csíksomlyó choir responded with angry and bewildered messages. The soprano named Emőke, who had praised intimate and calm liturgical participation in the choir's Tenth Anniversary Booklet, called the article, "Shameful and dirty!!!!!" Her husband wrote a lengthier note. He was not a singer but a familiar face at our performances, and had accompanied us on the Hungarian tour as a volunteer loading our luggage and equipment. He could have been Pál Péter Domokos, the interwar choir leader who had argued for an emotional over a linguistic basis of solidarity, when he wrote on my Facebook page (in English), "If you learn somebody's language, it's not enough to understand his feelings. Why do you think, that you learned Hungarian and lived in Szeklerland for a period, and now you are the big guru?"

I heard nothing from the men in the choir's bass section: The director Lajos, booklet editor Ferenc, or Attila, the man who had used his *bicska* Szekler pocketknife to turn the tour bus's air conditioning vent into a musical instrument. However, I did hear from a tenor, a middle-aged man who had been had too shy to speak to me during the years I spent in the choir. "I hope this isn't true," he wrote alongside a link to a far right-wing Hungarian political magazine that had covered my article. "If it is, then I hope that you never set foot in the Szekler Land again."

Father Pál did not offer any public comments, but his friend Father Albert emailed me with links to material that, so he hoped, would convince me to change my opinion about the Hungarian government's positions. I replied to express my gratitude for the tone of his message. He said he did not care about tone but rather that my opinion was seriously mistaken. He suggested that we should debate over email and then publish the correspondence in American and Hungarian Jesuit magazines. I recalled what my editor at *America* had said when he cut several paragraphs from my article: It is important to criticize right-wing positions, but the magazine was not interested in giving them publicity. I politely declined Father Albert's proposal.

Brother Csaba, who remains as savvy as ever about accessing right-wing and government-controlled media, was featured in a lot of the news coverage about Pope Francis's visit. The headline, "Brother Csaba will pray with Pope Francis," was featured on multiple media outlets, because government-controlled media outlets tend to repeat each other (Origo.hu 2019a, b). Father Pál was left out of the coverage of the pope's visit. However, a year later, he celebrated the reopening of his Black Sheep Foundation's headquarters after an extended renovation, which the Hungarian government had paid for. The gala ceremony featured speeches by Harghita County politicians and Hungarian government officials.

The Miercurea Ciuc mayor emphasized the precarious nature of ethnic minority's political institutions but praised the Hungarian state for its support. Despite efforts by Father Pál and Brother Csaba to turn touristic spiritual seekers into volunteers, the visiting Hungarian official, secretary for national politics Árpád János Potápi, urged his fellow Hungarian citizens to come to Transylvania because they can expect fairy-tale style magical experiences when they cross the border. "Transylvania is truly a magical garden," he said, "people shouldn't be fleeing this place but rather be coming here" (Korpos 2021).

Officials attached to Father Pál's Black Sheep Foundation continue to deny that he and Brother Csaba are rivals, although it is unclear if these statements disabuse the public or accomplish the opposite. In October 2019, the right-wing *Képmás Magazine,* a glossy publication "for readers who are committed to traditional, conservative family values," conducted an interview with Father Pál and one of his volunteers. The journalist prodded Father Pál to comment on the media coverage of the 25th anniversary of Brother Csaba's Saint Francis Foundation. To wit, "In the midst of gigantic media coverage, not to hear a single word about the Black Sheep Foundation."

The volunteer fielded the question. She seemed to echo the complaint of the former ward who, as I observed her asking Father Pál for help, had chided Brother Csaba for being too busy to answer her calls. "Brother Csaba has so many different kinds of orphanages, children, and teachers, while Father Pál wants everything to be close by because he likes to stay personally connected with everyone." She concluded by disagreeing with the interviewer's implication. "The two approaches fit well together and there is no competition" (Antal-Ferencz 2019).

After the 2016 American presidential election, which sent into office a right-wing and nationalist administration with ties to the Hungarian government, many anthropologists of Christianity who live and research in North America and Europe woke up to the reality that right-wing populism was growing in these areas. Some colleagues in the anthropology of Christianity, especially those who had spent time studying North American and European right-wing Catholic and Evangelical Christian communities, changed their research projects and veered off to study different regions and religious communities. They could not bear the disgust they felt that right-wing Catholics and Evangelical Christians—people they had come to know well—could feel such an affinity for authoritarianism.

Others remained to study the same right-wing Catholic and Evangelical Christian communities, but now took up the mantle of critique. Since 2016, I have read a number of academic books and articles unmasking the structures of power that grant right-wing Catholic and Evangelical Christian communities privileges that are not afforded to communities marginalized by virtue of their religion, race, class, ethnicity, sexual identity, gender, or immigration status. There has been an explosion of interest in critiquing Christian populist nationalism, justified because the typical anthropological approach to otherness—showing how people who are ostensibly different from us actually engage structures of power in much the same way as we do—has struck these colleagues as inadequate to meeting the right-wing challenge to open societies and democracy.

Based on my jarringly disparate experiences publishing in anthropology journals versus Christian magazines, I am skeptical of the stated goals of this new turn to critique among anthropologists of Christianity. I suspect that what I discovered is already widely known to anthropologists of Christianity, and how could it not be after decades of self-reflexive investigations about what anthropologists do and study: that the articles in anthropology journals and books in university presses reach only a small group of scholars. I also suspect that this audience of anthropologists is familiar with critical approaches to Christian populist nationalism.

Put bluntly, for exhortation's sake, why bother to criticize Christian populist nationalism in publications that everyday Christians and church leaders will not read? Do critical anthropologists of Christianity really want to change the minds of churches' decision-makers, raise Christians' awareness about moderate, progressive, radical, anarchist, and other voices, and more broadly change the public conversation in these institutions? If so, why have their complaints about Christian populist nationalism appeared in anthropology journals and not Christian magazines?

While several university-based research websites have emerged in recent years with the stated purpose of engaging a diverse audience and fostering fresh lines of conversation about the political influence of Christianity, I am also skeptical of such efforts to create new venues for this conversation when there is already a politically diverse and well-established world of Christian publishing that exists to serve this end. Perhaps the time and money that went into these websites would have been better spent training anthropologists about the existing landscape of Christian opinion journalism, and how to write effectively for Christian audiences. When I consider the stated goals of the critical anthropology of Christianity against its authors' decision to limit this critique to the pages of academic publications, it makes me wonder if anthropologists are either deluding themselves about convincing Christians of their critique or acting in bad faith.

I challenge anthropologists of Christianity to publish their research in Christian magazines that will reach readers in the countries where they teach and do research. I challenge anthropologists of Christianity to use these experiences in public scholarship to consider what they hope to accomplish with these projects, and what consequences they are willing to risk to their personal and professional lives by critiquing Christian populist nationalism. Have those anthropologists, so earnestly disturbed by right-wing Catholicism and Evangelical Christianity, received feedback from the people whom they thus critique? What professional and personal consequences have they suffered as a result of their critiques? Below, I have included a non-comprehensive list of English-language journals that reach Christian audiences. Until anthropologists actually publish their critique in journals that Christian church leaders will actually read and discuss, I will view the critique of Christian populist nationalism to be a riskless and solipsistic endeavor.

National Catholic Reporter
https://www.ncronline.org/
Commonweal
https://www.commonwealmagazine.org/
America: The Jesuit Review
https://www.americamagazine.org/
The Tablet
https://www.thetablet.co.uk/
The Catholic Herald
https://catholicherald.co.uk/
Sojourners
https://www.sojo.net
Christianity Today
https://www.christianitytoday.com/
The Christian Century
https://www.christiancentury.org/
Crux: Taking the Catholic Pulse
https://cruxnow.com/
Religion News Service
https://religionnews.com/
Religion Unplugged
https://religionunplugged.com/

NOTE

1. In subsequent articles, I have mentioned the Transylvanian Hungarian Roma pastoral ministry that has elevated Roma Catholic priests into positions of leadership in the Catholic Church (Loustau 2019). I have also highlighted the activism of Catholic theologian János Wildmann, who has opposed the Church hierarchy's silence in response to the Hungarian government's anti-LGBTQ policies (Loustau 2021).

REFERENCES

Antal-Ferencz, Ildikó. 2019. Tiszti, aki jövőt ad az árva csibészeknek. *Kepmas Magazin*, March 29. https://kepmas.hu/hu/tiszti-aki-jovot-ad-az-arva-csibeszeknek. Accessed 7 Jan 2019.

Dungaciu, Dan. 2019. Se va cânta imnul Ungariei la Şumuleu Ciuc? Dimensiunile vizitei Papei Francisc în România. *Histori.ro.* https://www.historia.ro/sectiune/general/articol/se-va-canta-imnul-ungariei-la-sumuleu-ciuc-dimensiunile-vizitei-papei-francisc-in-romania. Accessed 6 Jan 2021.

Giantin, Stefano. 2019. Il Papa in Romania con gli occhi puntati sulla comunità dei cattolici magiari. *Il Piccolo*, March 31. https://ilpiccolo.gelocal.it/trieste/cronaca/2019/05/31/news/il-papa-in-romania-con-gli-occhi-puntati-sulla-comunita-dei-cattolici-magiari-1.33209190. Accessed 6 Jan 2021.

Grieco, Marco. 2021. Le spaccature che complicano il viaggio del papa in Ungheria. *Domani*, September 8. https://www.editorialedomani.it/fatti/viaggio-papa-francesco-ungheria-budapest-viktor-orban-oml7fqmf. Accessed 7 Jan 2022.

Habsburg-Lothringen, Eduard. 2019. Francis in Romania. *America: The Jesuit Review*, May 17. https://www.americamagazine.org/faith/2019/05/17/letters. Accessed 7 Jan 2022.

Jezsuita.hu. 2019. A Magyar Jezsuiták Az America Magazin Cikkéről, May 22. https://jezsuita.hu/a-magyar-jezsuitak-ovatossagra-intik-a-ferenc-papa-csiksomlyoi-utjarol-cikkezo-america-magazint/?fbclid=IwAR0X_5x3nEkv6O5D0-cXgzEqQU8U1kDaa9SBDVMP9rPiKnneI5Ts4znsYvk. Accessed 7 Jan 2019.

Korpos, Attila. 2021. Átadták a magyar kormány támogatásával felújított csíksomlyói Fodor-házat, October 3. https://szekelyhon.ro/aktualis/atadtak-a-magyar-kormany-tamogatasaval-felujitott-csiksomlyoi-fodor-hazat. Accessed 7 Jan 2021.

Lázár, György. 2019. Hungary's Jesuits and Orbán's Attempt to Exploit Pope Francis's Visit to Romania. *Hungarianfreepress.com*, May 6. https://hungarianfreepress.com/2019/05/06/hungarys-jesuits-and-orbans-attempt-to-exploit-pope-franciss-visit-to-romania/. Accessed 6 Jan 2021.

Loustau, Marc R. 2019. A Message to Pope Francis: Be Wary of Right-Wing Populists When You Visit Romania. *America: The Jesuit Review*, April 19. https://www.americamagazine.org/politics-society/2019/04/19/message-pope-francis-be-wary-right-wing-populists-when-you-visit. Accessed 7 Jan 2021.

———. 2021. Belief Beyond the Bugbear: Propositional Theology and Intellectual Authority in a Transylvanian Catholic Ethnographic Memoir. *Ethnos: A Journal of Anthropology* 86 (3): 492–509.

Origo.hu. 2019a. "Böjte Csaba: Arra születtünk, hogy a szolgáló szeretet által az élet mellett döntsünk" ["Böjte Csaba: We Are Born to Stand on the Side of Life Through the Love of Service]. *Origo.hu*, September 6. https://www.origo.hu/itthon/20190906-bojte-csaba-arra-szulettunk-hogy-a-szolgalo-szeretet-altal-az-elet-mellett-dontsunk.html. Accessed 1 Dec 2019.

———. 2019b. Ferenc pápa és Böjte Csaba együtt imádkoznak Csíksomlyón, January 17. https://www.origo.hu/itthon/20190117-bojte-csaba-fogadja-ferenc-papat-csiksomlyon.html. Accessed 7 Jan 2022.

Rabolini, Luisa. 2021. As arestas que complicam a viagem do papa à Hungria. *Revista IHU On-Line*, September 10. https://www.ihu.unisinos.br/78-noticias/612737-as-arestas-que-complicam-a-viagem-do-papa-a-hungria. Accessed 7 Jan 2022.

Senèze, Nicolas. 2019. En Roumanie, le pape rejette toute vision nationaliste du christianisme. *La Croix*, June 1. https://www.la-croix.com/Religion/Catholicisme/Pape/En-Roumanie-pape-rejette-toute-vision-nationaliste-christianisme-2019-06-01-1201025992. Accessed 7 Jan 2022.

Žiugždaitė, Saulena. 2019. Išbandymas Rumunija: tarp manipuliacijų grėsmės ir ortodoksiškos žiemos. *Bernardinai*, May 30. https://www.bernardinai.lt/2019-05-30-isbandymas-rumunija-tarp-manipuliaciju-gresmes-ir-ortodoksiskos-ziemos/. Accessed 7 Jan 2022.

CHAPTER 8

Epilogue: Witnessing the Rosary's Voice

These are fieldnotes and a sermon about how I learned to pray the Rosary.
In both, I bear witness to the voice of Our Lady of Csíksomlyó. This epilogue takes up a challenge offered by anthropologist Michael Taussig to craft
an ethnographic account of divine presence, which in his view amounts to
bearing witness. But this ethnographic witness is necessarily a fugitive and
playful visual intervention. For Taussig, the embedded scientistic norms of
ethnographic journaling demand that bearing witness takes the shape of
amateurish drawings in his field notebook's margins. I too see, or rather
hear, Our Lady of Csíksomlyó's voice as a destabilizing and fugitive presence at the penumbra of my historically and culturally mediated perception.

During my fieldwork, I learned for the first time to pray the Rosary by
joining a weekly prayer group of middle-aged devotees who lived in my
urban neighborhood. These women took an evangelistic interest in this
prayer practice: praying the Rosary, they hoped, would help family members renew their faith. I suspect they taught me to pray the Rosary for a
similar reason. As I tuned my ear to the voice of the Rosary and allowed it
to reshape the muscles of my jaw and mouth, I came to understand that
the Rosary is polyvocal. The Rosary's voice sounds in, across, and between
my voice and the women's voices, as a way of giving voice to Our Lady of
Csíksomlyó for their family members. Simply put, I couldn't locate the
speaker. But this knowledge did not come right away. In the group, first I
used physical gyrations to search for a specific individual reciting the prayer

and then felt inner-ear vertigo when I could not. In these moments, the Rosary was reshaping and redisciplining my habitual aural and vocal practice, which had, up that point, been disciplined to insist that a voice should and does originate in a single individual. By writing about the Rosary, I bear witness to its in-between sound and the presence of Our Lady of Csíksomlyó within that ambiguous voice.

After groundbreaking historical research revealed that theology has played a significant role in shaping anthropology's theoretical terms and models (Larsen 2014), anthropologists have offered various characterizations of Christian intellectual reflection. Theology, in anthropologists' eyes, is an officializing discourse (Scott 2015), a cultural artifact (Chua 2015), a cosmology that permeates quotidian life (Du Boulay 2009; Carroll 2017), or a counter-hegemonic cultural resource (Antohin 2019).[1] Each of these anthropologists, in their own way, take theology to be an "ethnographic object" (Carroll 2017) deserving of anthropological study, a source of ethnographic data to be subjected to anthropological analysis to the end of contributing to anthropological understanding of Christian cultures.

But Timothy Carroll complicates these approaches that attempt to turn theology into an inert object to be subjected to anthropologists' study with a remark, in his essay "Theology as an Ethnographic Object: An Anthropology of Eastern Christian Rupture," that, "Christianity is, perchance, the most recursive subject (apart from Anthropology) for Anthropology to study" (2017: 5). Despite his title reference to theology being an ethnographic object, Carroll's observation that anthropology and theology are in some way recursively intertwined implies that this moment in the history of anthropology could turn out to be much more destabilizing than an effort to understand an object on anthropology's own terms.[2]

Carroll, like the others cited above, still imagines that anthropologists will benefit from dialogue with theologians by gaining greater self-awareness into anthropology's disciplinary history or the use of anthropology's theoretical and analytical tools.[3] However, before anthropological self-reflexivity reaches the abstract level of engagement with the discipline as a historical formation or the process of theory building and analysis, it is grounded in more primary modes of being with others like, for example, concrete encounters with subjects in the complex social situation of an ethnographic fieldsite. Likewise, before a reified and abstract construct called anthropology engages with an equally reified and abstract construct called theology, human beings who are anthropologists encounter human beings who are theologians in particular times and places. If, as Carroll notes, the theological-anthropological engagement is recursive, it is also recursive in an inescapably interpersonal mode. The anthropological engagement with theology is also an open-ended invitation for anthropologists to enter into the type of concrete and grounded encounters with theologians that are indeed generatively recursive and self-reflexive.

This seems to be one of the messages of Eloise Meneses and David Bronkema's edited collection, *On Knowing Humanity: Insights from Theology for Anthropology* (Meneses and Bronkema 2017). Meneses is an evangelical Christian; the volume's other authors also teach at her evangelical Christian college. This explains why a number of contributors use their chapters to witness about how their conversion experience of being reborn in Jesus Christ beneficially informs their anthropological research. While the volume is a welcome biographical intervention into anthropologists' abstract reflections on Christian theological concepts and anthropological theory, how Christian theology might offer themes, styles, motifs, and tropes to anthropologists' personal biographical narratives remains a question few anthropologists of Christianity have explored.

Joel Robbins, for example, wrote the conclusion to *On Knowing Humanity*, and he thanks the authors for inspiring him to follow their biographical reflections with his own. However, there is a befuddling disconnect between Robbins' response and the contributors' accounts. The latter are concerned with typical evangelical Christian conversion narrative fare like primary social experiences in natal families, wayward adolescences and young adulthoods, and spiritual rebirths after life and death encounters, but Robbins begins his story with his acceptance into graduate school and focuses almost entirely on describing the institutions that gave him his professional training as an anthropologist.

Writing in a volume so focused on being "born again," it is curious that Robbins should tell us nothing about his family of birth. In *Search for a Method*, Jean-Paul Sartre once noted a similar lacuna in the work of labor historians: "Today's Marxists," he wrote, "are concerned only with adults; reading them, one would believe that we are born at the age when we earn our first wages" (1963: 62). To paraphrase Sartre, reading anthropologists' attempts to engage theology in a personal and biographical self-reflexive mood, one would believe that they are born at the age when they earn their first graduate student stipend.

How can theology help anthropologists become self-aware in and through grounded ethnographic practice, which most especially includes, as Clifford and Marcus long ago pointed out, the practice of writing (Clifford and Marcus 1986)? Contributing to a journal Special Issue on

210 M. R. LOUSTAU

Anthropological Theologies: Engagements and Encounters, Malcolm Haddon provides an exciting departure point for such an inquiry by investigating the relationship between evangelistic discourse and ethnographic writing. When encountering a religious community dedicated to evangelizing toward conversion, Haddon argues, an ethnographic text can become subject to the proselytizer's discourse such that "[it] can actually speak through us and work its influence on readers through a textual/ ethnographic equivalent of 'speech mimesis'" (2013: 265). Speech mimesis is a concept that anthropologist Susan Harding used to explain how she came to speak about God's plans for her after listening to an American evangelical Protestant pastor's evangelistic testimony: "My language is powerless to resist this kind of transformation," is Haddon's gloss on Harding's experience (Haddon 2013: 265; Harding 2000, 2013: 266).

For all of Harding's influence on the anthropological study of evangelical Christians' testimonial practices, her commentary on the irresistible force of evangelizing discourse is also a fearful response to religious otherness. Evangelical language, in Harding's dreadful imaginary, is dangerous, violent, menacing, and overwhelming. Rather than prompting anthropologists to explore the experiential contradictions posed by doing fieldwork with evangelizing communities, talk about evangelizers' language often leads anthropologists to normalize the discipline's dominant secular Enlightenment imaginary that relies on an image of evangelical Christians as modernity's strange and antagonistic other.[4]

A more fruitful approach would be to treat the encounter with evangelizers as a refraction of the necessarily transformative experience of doing ethnographic fieldwork. Taussig says that this is why he felt compelled to bear witness to miracles in his fieldnotes. "The anthropologist is quintessentially a stranger in a foreign land," he writes,

asking for directions and, in the process, likely to be changed in some fundamental way. We could think of the great story in anthropology as how such a change is dealt with, whether it is recognized, and how it is acted upon in the rest of the anthropologist's life until death. (Taussig 2011: 144)

Evangelizing discourse's otherness is retained by shifting the transformative encounter into the existential domain of the anthropologist's life until death. It is certainly true that evangelizing language may change the ethnographic text independently of an anthropologist's intentions in a way that exceeds the norms and boundaries of biographical narration, but this only heightens anthropologists' need to address Taussig's questions. We might also become more self-aware about why anthropologists have been so compelled by alarmist warnings about a uniquely irresistible evangelizing discourse. Such warnings now appear as a way that anthropologists draw on secular Enlightenment discourses to act upon the transformative effect of doing fieldwork.

My strategy in this epilogue is twofold: First, I return to the primary experience of ethnographic writing: taking fieldnotes in a journal. I shift evangelizers' mimetic influence out of Haddon's alienated and atemporal domain in which textual logics seem to interact as disembodied objects by offering a meditation on my embodied voice as it is formed across multiple practices: reciting prayers, writing fieldnotes, and preaching sermons. That is, I explore how I grappled with the transformative effects of the Rosary *qua* evangelistic tool not only in my grounded ethnographic practice of field journaling but also in my homiletic practice of preaching sermons, which I was trained to do as a Unitarian Universalist seminary student in the mid-2000s.

Second, prayer, field journaling, and preaching all take shape in the temporal horizon formed first by concrete lived experience and only second by the dates on which I entered and left the field. This former existential dimension gestures back to Taussig's "life until death"; he writes that field journaling is a constant process of producing afterthoughts: writing, reading, adding to, and rereading the notes in one's notebook (Taussig 2011: 150).

In my field journaling, when I bore witness to the in-between voice of the Rosary, I wrote that the women in my group were ventriloquists. I remember laughing when I wrote this, amused by the idea that my prayer group friends were playing a joke on me by casting their voices around the circle. Taussig suggests that by embodying a playful attitude, anthropologists can bear witness and intervene in the authoritative modern scientistic discourse that defines the practice of field journaling. Field journaling, he writes, is a "type of modernist literature that crosses over into the science of social investigation" (2011: xi).

When it crosses over like this, scientism influences not only the objectivity of what is written by turning it into data, but also the subjectivity of the writer by productively disciplining the ethnographer to work. His drawings, in contrast, are fugitive witnesses to the presence of the divine, like the *ex-voto* pictures that Catholics hang in churches and that show the Virgin Mary performing miracles. "And that is how I regard drawings such as mine in my notebook," Taussig declares, "as play, to be contrasted with the text, which is work" (2011: 73).[5] Taussig claims that his own playful drawings likewise bear witness to divine presence and intervene in the middle-class and scientistic norms that make field journaling into work.

By comparing the Rosary's voice to a ventriloquist's joke, was I also playfully intervening in the scientism that shaped field journaling practice? Perhaps, but encountering divine presence as play is not the ahistorical intervention that Taussig implies. My very thought that this was a ventriloquistic joke reflected my own history—my formation in a North American tradition of using play to discipline divine presence.

According to Catholic historian Leigh Eric Schmidt, in the nineteenth century North American scholars of religion teamed with entrepreneurs of an emerging mass consumer culture to invent ventriloquism as a technology that disciplined the ear (1998: 273). Ventriloquists taught the masses how, through skill alone, individuals could cast their voices across rooms. I was also giving voice to nineteenth century North American consumer cultural entrepreneurs' attempts to productively discipline "popular Christianity's explosive vocality" and the moral dangers of the "protean malleability of personal identity" (1998: 274). My joke about ventriloquism not only bore witness to Our Lady of Csíksomlyó's voice but also testified to my own formation in this North American cultural history.

But times continue to change, and so also do the relationships that Protestants adopt toward Catholic practices like the Rosary that were once derided as unruly and explosive popular Christianity. In the contemporary urban North American cities where I grew up, many members of the European-descended white middle class who were once Catholic now attend Protestant churches, and Protestants are increasingly interested in the Rosary and other Catholic practices that they once derided.

In her research about American Christian pilgrims to the Holy Land, Hillary Kaell dramatizes this new state of affairs by describing Catholics who prepare for their trip with evangelical Protestant Bible study curricula (Kaell 2012: 137–8). Within these conditions, I synthesized Protestant practices of verbal witnessing with the Rosary's voice: I include a sermon that I preached about praying the Rosary in Transylvania to a Unitarian Universalist congregation in Boston, Massachusetts. This was one of Taussig's "back and forth" tacks with fieldnotes. And it was also a version of Taussig's "great story in anthropology" about how I grasped, sought acknowledgment of, and carried forward the change that the voice of the Rosary effected in my own.

Boston, MA, USA, January, 2022.

CSÍKSOMLYÓ, ROMANIA, SEPTEMBER 5, 2010

I was glad when Father Arthur opened the door to the monastery's library and raised his arm toward a table and two chairs for our interview. The shelves of books made for a quiet background, and I thought, "I won't have to listen to the same sentence five times in a row to make sense of it." Father Arthur also spoke slowly and clearly, which I appreciated, as he filled me in on his education, his ordination, and where he had served. He is doing doctoral research in biblical studies, something he called "source criticism." When we chatted, he was curious if I found it hard to have a conversation in Hungarian. Yes of course, I said, especially at parties or over dinner with multiple people talking at once.

I avoided the example of the Csíksomlyó sanctuary, though, where the echoes make priests' homilies sound like three separate speeches all at once. "It's easier to translate one-on-one interviews," I said, "because I can always tell who is speaking when I'm listening at home." Because I was interested in Csíksomlyó's recent history, he suggested I should come back tonight for the latest addition to the shrine's regular schedule of worship services. Some Franciscans had gone to the Lourdes shrine in France and seen the shrine's monthly candlelit evening procession. "They carry a brightly lit statue around, outside the main church," Arthur said, "so we will have a candlelit procession like it, just with people going behind a statue of the Virgin Mother of Csíksomlyó." He called the event a "Tribute to Mary," which I wrote down in my notes next to the name in Hungarian: Mária köszöntő.

I walked twenty minutes into the city to my apartment for dinner, before returning on foot again for the service. Coming back, I heard another layer of noise over the traffic passing me by: an amplified broadcast coming from the shrine. What was a vague and sibilant undertone resolved into words when I followed the bend in the road to see the Csíksomlyó church and, facing the big wooden doors, the square grassy park where I expected we would be parading with Mary's statue.

But still, I couldn't recognize the text, which began with "Mary" but had some other terms I didn't know and a strange version of the phrase "with you." Three buses that had passed me by from the city were stopped one after the other on the road, directly under the megaphones carrying the broadcast. The sound was directed back from where we came, as if the buses had been following a trail of sound to the site. The last bus's door opened just as I walked past, and I turned around when I heard voices reciting along with the megaphones from inside.

The first four women off took the final step to the sidewalk stiffly, holding onto the door for safety and reaching back to help the next companion down. The middle-aged women had short hair-dos, dark blouses, and slacks; a few elderly companions were in peasant-style flower-print headscarves and skirts. Besides purses, each woman paused to take hold of a low portable chair made of wooden slats that they slung against their thighs as they walked across the church's cobbled esplanade. I followed them to the church's three doors, dark and open to the summer evening air. I stopped for a moment to one side with my shoulder brushing the rough mortar of the exterior wall. The sunshine made it difficult to see inside. From here, the interior sound now overshadowed the loudspeakers. Especially when the woman speaking over the megaphone stopped for a moment, it became a garbled background noise of hundreds of female voices reciting together.

I pushed off the wall with my elbow and into the stream of women entering the church, following one group to the right and down the aisle. They stopped when they put their wooden folding chairs down on the stone floor in front of a side altar. As they set their purses underneath and got comfortable, I rested my hand on the low wooden platform in front of the altar and lowered myself to a sitting position. I didn't want to nudge the platform or shake the women kneeling at the altar, about a foot away from me. I settled in by tucking my backpack under my legs. A passerby's foot nudged my boot, and I whispered, "excuse me," while I pulled my shoes all the way back against the platform edge.

I glanced around to get my bearings—the sidelong view of the pews was different, showing the profiles of women's faces not the backs of their heads. I turned my head to the right and saw the main altar, brightly lit but empty. How long until the priests would come out for Mass? I reached into my pocket for my cell phone to check the time, but stopped at a longer pause in the broadcast.

Another woman took over leading the recitation. But I couldn't pinpoint where the new woman was sitting. I leaned out into the aisle and craned my chin around to see this side of the church, and then strained the position a bit further to see all the way to the back. I tipped my neck back to see the balcony, but the seats were mostly empty. I shoved my weight onto my feet for a moment to see across to the other side. I couldn't get high enough off the ground, so I rocked back even further. I felt the platform shift under me as I pitched myself forward. When I turned around, the woman kneeling at the altar was shaking her head at me. So was a woman on a folding stool to my right, who had noticed my gyrations. I felt embarrassed and judged: Too much curiosity, not enough piety. I gave up on pinpointing the voices and just listened for a while. The first thing I noticed was that the text was repeating. I also finally caught the start of one phrase and kept track of it until the end. I press my thumb against the tip of my index finger to mark the first iteration, thumb and middle finger for the second, and so on. I finished the fingers on one hand, and then through the next until I reach ten. Shaking my head and smiled down at the floor with surprise and exasperation, I remembered that Catholics pray a "decade" of the Rosary. Ten parts. "Did I just learn to pray the Rosary?" I asked myself, before reciting with the crowd, in Hungarian, *Üdvözlégy Mária…*

MIERCUREA CIUC, ROMANIA, NOVEMBER 1, 2010

Crossing the street to Anikó's apartment building, I squeezed onto the sidewalk through two cheek-to-jowl parked cars. I didn't want to take my hands out of my winter coat pockets; it was so cold. I slid my finger down the transparent plastic that shielded the list of Anikó's neighbors, a print-out of last names, apartment numbers, and doorbell buttons. Hungarian last names, mostly, but there was also an "I. Pop" on the sixth floor. Does Miercurea Ciuc have a district where its twenty percent Romanian popula-tion tends to live, I wondered? Or does every Hungarian have one or two Romanian neighbors? I considered asking Anikó as I found her name and heard the doorbell through the speaker. The sound was an artificial two-tone mix between an emergency siren and donkey's bray. If neon were a noise, I thought, this is how it would sound.

My hand stung so much from the cold that I let the buzzer go for barely a second before pulling on the white plastic handle. Inside, I turned right and up the slick concrete stairs, my hand on the metal handrail that vibrated with my footsteps. I pictured pulling the rail with both arms until the spindly attachments popped from the concrete. Would the noise make the neighbors open their doors, I wondered, or would they just call the police? Maybe it would take hours for the damage to be discovered. A naked lightbulb flicked on when I reached the landing for Anikó's floor, which I recognized for its sole decoration: an unframed collage of pictures of Catholic saints, Pope John Paul II, and Roman scenes, taped to each on cardboard backing. This was one more collage than my building across the street had, so the last time I had come I had asked Anikó about it.

"There are all kinds of people in the building," she had explained. "Sometimes we have the prayer group in my neighbor's apartment, and she's a Protestant."

"Do you want them to become Catholic?" I asked.

"The pictures are there just in case someone might need some help someday, so the person can know they can turn to God."

"How long have they been up on the wall?"

"Oh, I don't know, maybe ten years? That's a miracle, too, that they've lasted so long and no one has done anything to them."

I had just a moment to look again at the collage. I heard Anikó's door open to my left and then her half-whisper, "Marc, come in, come in." We kissed cheeks before she took the collar of my coat and helped me tug it off. I peeked through another open door into the living room where several other women were already seated on a plush mottled gray and black couch. Anikó answered my unasked question, "We haven't started yet," as she hung my coat above a slotted wooden stool, folded and leaning against the wall.

I found a spot opposite the women on a dining room chair with a velvety gold seat. Three more women came in together, one leading her seven-year old granddaughter by hand to a spot on the couch. The blind woman came in with her downstairs neighbor.

"I was the one who invited her first," Anikó had whispered proudly after last week's meeting.

Anikó took two steps across the circle, holding a wooden box with the Rosary I had used last time. She smiled when I responded by pulling the string of black beads from my pants pocket. I dangled the Rosary above my open palm. Lowering it slowly, I felt it pour gently into a curled pile. While Anikó left to answer the doorbell again, I balled up the beads into a loose fist and shook it gently. I did this sometimes with my keys, and the Rosary rattled against my fingers like a lighter and smoother version. Twenty minutes later, we were halfway through and I had hold of the end of the circle furthest from the crucifix, which I had left draped across my upper thigh. My attention wandered off the beads in my fingers to the words. But not the meaning of what we were saying.

I started paying attention to the way the prayer took a shape in my mouth, to my lips, jaw, and palate as I recited. It felt like I was relinquishing to the length of the first vowel, "a," in Mary. Mária, in Hungarian, pulled my tongue down, into a hollow formed as the word expanded and my bottom jaw circled down, back, and then out again. The "a" inflated, and then some more. The difference was perceptible, to my feeling, as I said over and over again "Máááária." But it wasn't as if I was exaggerating or parodying. I was still praying *with* the other women.

And starting then, after giving myself over the shape of this word, I began to feel a little dazed. Because Anikó was whispering the Rosary so perfectly in tune with her neighbor, I lost her voice. "Why is Anikó speaking with the other woman's voice," I wondered. I smiled at the thought that she had thrown it and cast it around the circle somehow. Like there was one voice, a detachable thing, getting passed around the Rosary circle.

When I began shifting my eyes back and forth between the women's lips, from right to left and back again, the effort brought a broad and gentle vertigo. For the next thirty seconds, as long as I could manage it, I kept my head and eyes swiveling to pin down the voice's source amid the distinctly uncomfortable spin that shifted not just the circle of women but the darkness, too, when I closed my eyes. Ten minutes later, I was holding onto the final beads in my Rosary while the crucifix bobbed against my pinky finger. With an audible sigh, Anikó finished and put her Rosary back in its box.

I slipped mine into my pocket as the woman next to me got up to retrieve the three Bibles stacked on the dining room table. Anikó said that the text was from Paul's Letter to the Romans. I was still flipping toward the back of my black, faux-leather bound mini-Bible when Anikó began reading. We patiently followed in our Bibles until Anikó began reading, "Likewise the Spirit helps us in our weakness; for we do not know how to pray as we ought, but that very Spirit intercedes with prayers too deep for words." Anikó pursed her lips when the blind woman's neighbor interrupted.

"Mine doesn't have 'to pray,'" she reported, "Read it again, Anikó, please?" Anikó repeated the sentence.

"In this version," she reported, holding up her Bible, "it says 'sighs unable to be poured into words.' Are there any other translations?"

Everyone else demurred at Anikó's strained expression. "Either way is fine," Anikó finally broke in before continuing on with her reading.

Anikó's husband, Csaba, opened the glass-paned door into the bedroom after she had stacked up the Bibles. He pulled his head out again and returned with a tray of glasses. Another trip out and he had a green sparkling water bottle and transparent plastic jug full of red wine. He took a chair next to me, the only other man in the group, while the other women poured the water and, more sparingly, the wine.

"Marc," the blind woman asked, "are you Catholic?" I smiled, shy from the sudden attention. I was relieved when Anikó answered for me.

"No," she grinned and pitched her voice a half-octave up, "but he will be." I laughed at the audacity, softened by the smile and winsome tone. "He will be," Anikó said again.

BOSTON, MA, USA, JUNE 23, 2017

"Sea Snakes and Rosaries," Sermon for King's Chapel Sunday Worship by Dr. Marc Roscoe Loustau

The American writer Mark Twain once quipped that, "In New York City, they ask, 'How much money does he have?' But in Boston they ask, 'How much does he know?'" With 45 colleges and universities near our city, Twain hits Boston's intellectual culture on the nose. But he has a deeper message for us. We might agree that it's foolish to be proud of money, but we need to be reminded that neither will knowledge make us virtuous of its own accord. Quite the opposite, visiting a library may just leave us free to engage in that peculiarly contemporary expression of pride: the book recommendation.

I have been known to make this mistake, saying to one friend, "Oh, you should really read this new book about spiritual parenting," even when I knew she had three young children and barely time to bathe. Knowledge, when overlaid on self-absorption, does not necessarily enhance our compassion; it can actually make it harder to see what another person truly needs.

Pride goes before a fall, so the saying goes; and Twain was right that we often think of a person's undoing in financial terms. But knowledge, just as much as money, can lead us to become arrogant. This is the lesson of the old seafarers' yarn, the Legend of the Flying Dutchman, who, so the story goes, was a real-life Dutch sea captain in the early 1800s. He was so clever a navigator that over the years he survived the worst storms. Knowledge of the seas brought confidence and pugnacity in equal measure; he sailed routes no other captain dared contemplate, not to ensure swift passage and earn greater profit but simply for the sport of it.

One day in a portside bar, the captain boasted that he would never back down from any weather should he have to stay on the waves for all time. The Devil promptly called his bluff, damning the Flying Dutchman to wander 'til Judgement Day'. A classic tale of hubris and comeuppance, the

Legend of the Flying Dutchman imparts an important lesson. Pride does indeed go before the fall, for the brightest as for the wealthiest.

I can't hold a candle to the Flying Dutchman for epic globetrotting, but since the last time I was in this pulpit, I have spent a good three years overseas. In 2006, I enrolled in a doctorate program where I learned how to do archival research. Then I departed for Transylvania, a region of Eastern Europe that is today part of Romania. Earlier in the 19th century, Transylvania was part of neighboring Hungary. Transylvania still has small ethnic enclaves where people speak Hungarian. I moved there in 2009 to learn Hungarian and study old sermons in basement church archives.

Every time I thumped my heavy Hungarian-English dictionary down in one of these archives, it felt like a thrill and a challenge. Month by month, my Hungarian got better and I understood more. The first time I read a sermon all the way through without flipping around in my diction-ary, I felt such a rush that I wrote an email to a graduate student colleague about my success.

Later that same week, I ran into one of my Transylvanian neighbors in my four-story apartment building. I had introduced myself to this retirement-age woman the day I moved in. Now she invited me to a prayer group she was hosting that evening. Once a week, she explained, women in the building got together for an hour to pray the Rosary.

"Would you like to come?" she asked.

"I need to translate a sermon," I replied, thinking of my recent success in the archive.

The Rosary is a very old prayer; the words date back to the 1200s. The text honors Mary, mother of Jesus, and begins, "Hail Mary, full of grace, the Lord is with thee." You pray the Rosary by saying the same paragraph over and over again, keeping track of the number of times on a string of beads, which is also called a Rosary.

The Rosary is old, but to some it also feels old-fashioned. Unfortunately, today rote memorized prayer has taken a backseat to having a conversation with God. Many folks today want a more dynamic prayer experience. We prefer the give and take of having a dialogue with God to reciting the same words over and over again.

This is true of both Transylvania and the US. I learned the Rosary from a group of retired women; younger Catholics in Transylvania think of the Rosary as something for retirees. Here in the US, a Catholic friend, a pro-fessor at a nearby university, recently told me that her ten-year-old daugh-ter's Sunday school teachers don't teach the Rosary anymore. She worried to me that young American Catholics might forget about the Rosary entirely. At the end of our conversation, my friend joked wryly that that if her daughter is ever likely to get a string of Rosary beads, she will probably buy them on eBay because a stranger wants to clean out his grandmother's attic.

Growing up a Unitarian Universalist, I had never prayed the Rosary before; it was new to me. I said yes to my neighbor next invitation, but I have to admit I quickly got bored. After a month, I stopped going to her prayer group. Afterwards, I patted myself on the back for being polite to my neighbors, but in reality I was more than a little arrogant. My arrogance gave me all the seemingly good excuses I made for dropping out: I was a Unitarian Universalist; the Catholic Rosary wasn't part of my tradition. I didn't come to Transylvania to study the Rosary. I preferred to pray by having a conversation with God. Once I learned what the Hungarian text meant in English, it didn't offer the kind of intellectual challenge that I could write home about. My pride was just as evident in what I said to convince myself praying the Rosary wasn't worth my time.

In the spring of 2014, about a year after I returned to Boston from Transylvania, I came down with a stomach flu. After I recovered, I still had a mild headache. So I stopped by my doctor's office. I didn't think much of it. In fact, I brought an overdue book to the appointment. My doctor's office was across the street from a library and I figured I could pop over.

The headache turned out to be something quite serious, an injury to my carotid artery. I landed in a hospital emergency ward, where a white-coated young man explained that with an injury like this, I could develop a clot in my artery.

The clot could go to your brain, he explained.

That could cause a stroke, he said.

To which I joked, "I guess I won't have time to return my book, then."

The doctor didn't laugh. He ordered an MRI, pointed me to a gurney to lie down on and a nurse who would push me there. When I got on the bed, I was still carrying my book.

"You're going to have to leave this," he explained and took the book out of my hand.

As the nurse wheeled me out into the maze of hallways, lying on the gurney I began repeating to myself, "They took away my book." That's all I could manage to say: "They took away my book." Over and over again.

I wasn't attached to that particular book. I can't even remember the title, although I remember having it open in my hands with my eyes trained on the page through the ambulance ride. The book was a symbol; the book was my knowledge. When the doctor took it away from me, I feared it was a presentiment. With a stroke and an injury to my brain, fate might take away my knowledge, my learning, my mind.

Looking at the book had been a welcome distraction from what was happening to me. In fact, this wasn't a one-off gesture; it was a habit. I had made a routine, not just in graduate school but before as well, of keeping my eyes trained on my books. Really, I had kept myself distracted. I had kept myself from seeing me for what I truly was. But in the hospital, I saw I was a mortal being, eventually destined to lose not only my mind, but my life.

I don't think I ever had my knowledge to begin with. If it wasn't this injury, even if this turned out to be nothing and I walked away from the hospital and back to my collection of Hungarian sermons, then simply the passing of time would render my accomplishments passé. Like a popular song that next year sounds shrill, or a bestseller whose style now reads overwrought.

Then, in the longer timeframe in which civilizations rise and fall, inevitably a hefty dissertation, an even heavier book, whatever the scholarly accomplishment, is destined to become dust scattered by the lightest breeze. I realized that, along with my life, my mind, which I thought had given my life meaning, could be taken away as easily as the doctor had taken my book.

As the nurse pushed my gurney forward, I was so terrified I was ready to make a run for it. I had no idea where I was in the hospital maze. Screw the clots, I thought, and I started looking for exit signs. Finally, the nurse stopped in an empty, nondescript hallway. She slid the gurney against a wall, and without a word walked away.

What ensued was a proverbial dark night of the soul, but in this case it was neon lit in a hospital hallway. Alone, without even a book to look at, I had only myself to see. I tried to pray, to have a conversation with God, but I was too afraid to speak. It seemed like I'd lost my ability to pray, and felt like God had wandered away like my nurse. I was in a hospital full of people, but I was as lonely as I've ever been.

Then, although I couldn't pray, I began praying – that is, I began praying the Rosary. I found myself repeating, "Hail Mary, mother of God, the Lord is with thee." And what was even more surprising, the words were in Hungarian, because after all the only time I had never prayed the Rosary was in Transylvania. I didn't say, "Hail Mary," but rather, "Üdvözlégy Mária.

As I recited these words, my fear didn't disappear, but I felt something else besides loneliness: resolve. I had no more thoughts of running for the exit as I reached the final words of the prayer. In Hungarian, "Imádkozzál érettünk, bűnösökért, most és halálunk óráján." "Pray for us, sinners, now and at the hour of our death." I pulled myself to a sitting position on the gurney, and squared my back against the wall. Whatever this experience might bring, I was going to meet it with my head up and eyes open.

In another seafarer's legend, Samuel Taylor Coleridge's "Rime of the Ancient Mariner," another prideful navigator suffers a fall. He shoots an albatross, a beautiful sea bird, for no other reason than to impress his crew with his marksmanship. Suddenly, the winds disappear and his ship is becalmed under a blasting sun, which inspired Coleridge's famous words: "Water, water, everywhere, Nor any drop to drink." In their final act before dying of thirst, the crew makes the captain bear the sign of his sin: "Instead of the cross," the captain recalls, "the Albatross/About my neck was hung."

The mariner sails on, languishing without hope, overwhelmed by his guilt. His soul is in agony. He cannot even pray. In his suffering, he is just as self-absorbed as before, only now instead of his cleverness, he is blinded by his ugliness, which mirrors the ugliness he sees in the world around him. "And a thousand thousand slimy things/Lived on," the mariner recalls, "and so did I."

Then, one day, he notices a school of water snakes swimming in the sun at the bow of his ship. They are just as slimy as the rest. The mariner confesses that no one would be inclined to call them lovely. Yet, without thinking, he remarks at the beauty of these humble creatures. At this moment, the albatross falls from the mariner's neck, and his journey begins anew. His shipmates return to life. The wind blows out their sails. And eventually they glide back into their home port, where the crew are happily raised into heaven.

Coleridge's tale reveals a profound psychological truth about pride's persistence. Pride goes before the fall, but its effects linger; pride can prevent us from being truly humble even after we've been humbled. After his condemnation, the Ancient Mariner was just as self-absorbed, only now the world's ugliness was a reflection of his all-encompassing awareness of his own. After fate had humbled me, I too was just as self-absorbed as before, only now I was terrified by the impermanence of the accomplishments that had given my life meaning. The ancient mariner in his boat on the ocean, me on my gurney in the hospital hallway, we were equally alone; but infinitely worse, we were trapped in ourselves.

The Ancient Mariner, in the end, is saved from himself, and the key that unlocks his heart and his salvation reveals a deep theological truth, one of the great paradoxes of Christian faith: Whatever it is that pride leads us to dismiss, God will use to save us. The sea snakes save the Ancient Mariner because out of a vision of his own ugliness, God makes something beautiful; God saves us from ourselves, yes, but with our own selves too.

At this point, the skeptical minds among us might be thinking, surely we're not talking about the same kind of sin. On the one hand, there is the captain cruelly taking the life of a beautiful bird just to show off. On the other hand, what harm is there in saying the Rosary is old-fashioned, not part of my tradition, or doesn't feel right for me?

Yet this is an act of pride, too. Pride finds different ways to express itself today than in Coleridge's time. Among Coleridge's beauty-obsessed contemporaries, who lived by the axiom penned by the fellow Romantic poet John Keats, "beauty is truth, truth beauty," to call something slimy was the most sneering of insults. Today, American Catholics do not dismiss the Rosary because the words are ugly. In our contemporary consumerist society, where so many take pride in discovering the latest trend and being up-to-date on the newest fad, the greater insult is to call something old-fashioned. I am not Catholic, but I had my own prideful reasons to dismiss the Rosary. I thought it was not worth my time, the text so simple it paled in comparison to the complex ideas I found in my archives of sermons.

In the end, the Ancient Mariner is saved from his self-absorption, and eventually returned home and to God, by seeing the beauty in all God's creatures. Coleridge has the Ancient Mariner recall how, at the moment he praises the lowly sea snakes, "A spring of love gushed from my heart/ And I blessed them unaware." To bless all God's creatures, great and small – another famous line from Coleridge's poem – is to love God's creatures, and only by loving others can we be saved from our self-absorption.

In the hospital hallway, I learned to bless Mary and the powerful, world-changing, history-making life she led as part of God's plan. For me, this is the meaning of the Rosary's words, "The Lord is with thee." By reciting the Rosary, I blessed Mary. A spontaneous expression of praise for this human being, so determined and strong in God's plan, opened my heart, pierced my self-absorption, and helped me to be determined as well.

In the end, I got lucky, and the MRI came back negative. No clot, no stroke. One year later, I turned in my dissertation. And today I teach at one of those 45 colleges and universities in the Boston area. My life goes on much as it did before that dark night of the soul in the emergency ward hallway, and when I stroll into a classroom five days a week, I look like so many other teachers and professors who make Boston an interesting place to live.

Pride goes before the dark night of the soul. I am willing to bet that no matter where you work – a classroom, cubicle, emergency ward, or simply your home office – each of us will have a dark night some time in their lives. Still, I cannot know what object of pride fate will take from our hands in that moment. For me, a professor, I nearly lost my knowledge, my mind. For you, it may be, like Mark Twain said, your money; the dark night of the soul may begin when your stock portfolio's graphline threatens to become a flatline.

Or the object of your pride could seem far nobler. If you are a social justice advocate, the object of your pride may be knowing the best community organizing strategy. As you tell a friend about the latest book riffing on Saul Alinsky or Paolo Freire, perhaps like me, you may not be seeing what she really needs is an offer to babysit a few hours one night this week. Pride is so insidious because it can hide even in the noblest pursuits that we truly believe make life better.

Even when we don't feel especially lost – when our life looks like it's going to plan – dark nights of the soul can reveal deeper truths. What looks like a purposeful life quest can actually be purposeless drifting: back and forth, day in day out from birth to death. Minding our own business, risking nothing, we spend years grinding our tires bald on familiar highways, always finding good excuses to speed past exit signs. For this reason, life crises offer a promise that the happiness of a list of checked-off accomplishments, no matter how long, can't equal. And then, with something we've already dismissed a thousand times over, with the least likely of blessings, God might just fulfill that promise of an open, humble, and determined heart.

MIERCUREA CIUC, ROMANIA, JULY 12, 2016

I went to see Anikó today. It was nostalgic and strange to walk up the stairwell in her apartment building. The bannister rattled with the same dull vibration, ticking through my forearm. Anikó put my coat on the wooden peg before ushering me into the kitchen for coffee. I asked about the women in our Rosary prayer group. She shared news about births, marriages, and trips abroad. I filled a pause after a report about one woman's recent eye procedure:

"I also ended up in the hospital."

"Oh, no," she exhaled.

I retold the story from the sermon, from the stomach flu to the ambulance and then the empty hospital hallway. She exhaled a mix of amazement and pleasure at crucial moments.

When it felt like my body was praying, "My God, it's like that for you, too."

When I prayed the Rosary, "Because it's the strongest prayer."

And at praying in Hungarian, "Our Lady of Csíksomlyó, you were praying to her!"

Her longest response came after I was done. "That's a powerful testimony," she declared, "Indeed. Amazing. And so you were able to calm down, then, right?" And then began her own story.

"You know, Marc, my husband Csabi, he had just this kind of big conversion. You know that he was never big on going to church. Until recently, he never went once to Mass. He said he couldn't pray. Not at all. He's not big on praying, not even now."

The statement that Csabi had converted left me a little confused, but I kept smiling: Anikó's husband, Csaba, was a born and baptized Catholic. He had started praying not changed faiths, even though Anikó used the word for "conversion" (*megtérés*). My story wasn't about switching faiths, either. But as she went on, I kept smiling because her joy was infectious, and because she had had so much praise for my story.

"But nowadays, you know, he started a new job driving a truck. And when he came home from a trip, he went to Csíksomlyó, to the Virgin Mother. I asked him, 'Did you go out to the Virgin Mother?' He said, 'Yes.' He told me that he had read the prayers that are written on a placard right next to the statue, and he said he read it aloud."

Anikó didn't need to give a full description of this placard; I could picture it perfectly from the hundreds of hours I had spent at the Our Lady of Csíksomlyó shrine. It was a printed text of the Rosary in three languages: Hungarian, German, and Romanian. The font is old-fashioned and blue, almost like it came from an oversized typewriter. The prayers are set under glass and edged with a narrow, gold painted wooden frame. "Why isn't it hung up somewhere to see," I remember thinking the first time I saw it, on the ground and leaning against the base of the statue of Our Lady of Csíksomlyó. "And then," Anikó continued, "he asked for help in his words, too. Because you know, Marc, one can pray beautifully in one's own words. Because your spirit is praying. The spirit is praying. He also converted, very much so, he converted."

NOTES

1. For these historical studies, see Robbins 2013; Asad 1993; Bloch 2002; and Cannell 2006a, b; Davies 2002.
2. Christian theologians are, after all, nothing more than Christian intellectuals, and as Zygmunt Bauman has observed, the chief certainty of any anthropological engagement with intellectuals is the relationality of the knowledge thereby produced (Bauman 1987: 8).
3. See Cannell 2005: 8. See also Carroll's exhortation that, "If, however, the discipline [of anthropology] is willing to critique its own analytical tools in the face of a new Other (e.g., modes of religiosity) and incorporate new analytical tools offered by the Other (e.g., kenosis), then the discipline may move forward" (2017: 9).
4. Harding herself offers this analysis in an essay published ten years before her book on conservative evangelical Protestants. See Harding 1991.
5. Scientism leaves room for anthropologists to bear witness only in unserious and playful forms of representation: "Such drawings have no place in the anthropologists' canon," Taussig writes (2011: 73).

REFERENCES

Antohin, Alexandra. 2019. Preserving the Intangible: Orthodox Christian Approaches to Spiritual Heritage. *Religions* 10 (5): 336–348.

Asad, Talal. 1993. The Construction of Religion as an Anthropological Category. In *Genealogies of Religion: Discipline and Reasons of Power in Christianity and Islam*, 27–54. Baltimore: Johns Hopkins University Press.

Bauman, Zygmunt. 1987. *Legislators and Interpreters: On Modernity, Post-Modernity and Intellectuals*. Cambridge: Polity Press.

Bloch, Maurice. 2002. Are Religious Beliefs Counterintuitive? In *Radical Interpretation in Religion*, ed. Nancy Frankenberry. Cambridge: Cambridge University Press.

Cannell, Fenella, ed. 2006a. *Anthropology of Christianity*. Durham: Duke University Press.

————. 2006b. The Christianity of Anthropology. *Journal of the Royal Anthropological Institute* 11 (2): 335–356.

Carroll, Timothy. 2017. Theology as an Ethnographic Object: An Anthropology of Eastern Christian Rupture. *Religions* 8 (7): 114–132.

Chua, Liana. 2015. Horizontal and vertical relations: Interrogating "in/dividualism" among Christian Bidayuhs. *Hau: Journal of Ethnographic Theory* 5 (1): 339–35.

Davies, Douglas. 2002. *Anthropology and Theology*. Oxford: Berg.

Du Boulay, Juliet, 2009. *Cosmos, Life, and Liturgy in a Greek Orthodox Village*. Athens: Denise Harvey.

Haddon, Malcolm. 2013. Anthropological Proselytism: Reflexive Questions for a Hare Krishna Ethnography. *The Australian Journal for Anthropology* 24 (3): 250–269.

Harding, Susan. 1991. Representing Fundamentalism: The Problem of the Repugnant Cultural Other. *Social Research* 58 (2): 373–393.

————. 2000. *The Book of Jerry Falwell: Fundamentalist Language and Politics*. Princeton: Princeton University Press.

Kaell, Hillary. 2012. Of gifts and grandchildren: American Holy Land souvenirs. *Journal of Mate- rial Culture* 17 (2): 133–51.

Larsen, Timothy. 2014. *The Slain God: Anthropologists and the Christian Faith*. Oxford: Oxford University Press.

Meneses, Eloise and David Bronkema, eds. 2017. *On Knowing Humanity: Insights from Theology for Anthropology*. New York: Routledge.

Robbins, Joel. 2013. Afterword: Let's keep it awkward: Anthropology, theology, and otherness. *The Australian Journal of Anthropology* 24 (3): 329–337.

Scott, Michael W. 2015. Cosmogony Today: Counter-Cosmogony, Perspectivism, and the Return of Anti-Biblical Polemic. *Religion and Society: Advances in Research* 6 (1): 44–61.

Taussig, Michael. 2011. *I Swear I Saw This. Drawings in Fieldwork Notebooks, Namely My Own*. Chicago: University of Chicago Press.

References

Abrahms-Kavunenko, Saskia. 2012. Religious 'Revival' After Socialism? Eclecticism and Globalisation Amongst Lay Buddhists in Ulaanbaatar. *Inner Asia* 14 (2): 279–297.

———. 2015. The Blossoming of Ignorance: Uncertainty, Power and Syncretism Amongst Mongolian Buddhists. *Ethnos* 80 (3): 346–363.

Ádám, Zoltán and András Bozóki. 2016. State and Faith: Right-wing Populism and Nationalized Religion in Hungary. *Intersections: East European Journal of Society and Politics* 2 (1): 98–122.

Anghel, Roxana, Maria Herczog, and Gabriela Dima. 2013. The Challenge of Reforming Child Protection in Eastern Europe: The Cases of Hungary and Romania. *Psychosocial Intervention* 22: 239–249.

Antal-Ferencz, Ildikó. 2019. Tiszti, aki jövőt ad az árva csibészeknek. *Kepmas Magazin*, March 29. https://kepmas.hu/hu/tiszti-aki-jovot-ad-az-arva-csibeszeknek. Accessed 7 Jan 2019.

Antohin, Alexandra. 2019. Preserving the Intangible: Orthodox Christian Approaches to Spiritual Heritage. *Religions* 10 (5): 336–348.

Apolito, Paolo. 1998. *Apparitions of the Madonna at Oliveto Citra: Local Visions and Cosmic Drama*. Trans. Jr. William A. Christian. University Park: The Pennsylvania State University Press.

Apor, Péter. 2013. Autentikus közösség és autonóm személyiség: 1989 egyik előtörténete [Authentic Community and Autonomous Personality: A Prehistory of 1989]. *AETAS* 28 (4): 22–39.

Asad, Talal. 1993. The Construction of Religion as an Anthropological Category. In *Genealogies of Religion: Discipline and Reasons of Power in Christianity and Islam*, 27–54. Baltimore: Johns Hopkins University Press.

———. 2003. *Formations of the Secular: Christianity, Islam, Modernity*. Stanford: Stanford University Press.

Bakó, Boglárka. 1998. Az érdekességeket kereső turisták és a turistákat kereső érdekességek. In *A turizmus mint kulturális rendszer*, ed. Zoltán Fejős, 129–139. Budapest: Néprajzi Múzeum.

Barabás, Hajnal. 2016. Várják a diákokat az új csíkszeredai kollégiumba. *Krónika Online*, August 31. https://kronikaonline.ro/erdelyi-hirek/varjak-a-diakokat-az-uj-csikszeredai-kollegiumba. Accessed 16 Jan 2020.

Barabási, László. 1996. *Balánbánya története* [History of Balánbánya]. Miercurea Ciuc: Barabási.

Bárdi, Nándor. 1996. A Keleti Akció – A romániai magyar intézmények anyaországi támogatása az 1920-as években [The Eastern Action – Homeland State Support for Hungarian Institutions in Romania in the 1920s]. In *Magyarságkutatás 1995–96*, ed. László Diószegi, 143–190. Budapest: Teleki László Alapítvány.

———. 2004. *Tény és Való: A budapesti kormányzatok és a határon túli magyarság kapcsolattörténete* [Fact and Reality: The History of Relations Between the Budapest Government and Cross-Border Hungariandom]. Pozsony: Kalligram.

———. 2013. *Otthon és haza: Tanulmányok a romániai Magyar kisebbség történetéről* [At Home, There and Here. Research on the History of the Hungarian Minority in Romania]. Miercurea Ciuc: Pro-Print.

———. 2015. A népszolgálat genezise és tartalomváltozása. In *Népszolgálat: A közösségi elkötelezettség alakváltozatai a magyar kisebbségek történetében* [Service to the People: The Elementary Forms of Community Commitment in the History of the Hungarian Minority], eds. Nándor Bárdi, Tamás Gusztáv Filep, and József D. Lőrincz, 11–48. Pozsony: Kalligram Kiadó.

Bárdi, Nándor, Tamás Gusztáv Filep, and József D. Lőrincz. 2015. Bevezető [Introduction]. In *Népszolgálat: A Közösségi Elkötelezettség Alakváltozatai A Magyar Kisebbségek Történetében* [Service to the People: The Elementary Forms of Community Commitment in the History of the Hungarian Minority], 2–10. Pozsony: Kalligram Kiadó.

Barna, Gábor. 1987. Egy szokáskör: a búcsújárás strukturális változásai kisalöüldi példák alapján [A Circle of Practice: The Structural Varieties of Pilgrimage on the Basis of an Example from Kisalöüld]. *Folklór és tradíció* 4: 228–237.

———. 1991. A magyarországi búcsújárás változásai [The Varieties of Hungarian Pilgrimage]. *Vigilia* 56 (5): 345–347.

———. 2001. *Búcsújárok: kölcsonhatások a magyar és más európai vallási kultúrákban* [Pilgrims: Exchanges of Influence Between Hungarian and Other European Religious Cultures]. Budapest: Lucidas.

Barszczewska, Agnieszka, and Lehel Peti. 2011. *Integrating Minorities: Traditional Communities and Modernization*. Cluj-Napoca: ISPMN.

Bártok, Béla. 1947. Gypsy Music or Hungarian Music? *The Musical Quarterly* 33 (2): 240–257.

Bauer, Stefan. 2021. The Uses of History in Religious Controversies from Erasmus to Baronio. *Renaissance Studies* 35 (1): 9–23.

Bauman, Zygmunt. 1987a. Intellectuals in East-Central Europe: Continuity and Change. *East European Politics and Societies and Cultures* 1 (2): 162–186.

———. 1987b. *Legislators and Interpreters: On Modernity, Post-Modernity and Intellectuals*. Cambridge: Polity Press.

———. 1992. Love in Adversity: On the State the Intellectuals, and the State of the Intellectuals. *Thesis Eleven* 31 (1): 81–104.

Bell, Daniel. 1973. *The Coming of Post-Industrial Society: A Venture in Social Forecasting*. New York: Basic Books.

Benjamin, Walter. 2019. *Origin of the German Trauerspiel*. Trans. Howard Eiland. Cambridge: Harvard University Press.

Bialecki, Jon. 2017a. *A Diagram for Fire: Miracles and Variation in an American Charismatic Movement*. Oakland: University of California.

———. 2017b. Eschatology, Ethics, and Ēthnos: Ressentiment and Christian Nationalism in the Anthropology of Christianity. *Religion and Society* 8 (1): 42–61.

Biró, Zoltán, and Bodó Julianna. 1992. A "hargitaiság" – egy régió identitásépítési gyakorlatáról. Átmenetek – a mindennapi élet antropológiája. *Kommunikációs Antropológia Munkacsoport* 1: 14–29.

Bloch, Maurice. 2002. Are Religious Beliefs Counterintuitive? In *Radical Interpretation in Religion*, ed. Nancy Frankenberry. Cambridge: Cambridge University Press.

Bodó, Julianna. 1991. Etnikai jelképek és identitás. In *Nemzetiség – Identitás*, ed. Zoltán Ujváry, Ernő Eperjessy, and András Krupa, 67–70. Békéscsaba/Debrecen: Ethnica.

———. 1996. *Elvándorlók? Vendégmunka és életforma a Székelyföldön*. Miercurea Ciuc: Pro-Print Könyvkiadó.

———. 2008. *Migrációs folyamatok – közösségi megjelenítések*. Miercurea Ciuc: Státus Kiadó.

Bögre, Zsuzsanna. 2016. Individual Religiosity, Secularization and Seekers Among Hungarian Youth. In *Seekers or Dwellers? Social Character of Religion in Hungary*, ed. Zsuzsanna Bögre, 195–212. Washington, DC: The Council for Research in Values and Philosophy.

Böjte, Csaba, and Éva Karikó. 2009. *Ablak a Végtelenre: Csaba testvér gondolatai Istenről, vallásról, életről, emberről* [Window onto the Infinite: Brother Csaba's Thoughts About God, Religion, Life, and the Human Being]. Budapest: Helikon Kiadó.

———. 2010. *Út a végtelenbe: Csaba testvér gondolatai Isten ajándékairól* [Path Toward the Infinite: Brother Csaba's Thoughts About God's Gifts]. Budapest: Helikon Kiadó.

———. 2011. *Iránytű a végtelenhez: Csaba testvér gondolatai az isteni parancsolatokról* [Signpost Toward the Infinite: Brother Csaba's Thoughts About the Divine Commandments]. Budapest: Helikon Kiadó.

———. 2012. *Párbeszéd a Végtelennel: Csaba testvér gondolatai az Istennel való mély és bensőséges kapcsolatról* [Dialogue with the Infinite: Brother Csaba's Thoughts About the Deep and Intimate Relationship with God]. Budapest: Helikon Kiadó.

Bollbuck, Harald. 2021. Searching for the True Religion: The Church History of the *Magdeburg Centuries* Between Critical Methods and Confessional Polemics. *Renaissance Studies* 35 (1): 100–117.

Boltanski, Luc, and Eve Chiapello. 2006. *The New Spirit of Capitalism*. New York: Verso.

Böröcz, József. 1993. Simulating the Great Transformation: Property Change Under Prolonged Informality in Hungary. *European Journal of Sociology* 34 (1): 81–107.

Bottoni, Stefano. 2008. *Sztálin a Székelyeknél. A Magyar Autonóm Tartomány Története (1952–1960)* [Stalin and the Székelys: History of the Hungarian. Autonomous Region]. Miercurea Ciuc: Pro-Print Könyvkiadó.

———. 2013. National Projects, Regional Identities, Everyday Compromises Szeklerland in Greater Romania (1919–1940). *Hungarian Historical Review* 2 (3): 477–511.

Bourdieu, Pierre. 1991. *Homo Academicus*. Stanford: Stanford University Press.

———. 1977. *Outline of a Theory of Practice*, translated by Richard Nice. Cambridge: Cambridge University Press.

Boyer, Dominic. 2003. Censorship as a Vocation: The Institutions, Practices, and Cultural Logic of Media Control in the German Democratic Republic. *Comparative Studies of Society and History* 45 (3): 511–545.

———. 2005. *Spirit and System: Media, Intellectuals, and the Dialectic in Modern German Culture*. Chicago: University of Chicago Press.

Boylston, Tom. 2012. The Shade of the Divine: Approaching the Sacred in an Ethiopian Orthodox Christian Community. Ph.D. Thesis, London School of Economics, London, UK.

———. 2018. *The Stranger at the Feast: Prohibition and Mediation in an Ethiopian Orthodox Christian Community*. Berkeley: University of California Press.

Bren, Paulina, and Mary Neuburger. 2012. *Communism Unwrapped: Consumption in Cold War*. New York: Oxford University Press.

Brubaker, Rogers. 1996. *Nationalism Reframed: Nationhood and the National Question in the New Europe*. Cambridge: Cambridge University Press.

———. 1998. Myths and Misconceptions in the Study of Nationalism. The State of the Nation: Ernest Gellner and the Theory of Nationalism. In *The State of the Nation: Ernest Gellner and the Theory of Nationalism*, ed. John Hall, 272–306. Cambridge: Cambridge University Press.

———. 2011. Religion and Nationalism: Four Approaches. *Nations and Nationalism* 18 (1): 2–20.

———. 2017. Between Nationalism and Civilizationism: The European Populist Moment in Comparative Perspective. *Ethnic and Racial Studies* 40 (8): 1191–1226.

Brubaker, Rogers, Margit Feischmidt, Jon Fox, and Liana Grancea. 2007. *Nationalist Politics and Everyday Ethnicity in a Transylvanian Town*. Princeton: Princeton University Press.

Buchowski, Michal. 2006. The Specter of Orientalism in Europe: From Exotic Other to Stigmatized Brother. *Anthropological Quarterly* 79 (3): 463–482.

Buck-Morss, Susan. 1989. *The Dialectics of Seeing: Walter Benjamin and the Arcades Project*. Cambridge: MIT Press.

Burdick, John. 1998. *Blessed Anastacia: Women, Race, and Popular Christianity in Brazil*. New York: Routledge.

Buzogány, Aron, and Mihai Varga. 2018. The Ideational Foundations of the Illiberal Backlash in Central and Eastern Europe: The Case of Hungary. *Review of International Political Economy* 6: 811–828.

Cameron, Euan. 2012. *The European Reformation*. Oxford: Oxford University Press.

Cannell, Fenella, ed. 2006a. *Anthropology of Christianity*. Durham: Duke University Press.

———. 2006b. The Christianity of Anthropology. *Journal of the Royal Anthropological Institute* 11 (2): 335–356.

Carroll, Timothy. 2017. Theology as an Ethnographic Object: An Anthropology of Eastern Christian Rupture. *Religions* 8 (7): 114–132.

———. 2018. *Orthodox Christian Material Culture: Of People and Things in the Making of Heaven*. London: Routledge.

Case, Holly. 2009. *Between States: The Transylvanian Question and the European Idea During World War II*. Stanford: Stanford University Press.

Chelcea, Liviu. 2002. The Culture of Shortage During State-Socialism: Consumption Practices in a Romanian Village in the 1980s. *Cultural Studies* 16 (1): 16–43.

Chesnut, Andrew R. 2003. *Competitive Spirits: Latin America's New Religious Economy*. Oxford: Oxford University Press.

Christian, William A. Jr. and Zoltán Krasznai. 2009. The Christ of Limpias and the Passion of Hungary. *History and Anthropology* 20: 219–242.

Chua, Liana. 2015. Horizontal and vertical relations: Interrogating "in/dividual-ism" among Christian Bidayuhs. *Hau: Journal of Ethnographic Theory* 5 (1): 339–35.

Coleman, Simon. 2002. Do You Believe in Pilgrimage? Communitas, Contestation and Beyond. *Anthropological Theory* 2 (3): 355–368.

———. 2014. Pilgrimage as Trope for an Anthropology of Christianity. *Current Anthropology* 55 (S10): S281–S291.

Coleman, Simon, and Marion Bowman. 2018. Religion in Cathedrals: Pilgrimage, Heritage, Adjacency, and the Politics of Replication in Northern Europe. *Religion* 50 (1): 1–23.

Coser, Lewis. 1965. *Men of Ideas: A Sociologist's View*. New York: Free Press.

Csibész Alapítvány. 2017. Rólunk [About Us]. http://www.csibesz.ro/word-press/en/about-us/. Accessed 2 Jan 2020.

Csordas, Thomas J. 1994. *The Sacred Self: A Cultural Phenomenology of Charismatic Healing*. Berkeley: University of California Press.

———. 1996. Imaginal Performance and Memory in Ritual Healing. In *The Performance of Healing*, ed. Carol Laderman and Marina Roseman, 91–114. London: Routledge.

———. 1997. *Language, Charisma, and Creativity: The Ritual Life of a Religious Movement*. Berkeley: University of California Press.

Daczó, Árpád. 2000. *Csíksomlyó titka: Mária-tisztelet a néphagyományban* [The Secret of Csíksomlyó: Marian Devotionalism in Folk Tradition]. Miercurea Ciuc: Pallas-Akadémia.

Dahlhaus, Carl. 1989. *Between Romanticism and Modernism: Four Studies in the Music of the Later Nineteenth Century*. Berkeley: University of California Press.

Davies, Douglas. 2002. *Anthropology and Theology*. Oxford: Berg.

Davis, Nathaniel. 1995. *A Long Walk to Church: A Contemporary History of Russian Orthodoxy*. Boulder: Westview.

Davis, R. Chris. 2019. *Hungarian Religion, Romanian Blood: A Minority's Struggle for National Belonging, 1920–1945*. Madison: University of Wisconsin Press.

DeHanas, Daniel Nilsson, and Marat Shterin, eds. 2018. *Religion and the Rise of Populism*. London: Routledge.

Deletant, Dennis. 1999. *Communist Terror in Romania: Gheorghe Gheorghiu-Dej and the Police State 1948–1965*. New York: St. Martin's Press.

della Dora, Veronica. 2014. Where the Tourist's Gaze Fades: Performing Landscape and the Sacred in Meteora. In *Christian Pilgrimage, Landscape and Heritage: Journeying to the Sacred*, ed. Avril Maddrell, Veronica della Dora, Alessandro Scafi, and Heather Walton, 67–87. New York: Routledge.

Demeter, Csanád. 2009. *Területfejlesztési- és modernizációs politika Székelyföld elmaradott régióiban* [The Politics of Regional Development and Modernization in Backwards Regions of the Szekler Land: Harghita and Covasna Counties in "the Multilaterally Developed Socialist Society"]. Ph.D. dissertation. Department of History, Babeş-Bolyai University, Romania.

———. 2010. "Városrendezés" Csíkszeredában ["Ordering the City" in Csíkszereda]. *Korunk* 2: 101–108.

———. 2011. Falusi urbanizáció és városi ruralizáció a Székelyföldön [Village Urbanization and Urban Ruralization in the Szekler Land]. *Korunk* 4: 101–107.

Dezső, László. 1997. *A kisebbségi élet ajándékai.* Cluj-Napoca: Minerva Kiadó.

Domokos, Pál Péter. 1938. A magyar népzene és énekkari műveltségünk [Hungarian Folk Music and Our Choral Cultivation]. *Erdélyi Iskola* 2: 135–143.

Du Boulay, Juliet, 2009. *Cosmos, Life, and Liturgy in a Greek Orthodox Village.* Athens: Denise Harvey.

Dulles, Avery. 1974. *Models of the Church.* New York: Doubleday.

Dungaciu, Dan. 2019. Se va cânta imnul Ungariei la Şumuleu Ciuc? Dimensiunile vizitei Papei Francisc în România. *Histori.ro.* https://www.historia.ro/secti-une/general/articol/se-va-canta-imnul-ungariei-la-sumuleu-ciuc-dimensiunile-vizitei-papei-francisc-in-romania. Accessed 6 Jan 2021.

Dunn, Elizabeth C. 2004. *Privatizing Poland: Baby Food, Big Business, and the Remaking of Labor.* Ithaca: Cornell University Press. Thomas J. Csordas. Body/meaning/healing. New York: Palgrave Macmillan, 2002.

Eade, John, and Michael Sallnow. 1991. *Contesting the Sacred: The Anthropology of Christian Pilgrimage.* Eugene: Wipf and Stock.

Eire, Carlos. 2014. *Singing the Right Way: Orthodox Christians and Secular Enchantment in Estonia.* Oxford: Oxford University Press.

———. 2016. *Reformations. The Early Modern World, 1450–1650.* New Haven: Yale University Press.

Engelke, Matthew. 2007. *A Problem of Presence: Beyond Scripture in an African Church.* Berkeley: University of California Press.

———. 2012. Angels in Swindon: Public *Religion* and *Ambient Faith* in England. *American Ethnologist* 39 (1): 155–170.

———. 2013. *God's Agents: Biblical Publicity in Contemporary England.* Berkeley: University of California Press.

———. 2018. *How to Think Like an Anthropologist.* Princeton: Princeton University Press.

Englund, Harri. 2011. *Christianity and Public Culture in Africa.* Athens: Ohio University Press.

Erdélystat.com. 2020. Csíkszentdomokos. (Sândominic). http://statisztikak. erdelystat.ro/adatlapok/csikszentdomokos/1446

Fassin, Didier. 2008. Beyond Good and Evil?: Questioning the Anthropological Discomfort with Morals. *Anthropological Theory* 8 (4): 333–344.

———. 2011. A Contribution to the Critique of Moral Reason. *Anthropological Theory* 11 (4): 481–491.

Fathi, Habiba. 2006. Gender, Islam, and Social Change in Uzbekistan. *Central Asian Survey* 25 (3): 303–317.

Faubion, James. 2001. Toward an Anthropology of Ethics: Foucault and the Pedagogies of Autopoiesis. *Representations* 74: 83–104.

———. 2011. *An Anthropology of Ethics.* Cambridge: University Press.

Fehérváry, Krisztina. 2013. *Politics in Color and Concrete: Socialist Materialities and the Middle Class in Hungary*. Bloomington: University of Indiana Press.

Feierman, Steven. 1990. *Peasant Intellectuals: Anthropology and History in Tanzania*. Madison, Wis.: University of Wisconsin Press.

Feischmidt, Margit. 2005. A magyar nacionalizmus autenticitás-diskurzusainak szimbolikus térfoglalása Erdélyben. In *Erdély – (de)konstrukciók*, ed. Margit Feischidt, 7–35. Budapest/Pécs: Néprajzi Múzeum – PTE Kommunikáció- és Médiatudományi Tanszék.

Fejérdi, András. 2016. *Pressed by a Double Loyalty: Hungarian Attendance at the Second Vatican Council, 1959–1965*. Budapest: Central University Press.

Forró, Gyöngyvér. 2010. Csíkszereda: húszéves a Csibész Alapítvány [Csíkszereda: The Black Sheep Foundation is 20 Years Old]. *Krónika Online*. January 13. https://kronikaonline.ro/erdelyi-hirek/csikszereda_huszeves_a_csibesz_alapitvany. Accessed 2 Jan 2020.

Foucault, Michel. 1990. Morality and Practice of the Self. In *History of Sexuality Vol. 2: The Use of Pleasure*, ed. Robert Hurley. New York: Vintage Books.

———. 1997a. Technologies of the Self. In *Ethics: Subjectivity and Truth*, ed. Paul Rabinow, 221–251. New York: The New Press.

———. 1997b. *Ethics: Subjectivity and Truth*, ed. Paul Rabinow. Trans. Robert Hurley. New York: New Press.

Fox, Jon. 2009. From National Inclusion to Economic Exclusion: Transylvanian Hungarian Ethnic Return Migration to Hungary. In *Diasporic Homecomings: Ethnic Return Migration in Comparative Perspective*, ed. Tsuda Takeyuki, 186–207. Stanford: Stanford University Press.

Frey, Nancy. 1998. *Pilgrim Stories: On and Off the Road to Santiago, Journeys Along an Ancient Way in Modern Spain*. Berkeley: University of California Press.

Froese, Paul. 2008. *The Plot to Kill God: Findings from the Soviet Experiment in Secularization*. Berkeley: University of California Press.

Fülöp-Székely, Botond. 2021. A Szent Korona felnagyított mását állították ki Székelyudvarhelyen [Exhibiting the Oversized Copy of the Holy Crown in Odorheiu Secuiesc]. *Szekelyhon.ro*, August 2. https://szekelyhon.ro/aktualis/a-szent-korona-felnagyitott-masat-allitottak-ki-szekelyudvarhelyen. Accessed 27 Dec 2021.

Füredi, Frank. 2017. *Populism and the European Culture Wars: The Conflict of Values Between Hungary and the EU*. London: Routledge.

Gal, Susan, and Gail Kligman. 2000. *The Politics of Gender After Socialism: A Comparative-Historical Essay*. Princeton: Princeton University Press.

Gazda, Árpád. 2007. Tiszti vállalja a sorsát [Father Pál Shoulders His Fate]. *Kronika Online*, July 4. https://kronikaonline.ro/erdelyi-hirek/tiszti_vallalja_a_sorsat_/print. Accessed 2 Jan 2019.

Gella, Aleksander. 1976. *The Intelligentsia and the Intellectuals: Theory, Method, and Case Study*. Beverly Hills: Sage.

Georgescu, Diana. 2011. Marrying into the European Family of Nations: National Disorder and Upset Gender Roles in Post-Communist Romanian Film. *Journal of Women's History* 23 (4): 131–154.

Ghodsee, Kristen. 2009. *Muslim Lives in Eastern Europe: Gender, Ethnicity, and the Transformation of Islam in Postsocialist Bulgaria*. Princeton: Princeton University Press.

Giantin, Stefano. 2019. Il Papa in Romania con gli occhi puntati sulla comunità dei cattolici magiari. *Il Piccolo*, March 31. https://ilpiccolo.gelocal.it/trieste/cronaca/2019/05/31/news/il-papa-in-romania-con-gli-occhi-puntati-sulla-comunita-dei-cattolici-magiari-1.33209190. Accessed 6 Jan 2021.

Giesen, Bernhard. 1998. *Intellectuals and the Nation: Collective Identity in a German Axial Age*. Cambridge: Cambridge University Press.

Gille, Zsuzsa. 2007. *From the Cult of Waste to the Trash Heap of History: The Politics of Waste in Socialist and Postsocialist Hungary*. Bloomington: University of Indiana Press.

Gog, Sorin. 2020. Neo-Liberal Subjectivities and the Emergence of Spiritual Entrepreneurship: An Analysis of Spiritual Development Programs in Contemporary Romania. *Social Compass* 67 (1): 103–119.

Gondola.hu. 2007. Csíksomlyó ragaszkodik plébánosához [Csíksomlyó Sticks to Its Priest]. *Gondola.hu*, July 4. https://gondola.hu/cikkek/55093-Csiksomlyo_ragaszkodik_plebanosahoz.html. Accessed 2 Jan 2020.

Gouldner, Alvin. 1979. *The Future of Intellectuals and the Rise of the New Class*. New York: Seabury.

Gramsci, A. 1972. *Selections from the Prison Notebooks of Antonio Gramsci*. New York: International Publishers.

Grieco, Marco. 2021. Le spaccature che complicano il viaggio del papa in Ungheria. *Domani*, September 8. https://www.editorialedomani.it/fatti/viaggio-papa-francesco-ungheria-budapest-viktor-orban-oml7fqmf. Accessed 7 Jan 2022.

Grzymala-Busse, Anna. 2015. *Nations Under God: How Churches Use Moral Authority to Influence Policy*. Princeton: Princeton University Press.

Gunderson, C. 2010. "The making of organic indigenous-campesino intellectuals: catechist training in the diocese of San Cristóbal and the roots of the Zapatista uprising", Coy, P.G. (Ed.) Research in Social Movements, Conflicts and Change (Research in Social Movements, Conflicts and Change, Vol. 31), Emerald Group Publishing Limited, Bingley, pp. 259–295. https://doi.org/10.1108/S0163-786X(2011)0000031011

Habsburg-Lothringen, Eduard. 2019. Francis in Romania. *America: The Jesuit Review*, May 17. https://www.americamagazine.org/faith/2019/05/17/letters. Accessed 7 Jan 2022.

Hackett, Helen. 1994. *Virgin Mother, Maiden Queen: Elizabeth I and the Cult of the Virgin Mary*. New York: St. Martin's Press.

Haddon, Malcolm. 2013. Anthropological Proselytism: Reflexive Questions for a Hare Krishna Ethnography. *The Australian Journal for Anthropology* 24 (3): 250–269.

Halemba, Agnieszka. 2015. *Negotiating Marian Apparitions: The Politics of Religion in Transcarpathian Ukraine*. Budapest: Central European University Press.

Hallam, Elizabeth, and Tim Ingold, eds. 2007. *Creativity and Cultural Improvisation*. London: Routledge.

Handman, Courtney. 2015. *Critical Christianity: Translation and Denominational Conflict in Papua New Guinea*. Berkeley: University of California Press.

Hanebrink, Paul. 2006. *In Defense of Christian Hungary: Religion, Nationalism, and Antisemitism, 1890–1944*. Ithaca: Cornell University Press.

Hann, Chris. 1990. Socialism and King Stephen's Right Hand. *Religion in Communist Lands* 18 (1): 4–24.

———. 2011. Moral Dispossession. *InterDisciplines* 2 (2): 11–37.

Hann, Chris, and Mathijs Pelkmans. 2009. Realigning Religion and Power in Central Asia: Islam, Nation-State and (Post)socialism. *Europe – Asia Studies* 61 (9): 1517–1541.

Harding, Susan. 1991. Representing Fundamentalism: The Problem of the Repugnant Cultural Other. *Social Research* 58 (2): 373–393.

———. 2000. *The Book of Jerry Falwell: Fundamentalist Language and Politics*. Princeton: Princeton University Press.

Harris, Ruth. 1999. *Lourdes: Body and Spirit in the Secular Age*. New York: Viking.

Haynes, Naomi. 2018. Theology on the Ground. In *Theologically Engaged Anthropology*, ed. J. Derrick Lemons, 112–135. Oxford: Oxford University Press.

Hegedűs, Rita, and Gergely Rosta. 2016. Seekers and Dwellers in the Light of Empirical Social Research. In *Seekers or Dwellers? Social Character of Religion in Hungary*, ed. Zsuzsanna Bögre, 213–235. Washington, DC: The Council for Research in Values and Philosophy.

Herzfeld, Michael. 1984. The Significance of the Insignificant: Blasphemy as Ideology. *JRAI* 19 (4): 653–664.

———. 1985. *The Poetics of Manhood: Contest and Identity in a Cretan Mountain Village*. Princeton: Princeton University Press.

———. 1987. *Anthropology Through the Looking-Glass: Critical Ethnography in the Margins of Europe*. New York: Cambridge University Press.

Hirschkind, Charles. 2006. *The Ethical Soundscape: Cassette Sermons and Islamic Counterpublics*. New York: Columbia University Press.

Hitchins, Keith. 2007. Erdelyi Fiatalok: The Hungarian Village and Hungarian Identity in Transylvania in the 1930s. *Journal of Hungarian Studies* 21 (2): 85–99.

Højer, Lars. 2009. Absent Powers: Magic and Loss in Post-Socialist Mongolia. *JRAI* 15 (3): 575–591.

Hungariancatholicmission.com. 2011. Hungarian Catholic Mission – Deva Foundations. http://www.hungariancatholicmission.com/charity/devafoundations.htm. Accessed December 3, 2021.

Huseby-Darvas, Éva. 2001. Hungarian Village Women in the Marketplace During the Late Socialist Period. In *Women Traders in Cross Cultural Perspective: Mediating Identities, Marketing Wares*, ed. L. Seligmann, 185–209. Palo Alto: Stanford University Press.

Imre, Lajos. 1938. *Hivatás és Élet: Elmélkedések, Prédikációk, Előadások* [Calling and Life: Reflections, Sermons, and Lectures]. Cluj: Minerva.

Irene Hilgers. 2009. *Why Do Uzbeks have to be Muslims? Exploring Religiosity in the Ferghana Valley*. Münster: Lit Verlag.

Jezsuita.hu. 2019. A Magyar Jezsuiták Az America Magazin Cikkéről, May 22. https://jezsuita.hu/a-magyar-jezsuitak-ovatossagra-intik-a-ferenc-papa-csiksomlyoi-utjarol-cikkezo-america-magazint/?fbclid=IwAR0X_5x3nEkv6O5D0-cXgzEqQU8U1kDaa9SBDVMP9rPiKnneI5Ts4znsYvk. Accessed 7 Jan 2019.

Jowitt, Ken. 1983. Soviet Neotraditionalism: The political corruption of a Leninist regime. *Soviet Studies* 35 (3): 275–297.

Kaell, Hillary. 2012. Of gifts and grandchildren: American Holy Land souvenirs. *Journal of Mate- rial Culture* 17 (2): 133–51.

Kaell, Hillary. 2014a. *Walking Where Jesus Walked: American Christians and Holy Land Pilgrimage*. New York: New York University Press.

———. 2014b. Age of Innocence: The Symbolic Child and Political Conflict on American Holy Land Pilgrimage. *Religion and Society: Advances in Research* 5: 157–172.

———. 2017. Seeing the Invisible: Ambient Catholicism on the Side of the Road. *Journal of the American Academy of Religion* 85 (1): 136–167.

———. 2020. *Christian Globalism at Home: Child Sponsorship in the United States*. Princeton: Princeton University Press.

Kaiser, Wolfram, and Helmut Wohnout, eds. 2004. *Political Catholicism in Europe 1918–45*. Abingdon: Routledge.

Kallius, Annastiina, Daniel Monterescu, and Prem Kumar Rajaram. 2016. Immobilizing mobility: Border ethnography, illiberal democracy, and the politics of the "refugee crisis" in Hungary. 43 (1): 25–37.

Kapaló, James. 2011. *Text, Context and Performance: Gagauz Folk Religion in Discourse and Practice*. Leiden: Brill.

Kaufman, Suzanne. 2007. *Consuming Visions: Mass Culture and the Lourdes Shrine*. Ithaca: Cornell University Press.

Keane, Webb. 2007. *Christian Moderns: Freedom and Fetish in the Mission Encounter*. Los Angeles: University of California Press.

Kereki, Judit. 2011. Bántalmazás a családban: Lehet-e verni a gyerekeket? [Violence in the Family: Are You Allowed to Beat Children]. *Koloknet.hu*,

January 7. https://www.koloknet.hu/csalad/tabu/eroszak/lehet-e-verni-a-gyerekeket/. Accessed 6 July 2021.

Kideckel, David. 2008. *Getting by in Postsocialist Romania: Labor, the Body, and Working-Class Culture*. Bloomington: Indiana University Press.

Kleinman, Arthur. 2006. *What Really Matters*. Oxford: Oxford University Press.

Kligman, Gail. 1988. *The Wedding of the Dead: Ritual, Poetics, and Popular Culture in Transylvania*. Berkeley: University of California Press.

———. 1998. *The Politics of Duplicity: Controlling Reproduction in Ceausescu's Romania*. Berkeley: University of California Press.

Kligman, Gail, and Katherine Verdery. 2011. *Peasants Under Siege: The Collectivization of Romanian Agriculture, 1949–1962*. Princeton: Princeton University Press.

Koesel, Karrie J. 2014. *Religion and Authoritarianism: Cooperation, Conflict, and the Consequences*. Cambridge: Cambridge University Press.

Köllner, Tobias. 2016. Patriotism, orthodox religion and education: Empirical findings from contemporary Russia. *Religion, State and Society* 44 (4): 366–386.

Korpos, Attila. 2021. Átadták a magyar kormány támogatásával felújított csíksomlyói Fodor-házat, October 3. https://szekelyhon.ro/aktualis/atadtak-a-magyar-kormany-tamogatasaval-felujitott-csiksomlyoi-fodor-hazat. Accessed 7 Jan 2021.

Kovács, Csaba. 2007. Apasággal vádolják Tisztit [Father Pál Is Accused of Being a Father]. *Kronika Online*, August 2. https://kronikaonline.ro/erdelyi-hirek/apasaggal_vadoljak_tisztit/print. Accessed 2 Jan 2019.

Kovács, Ágnes, and Gabriella Zsarnóczay. 2007. Protected Meat Products in Hungary – Local Foods and Hungaricums. *Anthropology of Food* 2 (2): 1–7.

Kozán, István. 2013. Népszámlálás: a hargitaiak 85 százaléka magyar [Census: Residents of Hargita County are 85 percent Hungarian]. *Szekelyhon.ro*. http://www.szekelyhon.ro/aktualis/csikszek/pontafolytatodhatnak-a-kitiltasok. Accessed 23 June 2014.

Kürti, László. 2000. *The Remote Borderland: Transylvania in the Hungarian Imagination*. Albany: State University of New York Press.

———. 2008. East and West: The Scholarly Divide in Anthropology. *Anthropological Notebooks* 14 (3): 25–38.

———. 2015. Neoshamanism, National Identity, and the Holy Crown of Hungary. *Journal of Religion in Europe* 8 (2): 235–260.

———. 2016. Nomadism and Nostalgia in Hungary. In *Memories on the Move: Experiencing Mobility, Rethinking the Past*, ed. Monika Palmberger and Jelena Tošić, 217–246. London: Palgrave Macmillan.

Laidlaw, James. 2002. For an Anthropology of Ethics and Freedom. *Journal of the Royal Anthropological Institute* 8: 311–332.

———. 2013. *The Subject of Virtue: An Anthropology of Ethics and Freedom*. Cambridge: Cambridge University Press.

Lajosi, Kristina. 2018. *Staging the Nation: Opera and Nationalism in 19th-Century Hungary*. Leiden: Brill.

Lambek, Michael. 2008. Value and virtue. *Anthropological Theory* 8 (2): 133–157.

———. 2010. Toward an Ethics of the Act. In *Ordinary Ethics: Anthropology, Language, and Action*, ed. Michael Lambek, 39–63. New York: Fordham University Press.

———. 2012. Facing Religion, from Anthropology. *Anthropology of This Century* 4.

Lampland, Martha. 1995. *The Object of Labor: Commodification in Socialist Hungary*. Chicago: University of Chicago Press.

Lange, Barbara Rose. 2014. "Good Old Days:" Critiques of Masculinity in the Hungarian Folk Revival. *The World of Music* 3 (2): 39–58.

Larsen, Timothy. 2014. *The Slain God: Anthropologists and the Christian Faith*. Oxford: Oxford University Press.

Lázár, György. 2019. Hungary's Jesuits and Orbán's Attempt to Exploit Pope Francis's Visit to Romania. *Hungarianfreepress.com*, May 6. https://hungarianfreepress.com/2019/05/06/hungarys-jesuits-and-orbans-attempt-to-exploit-pope-franciss-visit-to-romania/. Accessed 6 Jan 2021.

Lempert, Michael. 2015. Ethics Without Immanence: A Reply to Michael Lambek. *Anthropological Theory* 15: 13–40.

Lester, Rebecca. 2005. *Jesus in Our Wombs: Embodying Modernity in a Mexican Convent*. Berkeley: University of California Press.

Levy, David. 2018. The Impulse to Orthodoxy: Why Illiberal Democracies Treat Religious Pluralism as a Threat. In *Religion and the Rise of Populism*, ed. Daniel Nilsson DeHanas and Marat Shterin, 58–72. New York: Routledge.

Lindquist, Galena. 2006. *Conjuring Hope: Magic and Healing in Contemporary Russia*. New York: Berghahn Books.

Linton, Ralph. 1936. *The Study of Man: An Introduction*. New York: Appleton-Century-Crofts.

Livezeanu, Irina. 1995. *Cultural Politics in Greater Romania: Regionalism, Nation Building & Ethnic Struggle, 1918–1930*. Ithaca: Cornell University Press.

Losonczy, Anne-Marie. 2009. Pilgrims of the "Fatherland": Emblems and Religious Rituals in the Construction of an Inter-Patriotic Space Between Hungary and Transylvania. *History and Anthropology* 20 (3): 265–280.

Loustau, Marc R. 2019. A Message to Pope Francis: Be Wary of Right-Wing Populists When You Visit Romania. *America: The Jesuit Review*, April 19. https://www.americamagazine.org/politics-society/2019/04/19/message-pope-francis-be-wary-right-wing-populists-when-you-visit. Accessed 7 Jan 2021.

———. 2020. Transgressing the Right to the City: Urban Mining and Ecotourism in Post-Industrial Romania. *Anthropological Quarterly* 93 (1): 1555–1578.

————. 2021. Belief Beyond the Bugbear: Propositional Theology and Intellectual Authority in a Transylvanian Catholic Ethnographic Memoir. *Ethnos: A Journal of Anthropology* 86 (3): 492–509.

Luehrmann, Sonja. 2005. Recycling Cultural Construction: Desecularisation in Postsoviet Mari El. *Religion, State, and Society* 33 (1): 35–56.

————. 2011. *Secularism Soviet Style: Teaching Atheism and Religion in a Volga Republic.* Bloomington: Indiana University Press.

Luhrmann, Tanya. 2012. *When God Talks Back: Understanding the American Evangelical Relationship with God.* New York: Alfred A. Knopf.

MacIntyre, Alasdair. 1984. *After Virtue: A Study in Moral Theory.* Notre Dame: University of Notre Dame Press.

Magdó, Zsuzsanna. 2016. "Romanian Spirituality in Ceaușescu's 'Golden Epoch': Social Scientists Reconsider Atheism, Religion, and Ritual Culture." In *Science, Religion, and Communism in Cold War Europe*, eds. Paul Betts and Stephen A. Smith. London: Palgrave, 77–101.

Magnificat.ro. 2010. Böjte atya: Ha egymillió ember csak 1 eurót adományozna…. *Magnificat.ro.* https://www.magnificat.ro/portal/index.php/hu/szent-ferenc-alapitvany/rk-mainmenu-315/sajtinmenu-311/5335-boejte-atya-ha-egymillio-ember-csak-1-eurot-adomanyozna. Accessed 25 Nov 2020.

Magyar, Zoltán. 2001. *Halhatatlan és visszatérő hősök. Egy nemzetközi mondatípus Kárpát-medencei redakciói.* Budapest: Akadémiai Kiadó.

Mahmood, Saba. 2004. *Politics of Piety: The Islamic Revival and the Feminist Subject.* Princeton: Princeton University Press.

Makkai, Sándor. 1931. *Magunk revíziója* [A Revision of Our Own]. Miercurea Ciuc: Pro-Print Könyvkiadó. Available online at http://mek.oszk.hu/10900/10935/10935.htm

Makkay, József. 2016. Csíksomlyói árva csibészek [The Orphan Black Sheep of Csíksomlyó]. *Erdélyi Napló*, March 25. https://erdelyinaplo.ro/aktualis/riportok/csiksomlyoi-arva-csibeszek. Accessed 10 Jan 2019.

Malkki, Liisa H. 2015. *The Need to Help: The Domestic Arts of International Humanitarianism.* Durham: Duke University Press.

Márk, Boglárka. 2016. "Tusványos: megalakult a Székelyföldi Értéktár Bizottság" ["The Tusványos Festival: The Committee to Preserve Szeklerland Cultural Treasures Has Been Formed." *Maszol.hu.* https://maszol.ro/kultura/67408-tusvanyos-megalakult-a-szekelyfoldi-ertektar-bizottsag. Accessed 22 Dec 2021.

Márton, Áron. 1933. A kiszélesített iskola [The Expanded School]. *Erdélyi Iskola* (1): 5–8. Available online at https://ersekseg.ro/hu/node/3363

————. 1934. Ugartörés előtt. *Erdélyi Iskola* (2): 1–2. Available online at https://ispmn.gov.ro/uploads/012Marton_Aron_Ugartores_elott.pdf

————. 1935. Az eszmény nyomán [On the Path of an Ideal]. *Erdélyi Iskola* 3 (5): 134–135. Available online at https://ispmn.gov.ro/uploads/014Marton_Aron_Az_eszmeny_nyoman.pdf

Marzouki, Nadia, Duncan McDonnell, and Olivier Roy, eds. 2016. *Saving the People: How Populists Hijack Religion*. New York: Oxford University Press.

Mattingly, Cheryl. 2012. Two Virtue Ethics and the Anthropology of Morality. *Anthropological Theory* 12 (2): 161–184.

———. 2013. Moral Selves and Moral Scenes: Narrative Experiments in Everyday Life. *Ethnos: Journal of Anthropology* 78 (3): 301–327.

Mauss, Marcel. 1990. *The Gift: The Form and Reason for Exchange in Archaic Societies*, translated by W.D.Halls. New York: Routledge.

McBrien, Julie, and Mathijs Pelkmans. 2008. Turning Marx on His Head: Missionaries, 'Extremists' and Archaic Secularists in Post-Soviet Kyrgyzstan. *Critique of Anthropology* 28 (1): 87–103.

McKenny, Gerald. 2021. *Karl Barth's Moral Thought*. Oxford: Oxford University Press.

McManus, Frederick R. 1987. *Thirty Years of Liturgical Renewal: Statements of the Bishops' Committee on the Liturgy*. Washington, DC: United States Catholic Conference.

Meneses, Eloise and David Bronkema, eds. 2017. *On Knowing Humanity: Insights from Theology for Anthropology*. New York: Routledge.

Mevius, Martin. 2005. *Agents of Moscow: The Hungarian Communist Party and the Origins of Socialist Patriotism, 1941–1953*. Oxford: Oxford University Press.

Meyer, Birgit. 2015. *Sensational Movies: Video, Vision, and Christianity in Ghana*. Berkeley: University of California Press.

Miele, Mara. 2008. CittàSlow: Producing Slowness Against the Fast Life. *Space and Polity* 12 (1): 135–156.

Mihăilescu, Vintilă, Ilia Iliev, and Slobodan Naumović. 2008. *Studying Peoples in the People's Democracies II: Socialist Era Anthropology in South-East Europe*. Berlin: LIT-Verlag.

Miner, Steven M. 2003. *Stalin's Holy War: Religion, Nationalism and Alliance Politics, 1941–1945*. Chapel Hill: University of North Carolina Press.

Minkenberg, Michael. 2015. *Transforming the Transformation? The East European Radical Right in the Political Process*. London: Routledge.

Mishkova, Diana, Marius Turda, and Balázs Trencsényi, eds. 2014. *Discourses of Collective Identity in Central and Southeast Europe (1775–1945): Texts and Commentaries*, Volume IV: Anti-Modernism. Radical Revisions of Collective Identity. Budapest: CEU Press.

Mohay, Tamás. 2009. A Csíksomlyói Pünkösdi Búcsújárás: Történet, Eredet, Hagyomány [The Csíksomlyó Pentecost Pilgrimage: History, Origin, Tradition]. Budapest: L'Harmattan.

Muehlebach, Andrea. 2012. *The Moral Neoliberal: Welfare and Citizenship in Italy*. Chicago: The University of Chicago Press.

Mutschlechner, Martin. 2022. A Diversity of Confessions. *www.habsburger.net*. https://ww1.habsburger.net/en/chapters/diversity-confessions. Accessed 28 Nov 2020.

Nabhan-Warren, Kristy. 2005. *The Virgin of El Barrio. Marian Apparitions, Catholic Evangelizing, and Mexican American Activism.* New York: NYU Press.
———. 2013. *The Cursillo Movement in America: Catholics, Protestants, and Fourth-day Spirituality.* Chapel Hill: University of North Carolina Press.
Nagy, István. 2014. "Az elhivatottságot megtörni nem lehet...Életsorsok: Gergély István "Tiszti". [It's not possible to destroy a calling: Life and destinies: István Gergély "Tiszti."]. http://szjptk.iif.hu/toronyor/V_evf_4/tiszti.htm. Accessed December 1, 2021.
Napolitano, Valentina. 2015. *Migrant Hearts and the Atlantic Return: Transnationalism and the Roman Catholic Church.* New York: Fordham University Press.
Naumescu, Vlad. 2012. The End Times and the Near Future: The Ethical Engagements of Russian Old Believers in Romania. *Journal of the Royal Anthropological Institute* 22 (2): 314–331.
Negruți, Sorin. 2014. The Evolution of the Religious Structure in Romania Since 1859 to the Present Day. *Revista Română de Statistică* 6: 46–70.
Nérath, Mónika. 2008. *A jelen lévő Isten: Pál Ferenccel beszélget Néráth Mónika* [The Presently Existing God: Mónika Néráth Talks with Ferenc Pál]. Budapest: Kairosz.
Nikunen, Kaarina. 2018. *Media Solidarities: Emotions, Power and Justice in the Digital Age.* London: SAGE Publications Ltd.
Novák, Csaba Zoltán. 2005. A Párt szolgálatában: Kádersors a Székelyföldön [In the Service of the Party: A Cadre's Life in the Szekler Land]. *Múltunk* 4: 100–127.
O'Neill, Kevin Lewis. 2009. *City of God: Christian Citizenship in Postwar Guatemala.* Berkeley: University of California Press.
O'Sullivan, Michael. 2018. *Patrick Leigh Fermor: Noble Encounters Between Budapest and Transylvania.* Budapest: Central European University Press.
Oláh, Sándor. 1996. A székelyföldi migráció előtörténetének áttekintése [A Sketch of the Pre-History of Migration from the Szekler Land]. In *Elvándorlók? Vendégmunka és életforma a Székelyföldön* [Emigrants? Labor Migration and Lifestyle in the Szekler Land], ed. Juliánna Bodó, 15–36. Miercurea Ciuc: Pro-Print Könyvkiadó.
Omer, Atalia. 2015. Modernists Despite Themselves: The Phenomenology of the Secular and the Limits of Critique as an Instrument of Change. *Journal of the American Academy of Religion* 83 (1): 27–71.
Origo.hu. 2019a. "Böjte Csaba: Arra születtünk, hogy a szolgáló szeretet által az élet mellett döntsünk" ["Böjte Csaba: We Are Born to Stand on the Side of Life Through the Love of Service]. *Origo.hu*, September 6. https://www.origo.hu/itthon/20190906-bojte-csaba-arra-szulettunk-hogy-a-szolgalo-szeretet-altal-az-elet-mellett-dontsunk.html. Accessed 1 Dec 2019.

———. 2019b. Ferenc pápa és Böjte Csaba együtt imádkoznak Csíksomlyón, January 17. https://www.origo.hu/itthon/20190117-bojte-csaba-fogadja-ferenc-papat-csiksomlyon.html. Accessed 7 Jan 2022.

Orsi, Robert A. 1985. *The Madonna of 115th Street: Faith and Community in Italian Harlem, 1880–1950*. New Haven, Conn.; London: Yale University Press.

———. 1996. *Thank You, Saint Jude: Women's Devotion to the Patron Saint of Hopeless Causes*. New Haven: Yale University Press.

Orta, Andrew. 2004. *Catechizing Culture: Missionaries, Aymara, and the "New Evangelization"*. New York: Columbia University Press.

Ozsváth Judit. 2012. Az Erdélyi Iskola című oktatásügyi és népnevelő folyóirat. Magiszter 10 (3): 68–83.

———. 2013. Márton Áron – a kolozsvári egyetemi lelkész és lapszerkesztő [Áron Márton – The Journal Editor and University Chaplain in Cluj]. In *Az idők mérlegén: Tanulmányok Márton Áron püspökről*, ed. Márta Bodó, Csilla Lázár, and János Lázár Lövétei, 19–35. Budapest: Szent István Társulat-Verbum.

———. 2017. Márton Áron és Domokos Pál Péter népnevelői munkássága a két világháború közötti időben [Márton Áron and Domokos Pál Péter Educational Work in the Interwar Period]. *HUCER*: 370–381.

Palonen, Emilia. 2018. Performing the Nation: The Janus-Faced Populist Foundations of Illiberalism in Hungary. *Journal of Contemporary European Studies* 3: 308–321.

Parsons, Talcott. 1969. 'The Intellectual': A Social Role Category. In *On Intellectuals*, ed. Peter Rieff, 3–26. Garden City: Doubleday.

Pelkmans, Mathijs, ed. 2009. *Conversion After Socialism: Disruptions, Modernisms and Technologies of Faith in the Former Soviet Union*. New York: Berghan.

Peña, Elaine A. 2011. *Performing Piety: Making Space Sacred with the Virgin of Guadalupe*. Berkeley: University of California Press.

Péter, László. 2003. The Holy Crown of Hungary, Visible and Invisible. *Slavonic and East European Review* 81 (3): 421–510.

Peti, Lehel. 2009. Collective Visions in the Moldavian Villages. *Acta Ethnographica Hungarica* 54 (2): 287–308.

———. 2020. *"Krisztus ajándéka van bennünk." Pünkösdizmus moldvai román, roma és csángó közösségekben* ["The Gift of Christ Is Within Us." Pentecostalism in Romanian, Roma, and Csángó Communities in Moldavia]. Budapest-Cluj-Napoca: Balassi Kiadó--Erdélyi Múzeum Egyesület.

Peyrouse, Sebastien. 2004. Christianity and Nationality in Soviet and Post-Soviet Central Asia: Mutual Intrusions and Instrumentalizations. *Nationalities Papers* 32 (3): 651–674.

Pius XI. "Divini Illius Magistri." The Holy See, December 31, 1929, https://www.vatican.va/content/pius-xi/en/encyclicals/documents/hf_p-xi_enc_31121929_divini-illiusmagistri.html

Pius XI. 1939. Pope Pius XI and Education. *Christian Education* 22 (4): 249–254.

Pozniak, Kinga. 2013a. Generations of Memory in the "Model Socialist Town" of Nowa Huta, Poland. *Focaal—Journal of Global and Historical Anthropology* 66: 58–68.

———. 2013b. Reinventing a Model Socialist Steel Town in the Neoliberal Economy: The Case of Nowa Huta, Poland. *City & Society* 25 (1): 113–134.

Pusztai, Bertalan. 2004. *Religious Tourists: Constructing Authentic Experiences in Late Modern Hungarian Catholicism*. Jyväskylä: University of Jyväskylä.

Rabolini, Luisa. 2021. As arestas que complicam a viagem do papa à Hungria. *Revista IHU On-Line*, September 10. https://www.ihu.unisinos.br/78-noticias/612737-as-arestas-que-complicam-a-viagem-do-papa-a-hungria. Accessed 7 Jan 2022.

Rada, János. 2020. Antiklerikális röpiratok vallással kapcsolatos attitűdjei a dualizmus idején: 1867-től 1895-ig. *Aetas* 35 (1): 18–39.

Rama, Angel. 1994. *The Lettered City*. Durham: Duke University Press.

Rédai, Botond. 2011. Nem gyakorolhatja papi hivatását Gergely István [Father Pál Cannot Practice His Priestly Calling]. *Szekelyhon.ro*, April 19. https://szekely-hon.ro/aktualis/csikszek/nem-gyakorolhatja-papi-hivatasat-gergely-istvan. Accessed 2 Jan 2020.

Rivkin-Fish, Michele. 2005. *Women's Health in Post-Soviet Russia: The Politics of Intervention*. Bloomington: Indiana University Press.

Robbins, Joel. 2004. *Becoming Sinners: Christianity and Moral Torment in a Papua New Guinea Society*. Berkeley: University of California Press.

———. 2007. Between Reproduction and Freedom: Morality, Value, and Radical Cultural Change. *Ethnos* 72 (3): 293–314.

———. 2008. On Not Knowing Other Minds: Confession, Intention, and Linguistic Exchange in a Papua New Guinea Community. *Anthropological Quarterly* 81 (2): 421–429.

———. 2013. Afterword: Let's keep it awkward: Anthropology, theology, and otherness. *The Australian Journal of Anthropology* 24 (3): 329–337.

———. 2017. Anthropology in the Mirror of Theology: Epistemology, Ontology, Ethics (an Afterword). In *On Knowing Humanity: Insights from Theology for Anthropology*, ed. Eloise Meneses and David Bronkema, 222–240. New York: Routledge.

Rogers, Douglas. 2009. *The Old Faith and the Russian Land: A Historical Ethnography of Ethics in the Urals*. Ithaca: Cornell University Press.

Said, Edward. 1994. *Representations of the Intellectual: The 1993 Reith Lectures*. London: Vintage.

Santiago, Jose. 2012. Secularisation and Nationalism: A Critical Review. *Social Compass* 59 (1): 3–20.

Schegloff, Emanuel A., Gail Jefferson, and Harvey Sacks. 1977. The Preference for Self-Correction in the Organization of Repair in Conversation. *Language* 53 (2): 361–382.

Scheppele, Kim Lane. 2017. The Social Lives of Constitutions. In *Sociological Constitutionalism*, ed. Paul Blokker and Chris Thornhill, 35–66. Cambridge: Cambridge University Press.

Scherz, China. 2014. *Having People, Having Heart: Charity, Sustainable Development, and Problems of Dependence in Central Uganda.* Chicago: University of Chicago Press.

Schweizer, Peter. 1988. *Shepherds, Workers, Intellectuals: Culture and Centre-Periphery Relationships in a Sardinian Village.* Stockholm: University of Stockholm Press.

Scott, Michael W. 2015. Cosmogony Today: Counter-Cosmogony, Perspectivism, and the Return of Anti-Biblical Polemic. *Religion and Society: Advances in Research* 6 (1): 44–61.

Seasoltz, Kevin. 1980. *New Liturgy, New Laws.* Collegeville: The Liturgical Press.

Senèze, Nicolas. 2019. En Roumanie, le pape rejette toute vision nationaliste du christianisme. *La Croix*, June 1. https://www.la-croix.com/Religion/Catholicisme/Pape/En-Roumanie-pape-rejette-toute-vision-nationaliste-chris tianisme-2019-06-01-1201025992. Accessed 7 Jan 2022.

Shils, Edward, ed. 1972. *The Intellectuals and the Powers, and Other Essays.* Chicago: University Chicago Press.

Spivak, Gayatri Chakravorty. 1988. Can the Subaltern Speak? In *Marxism and the Interpretation of Culture*, ed. Cary Nelson and Lawrence Grossberg, 271–313. London: Macmillan.

Ssorin-Chaikov, Nikolai. 2008. Evenki Shamanistic Practices in Soviet Present and Ethnographic Present Perfect. *Anthropology of Consciousness* 12 (1): 1–18.

Steinberg, Mark D., and Catherine Wanner, eds. 2008. *Religion, Morality, and Community in Post-Soviet Societies.* Bloomington: University of Indiana Press.

Strathern, Marilyn. 2000. The Tyranny of Transparency. *British Educational Research Journal* 26 (3): 309–321.

Sutcliffe, Steven J. 2008. The Dynamics of Alternative Spirituality: Seekers, Networks, and 'New Age'. In *The Oxford Handbook of New Religious Movements*, ed. James Lewis. Oxford: Oxford University Press.

Székely János Pedagógus Társas Kör. 2014. Az elhivatottságot megtörni nem lehet...Életsorok: Gergely István "Tiszti" [It's Impossible to Destroy a Calling...Lives and Destinies: Father Pál]. http://szjptk.iif.hu/toronyor/V_evf_4/tiszti.htm. Accessed 5 Jan 2020.

Szilágy, Tamás. 2011. Quasi-Religious Character of the Hungarian Right-Wing Radical Ideology. An International Comparison. In *Spaces and Borders: Current Research on Religion in Central and Eastern Europe*, 251–264. Berlin: Walter de Gruyter.

Szilágyi, Eszter. 2007. "Gyimes kevésbé devalvált vidék..." A gyimesi turizmus antropológiai megközelítése. In *A Miskolci Egyetem Bölcsészettudományi Kara tudományos diákköri közleményei*, ed. Csaba Fazekas, 271–289. Miskolc: Miskolci Egyetem.

Taussig, Michael. 1987. *Shamanism, Colonialism, and the Wild Man.* Chicago: Univesity of Chicago Press.

———. 1999. *Defacement: Public Secrecy and the Labor of the Negative.* Stanford: Stanford University Press.

———. 2011. *I Swear I Saw This. Drawings in Fieldwork Notebooks, Namely My Own.* Chicago: University of Chicago Press.

Tavaszy, Sándor. 1936. Nemzeti léttünk kérdései: A prófétai nemzetszemlélet [The Questions of Our National Existence: The Prophetic National Perspective]. *Pásztortűz* 21.

———. 1940. Az erdélyi szellem új hajnala [The New Dawn of the Transylvanian Spirit]. *Pásztortűz* 8–9: 365–367.

Thompson, Craig J., and Ankita Kumar. 2018. Beyond Consumer Responsibilization: Slow Food's Actually Existing Neoliberalism. *Journal of Consumer Culture* 0 (0): 1–20.

Throop, Jason, and Cheryl Mattingly. 2018. The Anthropology of Ethics and Morality. *Annual Review of Anthropology* 47: 475–492.

Tismaneanu, Vladimir. 2003. *Stalinism for All Seasons: A Political History of Romanian Communism.* Berkeley: University of California Press.

Trapl, Miloš. 1995. *Political Catholicism and the Czechoslovak People's Party in Czechoslovakia, 1918–1938.* Boulder: Social Science Monographs.

Trencsényi, Balázs. 2010. Imposed Authenticity: Approaching Eastern European National Characterologies in the Inter-War Period. *Central Europe* 8 (1): 20–47.

———. 2011. Civilization and Originality: Perceptions of History and National Specificity in Nineteenth-Century Hungarian Political Discourse. In *Encountering Otherness. Diversities and Transcultural Experiences in Early Modern European Culture*, ed. Guido Abbattista, 305–338. Trieste: Trieste University Press.

———. 2014. Beyond Liminality? The Kulturkampf of the Early 2000s in East Central Europe. *Boundary* 41 (1): 135–152.

Turda, Marius. 2001. Deciding the National Capital: Budapest, Vienna, Bucharest and Transylvanian Romanian Culture. In *Tradition and Modernity in Romanian Culture and Civilization*, ed. Kurt W. Treptow, 95–114.

———. 2007. From Craniology to Serology: Racial Anthropology in Interwar Hungary and Romania. *Journal of the History of the Behavioral Sciences* 43 (4): 361–377.

Urry, John. 2000. *Sociology Beyond Societies.* London: Routledge.

Valtchinova, Galia. 2009. Introduction: Ethno-Graphing "Divine Intervention". *History and Anthropology* 20 (3): 203–218.

Venczel, József. 1935. Collegium Transilvanicum. *Erdélyi Iskola* 5 (6): 180–184.

———. 1938. Márton Áron Püspök Népnevelő Rendszere [Bishop Áron Márton's Educational System]. *Erdélyi Iskola* 6 (6): 361–371.

———. 1991. "Metamorphosis Transylvaniae." In Albert T. (ed.) *Hitel, Cluj 1935–1944. Studii*, pp. 65–72. Budapest: Bethlen Gábor.

Verdery, Katherine. 1983. *Transylvanian Villagers: Three Centuries of Political, Economic, and Ethnic Change*. Berkeley: University of California Press.
———. 1991. *National Ideology Under Socialism: Identity and Cultural Politics in Ceaușescu's Romania*. Berkeley: University of California Press.
———. 1996. *What Was Socialism, and What Comes Next?* Princeton: Princeton University Press.
———. 2000. *The Political Lives of Dead Bodies: Reburial and Postsocialist Change*. New York: Columbia University Press.
———. 2003. *The Vanishing Hectare: Property and Value in Postsocialist Transylvania*. Ithaca: Cornell University Press.
———. 2013. *Secrets and Truths: Ethnography in the Archive of Romania's Secret Police*. Budapest: Central European University Press.
Visnovitz, Péter. 2008. "Saját szigetről álmodnak és zsíroskenyeret kennek a magyar lovagok." *Origo.com*, October 9. https://www.origo.hu/itthon/20081008-lovagrendek-magyarorszagon-lovagi-cimek-karitativ-tevekenyseg-maltai-lovagrend-es-tarsai.html. Accessed 7 Jan 2022.
Voigt, Vilmos. 2004. *A vallási élmény története. Bevezetés a vallástudományba* [The History of Religious Experience: An Introduction to the Study of Religion]. Budapest: Timp Kiadó.
von Klimo, Arpad. 2003. *Nation, Konfession, Geschichte. Zur nationalen Geschichtskultur Ungarns im europaischen Kontext (1860–1948)*. Munich: R. Oldenbourg Verlag.
Vörös, Gabriella. 2005. A szakrális, a nemzeti közösség és az egzotikum élménye: a magyarországiak részvételének motivációiról a csíksomlyói pünkösdi búcsúban. In *Erdély-(de)konstrukciók*, ed. Margit Feischidt, 69–84. Budapest: Néprajzi Múzeum, PTE Kommunikáció, és Médiatudományi Tanszék.
Wanner, Catherine. 2007. *Communities of the Converted: Ukrainians and Global Evangelism*. Ithaca: Cornell University Press.
Warren, Kay. 1998. *Indigenous Movements and Their Critics: Pan-Maya Activism in Guatemala*. Princeton: Princeton University Press.
Weber, Samuel. 2008. *Benjamin's -Abilities*. Cambridge: Harvard University Press.
Wessely, Anna. 2002. Travelling People, Travelling Objects. *Cultural Studies* 16 (1): 3–15.
Zigon, Jarrett. 2007. Moral Breakdown and the Ethical Demand: A Theoretical Framework for an Anthropology of Moralities. *Anthropological Theory* 7 (2): 131–150.
———. 2008. *Morality: An Anthropological Perspective*. London: Bloomsbury Academic.
———. 2009a. Developing the Moral Person: The Concepts of Human, Godmanhood, and Feelings in Some Russian Articulations of Morality. *Anthropology of Consciousness* 20.1 (March): 1–26.
———. 2009b. Morality and Personal Experience: The Moral Conceptions of a Muscovite Man. *Ethos* 37.1 (March): 78–101.

————. 2009c. Morality Within a Range of Possibilities: A Dialogue with Joel Robbins. *Ethnos* 74.2 (June): 251–276.

————. 2009d. Phenomenological Anthropology and Morality. *Ethnos* 74.2 (June): 286–288.

————. 2010. *HIV is God's BlessingRehabilitating Morality in Neoliberal Russia.* Berkeley: University of California Press.

————. 2013. On Love: Remaking Moral Subjectivity in Postrehabilitation Russia. *American Ethnologist* 40.1 (February): 201–215.

————. 2014. Attunement and Fidelity: Two Ontological Conditions for Morally Being-in-the-World. *Ethos: A Journal of Anthropology* 42 (1): 16–30.

Zigon, Jarrett, and C. Jason Throop. 2014. Moral Experience: Introduction. *Ethos: Journal of the Society for Psychological Anthropology* 42 (1): 1–15.

Zimdars-Swartz, Sandra L. 1991. *Encountering Mary: From LA Salette to Medjugorje.* Princeteon: Princeton University Press.

Žiugždaitė, Saulena. 2019. Išbandymas Rumunija: tarp manipuliacijų grėsmės ir ortodoksiškos žiemos. *Bernardinai*, May 30. https://www.bernardinai. lt/2019-05-30-isbandymas-rumunija-tarp-manipuliaciju-gresmes-ir-ortodoksiskos-ziemos/. Accessed 7 Jan 2022.

Zubrzycki, Genevieve. 2006. *The Crosses of Auschwitz: Nationalism and Religion in Post-Communist Poland.* Chicago: University of Chicago Press.

Zúquete, Jose Pedro. 2017. Populism and Religion. In *Oxford Handbook of Populism*, ed. Cristobal Rovira Kaltwasser, Paul A. Taggart, Paulina Ochoa Espejo, and Pierre Ostiguy, 445–466. Oxford: Oxford University Press.

INDEX[1]

[1] Note: Page numbers followed by 'n' refer to notes.

© The Author(s), under exclusive license to Springer Nature   251
Switzerland AG 2022
M. R. Loustau, *Hungarian Catholic Intellectuals in Contemporary
Romania*, Contemporary Anthropology of Religion,
https://doi.org/10.1007/978-3-030-99221-7

Germany, 23n16, 45, 86, 225
Gheorgheni, 155
Ghimeş, 54, 56, 76, 77
Giesen, Bernhard, 3, 8, 33, 34, 43, 44, 46, 48–50
Globalization, 126
God, 97n9, 221, 223
Goulash communism, 52, 89
Government
  and non-governmental
    organizations (NGOs), 118
Grace, 33, 44, 73
  See also Collaborative presence
Greater Hungary, 163, 164, 188
Great Lady of Hungary, see Mary
Groupness, 7
Grundtvig, Frederik, 41, 42, 57
Gusti, Dimitrie, 37

H
Habsburg Empire, 18, 120
Habsburg-Lothringen, Eduard, 199
Haddon, Malcolm, 210
Halemba, Agnieszka, 13, 23n13, 97n8
Hallam, Elizabeth, 14, 46
Handman, Courtney, 6, 7, 87
Hanebrink, Paul, 42, 43, 59n7, 137, 185
Hann, Chris, 13, 60n21, 136, 137, 139, 158n3, 158n12, 159n19, 185
Harding, Susan, 210, 226n4
Hard work, 38, 52, 57, 70, 81, 149, 181
Harghita County, 101, 104, 105, 110, 112, 113, 167, 168, 200
Harghita Mountains, 54, 97n6
Harvard Divinity School, 19
Hedeşan, Otilia, 110, 111
Heller, Ágnes, 60n23

Herod, 82
Herzfeld, Michael, 58n1, 155, 156, 182
Historical ethnography, 13
Hitchins, Keith, 37, 59n5
Holy Crown of King Stephen, 137, 158n11
  and religio-political spectacles, 128
  and the Virgin Mary, 136, 139, 140, 185, 189
Holy See, the, 199
Honor, 138
Hospitality, 154
  and care, 136, 154–156
  and masculinity, 155, 156
House of Culture, 17, 112–115, 133, 134, 149, 151, 152, 157
Human rights, 83, 84, 89, 198
Humility, 38, 57, 222, 224
Hungarian educational system in Transylvania, 33, 142, 147, 148
Hungarian Ethnic Autonomous Region, 147
Hungarian ethnic minority in Romania, 1–3, 19, 31, 35, 41, 50, 54, 55, 68, 72, 81, 84, 138, 143, 150, 187, 197, 198, 219
  as exiles in socialist Hungary, 54
  and labor migration, 55
  See also Szekler cultural revival, the
Hungarian National Museum, see Museums
Hungarians from Hungary, 6
  and charity, 77, 90
  and consumer culture, 6, 7, 9, 12, 52, 129n9, 187, 189
  and right-wing political views, 119, 120, 187, 200
  and tourism, 7, 53, 56, 57, 69, 92, 171, 187, 189
  and views on confession, 192

King Stephen, 109, 135, 137,
139, 156
and the Holy Crown, 18, 163, 191
and royal court, 138, 140
and succession, 53
and the Virgin Mary, 136, 139, 140,
158n11, 158n12
and virtue, 138, 157
See also King Stephen
Kligman, Gail, 5, 13, 104, 117, 150,
155, 166–168, 192n3,
192n4, 192n5
Knighthood Order of the Holy
Crown, 2, 16, 17, 43, 128, 135,
136, 138–140, 143, 152–157,
165, 185
Knighthood orders, 2, 16, 128, 135,
136, 138–140, 143, 152–154,
156, 157, 185
See also Chivalric associations
Kürti, László, 54, 55, 61n24, 79,
137, 138

L
Labor unions, 147, 149
See also Miners
Lajosi, Kristina, 119
Lake Saint Anna, 54, 56
Lange, Barbara Rose, 111
Laypeople, 109, 110
Legend of the Flying Dutchman, 218
Legitimacy, 9, 52, 58n1, 150
Lindquist, Galina, 13, 55
Liszt, Franz, 115
Lithuania, 199
Liturgy, 107, 115
and liturgical renewal
movement, 111
and liturgical revival movement,
102, 107, 126; and pedagogy,
103, 107

and pedagogy, 110, 116 (see also
Mass, the)
Losonczy, Anne-Marie, 56, 92
Love, 16, 38, 74, 108, 166–173, 179
See also Charity
Loyalty, 12, 33, 36, 38, 45, 138
Luehrmann, Sonja, 14, 15, 108, 111,
135, 170
Luhrmann, Tanya, 116

M
Makkai, Sándor, 38, 59n7, 60n18
Marcus, George E., 209
Marian devotionalism, 77, 143
See also Petitionary prayer
Mark, József, 105
Márton, Áron, 15, 31–34, 38, 40–51,
57, 67, 69, 73, 128, 134, 135,
142, 181
Mary, 157n1, 158n4, 158n11,
158n12, 175, 216, 223
apparitions, 142
dreams, 179
Mary, Queen of Light, 159n13
Our Lady of Csíksomlyó, 20, 108,
141, 207, 208, 212, 225, 226
Our Lady of Fatima, 159n13
Our Lady of Lourdes, 159n13
and the Rosary, 219
Masculinity, 158n12
pater familias, 167, 168, 192n4
soldiers, 115
and the Szekler cultural revival, 111
Mass, the, 80, 107, 109, 110, 116,
170, 171, 178, 180–184, 192,
214, 225
See also Liturgy
Mauss, Marcel, 90
McIntyre, Alasdair, 21n5
Media, 69, 70, 72, 83, 128, 165,
200, 201

CPSIA information can be obtained
at www.ICGtesting.com
Printed in the USA
LVHW021809310323
743029LV00019B/332